Praise for

This is an incredible story of ... and a determined single woman that faces an insurmountable task. This is the toughest dog journey as dog and people trainer of more than eighteen years of my life. Enter this amazing journey.

—BILL BARTEN, *BJ's Dog Training, Professional Gun Dog Trainer*

Saxon was a smart, beautiful, and amazingly kind golden retriever who had the innate sense of giving people his healing spirit in a way that very few humans can understand. Although his life was shortened by hemangiosarcoma, as his caregiver, I know he was on this earth, with Bonnie, at exactly the right time in her life. As I read this heartfelt memoir, I could feel the warmth that he exuded and visualize the gorgeous dog that I remembered. At the same time, it brought back memories of dogs that I have loved and have had to send over the rainbow bridge.

Thank you, Bonnie, for sharing your intimate and honest journey. I can't imagine a more loving way to cherish the memory of a beloved soul.

—DR. KEVIN LANDORF, *DVM*

Bonnie Wright's journey from a dysfunctional childhood of shaming carries into her adult life drives her deeper into dysfunctional relationships until a special golden retriever named Saxon mirrors the dysfunction back to her. Her need to "fix" Saxon drove her into uncharted territory opening doors of possibilities to healing. In the end, through faith, both are set free to live from their hearts' truth.

—LINDA LEDBETER, *Lightwinds Healing*

I am astounded at the power of the human spirit to transcend pain and suffering. This is a story of survival, one in which this author shares her wretched childhood, victim to the DNA that has predicted her future. Somehow, her faith and her ability to see strength and perseverance in other species, give her hope and determination to rise above all odds. This writer discovers how her canine friend mirrors her own internal struggle. Their scars are not unlike one another. Determined to escape her hopeless past, she shares her journey of peeling away the layers of shame and abuse. She recognizes the power of her own spiritual being in providing hope and healing. She breaks the chain, and chooses to be set free. Her past remains unforgettable, but also no longer holds her a prisoner.

—MARCIA DANZINGER, *Registered Nurse*
& Energy Healing Practitioner

Shame causes us to live two lives, an inner life and an outer life. The one we want the world to see and the one we dare not show because it's too painful.

—ANONYMOUS

A friend who is a psychiatrist, and who specializes in family problems said he always asked the family that if they had a dog, to bring the dog with them when they came in for therapy. When I asked why, he commented that the family dog always told him which member of the family was in the most emotional pain, as the dog indicated it to him. *Diggin' Up Bones* is about the emotional pain both human and dog were suffering from, and how they helped one another mend spiritually, aligning the inner and outer life as one.

—GLENDA BROWN, *Associate Editor/Field,*
Golden Retriever News Magazine, *Golden*
Retriever Club of America, Inc.

With brutal honesty and searing emotion, Bonnie Wright has used her personal life experiences to portray a healing undertaking of survival. I love how she credits her canine companions for the power of love, courage and joy they gave her so willingly. Each relationship was mutually beneficial, but that's what dogs do. Unconditional love is a powerful tonic for healing. What is remarkable is how she transformed her rough beginning into a life mission of helping others, both people and animals. Great work, Bonnie!

—MARY STOFFEL, *Author of,* The Practical Power of Shamanism,
Heal your life, loves and losses, *Animal Communicator,*
Shaman, Master Avatar

DIGGIN' UP BONES

DIGGIN' UP BONES

*ONE WOMAN'S SPIRITUAL STRUGGLE
AND HER GOLDEN RETRIEVER WHO LEADS
HER OUT OF A LIFE OF UNCONSCIOUS,
TRANSGENERATIONAL SHAME*

BONNIE WRIGHT

For information about this title or to order other books and/or electronic media, contact the publisher:

SS Safari All-Star Press
bonniewrightwrites.com
bonnie@bonniewrightwrites.com

ISBNs:
978-0-9891451-0-7 (softcover)
978-0-9891451-1-4 (eBook)

Printed in the United States of America

Cover and Interior design: 1106 Design

Dedication

To my Lord and Saxon who taught me how to choose a life with meaning and purpose by uprooting unconscious transgenerational shame. Teaching me to follow His path. To my mother who read the scriptures and taught me the importance of living a life of faith. Her reminder was to always be kind and have a pure heart. This book is my committed promise and labor of love to them to walk forward with steadfast faith, true intent, having an open mind, and compassionate heart. For it is in loving, serving and forgiving others we find our true self. It's why we are here.

We are survivors, the once-broken misfits whom God will use to help others, because we have walked by faith across the burning coals, tested through life's fire, to the other side, smiling in the radiant light of the Savior's love, our souls restored, our hearts' desires changed, and our mind follows truths versus being fed lies. Daring, we took the step of faith to rise above shame's ruthless destruction, while standing up against its sting, freeing ourselves of its clutches. Disharmony is replaced with harmony.

—Bonnie M. Wright

Table of Contents

Foreword

How does one build a bridge out of shame?

Shame, learned at home, specifically at the words and hands of a family of origin, permeates muscle memory, singes the soul, and creates for the bearer a life of burden that little, if anything, can touch. Deep, loud, and painful, shame inhabits territory and swamps it with dank messaging that allows no alternate sound or light.

Shame creates victimhood, fostering a fear-based response to the world's otherwise delightful invitation to live and breathe, explore and learn. It closes the heart to intimacy, love, and rapture. Shame allows for little curiosity and preys on the innocent by replicating itself and being passed along in the double helix of our emotional DNA.

But then there are dogs, whose species has developed to assist humans in our earthly pursuits. Perhaps this was not the original intent for *Canis familiaris*, but perhaps dogs recognized our all-too-obvious human needs and, as we domesticated them, they, in turn, domesticated us against our own worst selves.

In this breathtaking account of healing from shame, Bonnie Wright takes us on her lifelong travel to map herself a new territory where shame has no place.

The book in your hand is the true story of interspecies healing. In this story, the human and the dogs share their pain while undergoing the discipline of healing what's wrong in their combined lives. Along the way, the reader sees how we can leave our own pained countries of origin and, with faith and the loving support of our best companions, come to healing together.

Do not mistake this for a mere dog tale. It is nothing of the sort. Nor is it merely a memoir of spiritual healing. This is the true story of a spiritual struggle, of its price, and of an honest win over some of the greatest forces of evil any of us can know.

Read and learn. If you have a dog, read it alongside that best companion. And then, as the writer did, look deeply into those canine eyes and find what's there to inform you on your own path home.

—*Marion Roach Smith*

Introduction

Living a divided life is a lie. While I appeared normal to the world, I hid the dark shadow of trauma. It got inside me and followed me. Shrinking out of sight, I felt small and unworthy. After repeated rejection, I was begging to belong. I was always conflicted, wanting to be loved but not understanding love. Home was an inescapable rural prison of raw degradation, never feeling safe, valued, or wanted. Each verbal, emotional, and physical blow was a violent intrusion of a soul under siege, stealing my innocence, muzzled, chipping away hope, life's purpose, identity, made to feel invisible, and leaving a vulnerability.

This is how my emotional childhood foundation was formed. I believed what I was told and kept telling myself the same repeated tales.

Ah! The soul fires flashbacks to the conscious mind to take action and right itself. Hearing, this is not who you are. I battled to be perfect and accepted, but I was never good enough, no matter how hard I tried to prove myself. My soul crumbled like dirt under the pressure of a shoe. My anxiety-laden gut was constantly churning. I felt hopeless and scattered. This is how unconscious shame messes with reality, destroying my soul bit by bit from the inside. And, it doesn't care.

My awakening began the day two golden retrievers entered my life. Saxon and Sadie balanced me, so I might see—and change—the subconscious destructive patterns and dysfunctional formation rooted in me. They were my teachers, ministering and guiding me out to emotional healing and leading me to learn about love. Saxon experienced the same fractured start as a puppy that left deep-seated anger. We rewired one another and pieced together our shattered souls. When Saxon died and I had to face the reality of my broken self, God lifted me up, reframing healthy life patterns for serving the greater good. This began the unconscious unraveling of childhood traumas reverting to spiritual roots, clinging to the tree of life, being the cross.

It was my promise to Saxon when he took his last breath that I would help animals and people heal their souls' fragments and become whole again.

Diggin' Up Bones is a spiritual love story that is meant to inspire and awaken deep, subconscious wounds knitted in one's fiber. Because God and the dogs teach unconditional love, one can courageously face the soul damage being courageously supported walking through grief. Grief is God's process toward healing. You will be stronger and wiser, knowing that emotional pain's control fades as your faith rises through God's grace.

Child maltreatment will always be a part of me, but words like dummy, stupid, fatty-fatty, and pathetic are not my name. It doesn't have power over me anymore. I am no longer bullied into an altered mental state. Healthy boundaries, not barriers keep me balanced. The person the world now sees is whole, living in the present. I can now recognize trauma in others and support them on their road, based upon their willingness to grow spiritually. One person's trauma is neither measurable nor comparable to another's, as pain is unique to the individual. The animals have taught me to live in oneness, in interdependence, no longer in codependence. They've shown me how to stay balanced.

My well-being owes a great deal to what I have observed and studied about how adaptable the mind and body can be both wounded and healed. I have tapped into traditions of other cultures along with the advances of contemporary society. I have drawn strength from my experiences with Native

Americans and the Maasai tribe in Africa for whom harmony and unity with nature and spirituality are fundamental. Reading about the findings of modern neuroscience and medical research has shaped my understanding of how trauma affects the brain and people's overall health. A thirst for learning, I participated and read many of the great motivational speakers like Dr Alan Zimmerman, Zig Ziglar, Lou Holtz, Normam Vincent Peale and Scott Peck. I have taken seminars and hands-on courses led by teachers who have honed innovative techniques for communicating with and healing animals based on the principles of life's energy. I have incorporated into my own beliefs the wisdom of all these ways by which humans seek knowledge about our existence and coexistence with other species.

Herbert Ward, who led St. Jude's Ranch for Children for thirty years, said, "Child abuse casts a shadow the length of a lifetime. The child is given a life sentence." But I will no longer live as a psychological prisoner, a victim to be taken advantage of, disrespected, demeaned, and berated. I will endure no more mean-spirited pranks or unhealthy, disjointed relationships. Being told to shut up and stay in my box is intolerable. Shame doesn't control me.

The stories I tell myself now are filled with bright hope coming from a place of love and inner peace. My soul is whole. I am a thriving survivor and a child of God.

Prologue

Saxon and I are standing on a mound behind a camouflage holding blind at the hunt test line for the 2008 Master National Retriever Competition in Virginia, Minnesota. I'm looking over the test concepts, which even two years ago were unknown and inconceivable. We had failed to run in contention back then, but the honor of being selected as the test dog team for this prestigious event overshadowed our initial failure to qualify. Saxon's Master Hunter passes had been judged in Minot, North Dakota, by the competition's regional vice president. He knew about Saxon's aggression and thought Bill, my trainer, was wasting his time with what he called a "swamp collie." Others were mocking and ridiculing Saxon, saying he was worthless and the best thing would be to kill him. Friends criticized me for wasting my life with him.

Some nine years ago as an adolescent golden retriever, Saxon would have annihilated any dog he sighted within a quarter mile. Hearing his guttural growl and seeing his wild lunges terrified me. The more he was silenced, the quicker he'd strike without warning. Never understanding the root cause, I was clueless to help him. He and I triggered the traumas of each other. On the surface was Saxon's ability to perform to the hunt test standard. Underneath was his lack of impulse control and the need to counter his fear-aggression. It was risky. Could we hold it together? It was also gutsy. Could we survive our shared secret? We were driven to solve the problem. Saxon overcame his rage and outperformed himself. Restoring his identity, he transformed his anger, rising above it, living, and serving from a place of love. Together, we succeeded.

Now just being at the 2008 competition is a grand accomplishment. It superseded taking home a silver plate award. Nine years later, we are standing among the most esteemed performance field dogs in the United States. Saxon is respected. He is the star for Flight B. He is my boy and the love of my life. We believed! Together, faith carried us through seemingly near death encounters and impossible struggles.

This was joint soul work. Saxon's behavior modification led to healing my childhood patterns. He mirrored me, revealing my poor choices and ripping off the scars. God put him in my life to uncover years of emotional maltreatment. Saxon's transformation led me across the bridge of faith.

We are awaiting the judge's call to the hunt test line to demonstrate the water-land test for the best three hundred Master Hunters in the nation. Most of them are black Labs that live to possess their birds.

"All master handlers, we are running the test dog," the judges announce and call for the gunners. "Guns up!" Saxon and I come out of the holding blind. I give him a minute to sit at heel and assess the test across the landscape. Then I visualize it in my mind. Telepathically, we connect. Saxon sees my thoughts. He conceptualizes, seeing the bigger picture. Visualization and thought transference is a strategy we use to our advantage during the hunt tests. This is a spiritual skill, and Bill realizes Saxon has it.

Saxon identifies the orange marker on the other mound across the water. His tail slowly swishes behind him, fanning and raising dust. He confidently looks at me, almost winking as if to say, *I got this, Mom. You are just along for the ride. Just send me.*

I smile calmly, proud to be just standing next to him, knowing how far we've come. He more than me. As I send him down the slope to the water, he pauses and turns to look back at me. It is as if his heart skips a beat. Mine does too. I am breathless and bewildered after such a look of affirmation. I am unaware of the future, but he is wise to it as a fierce reality erupts inside him.

The test continues as we challenge the blind retrieve. Using hand signals and a whistle, I steer him across the 118 yards of water and land transitions. Three casts and he's on it. Cheers come from the gallery that applauds his excellent performance. The judges compliment him.

Remembering and retrieving the marks is next. The second mark is difficult to get, but he remembers exactly where the bird fell. Telepathy! As he swims across the channel, the combination of his waterlogged golden retriever coat, high bank, and hip dysplasia hampers his ability to get up on land. The handlers, who nicknamed him Mr. Happy Feet, see his determination to get the duck. They cheer him on. "Come on, Saxon, you can do this. Get the bird!" He captures their hearts. Using his powerful chest and front legs, he hoists himself, fighting gravity's forces, onto the bank, snatches the bird, swims back across, comes rear pigeon-toed to heel, and delivers to my hand. Whistles and thunderous applause resound, affirmation for Saxon's style that is both methodical and joyful in the field.

The first dog in contention is a black Lab waiting excitedly in the holding blind. Saxon calmly and proudly heels off line beside me. He brushes past the blind, disregarding the Lab's exuberance. He focuses on my face, prancing and smiling as I wink and smile back. We nailed it.

Sagacity fits Saxon in so many ways. His spiritual intuition knew my subconscious before I did. He zeroed in on my soul, serving as my looking glass, uprooting my childhood smothered in shame and emotional abuse. He and I were broken from the beginning. He chose me. We were destined to be together. In our hearts we understood the saying, *You're a little broken, eh? I understand, I am a little broken too. We'll get there.* It was up to me to discover my spiritual healing path. I needed to resurface, unshackle, unlearn, and flush out shame's transgenerational grip of self-destructive patterns and beliefs, and put them behind. Chaos, division, anger, fear, insecurity, codependence, and unworthiness are gone. I have a voice now. I stopped feeding myself lies.

Forming Roots

What startles me is the fierceness of my memory and the ferocious bond I now share with my dogs. My human eyes look at them with respect and gratitude for their sagacity and ability to tap into my subconscious, reading every thought and emotion, leaving me to feel naked and small to the raw truth. They demonstrate to me what I did not understand: love. Their love supported me after my family beat me down, every blow layering and compounding itself. I was wired for shame, but not toxic shame. I was the youngest and most vulnerable, the loser. My innate need to belong was met with rejection, verbal attacks, and volatile repressed anger. My ability to grow and thrive was stripped away. I felt powerless. My lack of nurturing formed a defective self-image, causing me to live a false sense of who I am. My identity was lost. I buckled under shame's weight. A hollow longing prevailed. My dogs felt and saw what I did not. Their instinctive animal-knowing recognized that I was wired to hoist myself up out of shame while others may choose to remain stuck. They showed me a spiritual life full of love and free of hostility. It was my decision to stay or move forward. My animal angels stood by me, holding a space of love, so I could evolve.

My spiritual battle for the soul began at birth. It was flesh versus faith, the time when the enemy preys upon the innocent, having the greatest influence to steal a fresh mind. I asked God what my purpose was for being born. Meaning in my life was lost. I just didn't realize it across my childhood and adulthood. I was chasing, grasping, and coming up empty. I was faltering, flailing, and going it on my own rather than reaching out for spiritual healing. I thought I could climb out of this rabbit hole and meet society's expectations. I wanted to live the American dream, a fairy tale, happy ever after. Every time I tried, I was dissatisfied and disappointed. The unconscious enemy, being shame already has control and thrives on division. Faith fights against it in spiritual warfare.

My home environment was confusing, conflicting, and complicated in patterns perpetuated by smoldering turmoil. Repetitive traumatic events pressured me to live a disassociated life from reality. The unrelenting lambasting made it easier to pretend and mentally escape. I created in a fictitious world a safe place out of my mind and body to exist. Unbeknown to me was an abnormal normal that my brain recorded as being the truth. But my soul fired a wake-up shot, and I was hell-bent to change what seemed wrong, even if it took the rest of my life.

My way of combating shame's detrimental effects was to bolt and hide. This was my coping mechanism, my automatic survival alarm system. But self-preservation conditioning such as this results in a lost identity of self. The emotional trauma bore in at a cellular level of my core.

Shame's dictatorial presence is tethered across generations and deeply rooted in my family's DNA. The tentacles of shame strangled my family. Shame lodged in me against my will. For every stream of light that entered my life, darkness rushed in to extinguish it. Isolation on a farm provided no outside comparison or social contact. Innocent and vulnerable, I believed what I was told. Farm life blanketed abuse in a cult-like environment. Animals suffer and die. The animal cruelty I witnessed was trapped in my somatic nervous system. Those degrading lies from my parents and sister formed my poor self-image and lack of self-worth. Rising from within was my inner critic who saw me being defective, worthless, and incapable. Feeling undeserving of love, I looked through an inward lens of loneliness and a heavy heart of hopelessness. Depression was layered in me.

Shame's outcroppings disguised themselves as emotional and sexual abuse, and later witnessing elder abuse. Torrential torment took the form of verbal passive-aggressive sibling maltreatment. My survival instinct materialized early and stays across my life, determined not to let this enemy strangle me. Breaking its choke hold, I free myself, rewiring my mind, releasing the layers from my body, and restoring a wounded heart, celebrating a changed heart and life on the other side of shame. I am one life's example of many who suffer from the mental maladies imposed upon us.

This Is Home

I only know what I am told. There are things I am not supposed to know as a child. This is my take on it. My sister can refute this. We are six years apart and she is the privileged older sibling.

White trash was what my father was born into in 1905. He and two brothers were the sons of a poor, alcoholic Alabama coal miner. He lived through the Spanish Flu, and many social and cultural atrocities in the sixteen years he stayed there. Atrocities, ruthless racial unrest, and lynchings were widespread during the resurfacing of the KKK and the prevalence of Jim Crow. Vigilante law prevailed. Diabolical hatred permeated communities. Respect for human life was minimal. Fear and intimidation were wielded to dismantle people's soul. People of color and children were left hanging as a warning and instilling fear. Child slavery in the mines was common. Women, children, and animals were used and abused as a man's property.

My father fled his home. He rebelled against authority. With a sixth-grade education, no spiritual imprinting, and few life skills, he became a hobo, riding the rails, carousing, and engaging in ruthless behavior. He spiraled downward, floundering, and failed miserably. He lived hand to mouth, panhandling in the streets of Chicago. An internal rebellion sprung up from his core. Either entitlement or the will to survive drove him to steal, lie, cheat, womanize, and drink, making him incapable of steady employment and following any rules. That was, in part, what put us on a dairy farm in Wisconsin after he married my mother. A good-hearted woman who felt sorry for him.

As a toddler at home and behind closed doors, I saw my father as an angry, sneaky, secretive, mean-spirited, conniving, unkempt, and emotionally distant man without scruples. He deemed himself blameless, laughed off bad behavior, and deflected truth with jokes. Always on guard, at any moment his jaded behavior was unpredictable and untrustworthy.

He hated the farm but was obligated to work it because of the children he sired, and he was held accountable by my mother's entrepreneurial father who provided the money to buy the farm. He was stuck, a prisoner forced to be Grandpa's underling. My grandfather treated my father like an aggressive stray dog and reckoned the only place to let such an animal live out his life was on a farm.

The two men were complete opposites. Grandpa was a successful finishing carpenter and an accomplished Norwegian farmer from Oslo. Dad seethed with resentment for being under his thumb. Pursed lips and shifty eyes molded his facial expressions. Head held down, hunched, he walked with a hobble due to arthritis. His upbringing had impaled a grapple hook in him, despite his best intentions to better himself.

Prior to her involvement with my Dad, my mother was a happy blossoming woman of upward potential, now anchored to a life of despair, strapped with the weight of raising two girls, stripped of the capacity for thriving. Yet she was the brains of the farm. Grandpa taught her how to operate and manage it. He loved my mother and was generous to her. Providing the farm (he was the cosigner) was his way of protecting and holding the family together, although it was my mother who made certain the farm succeeded, and the financial obligation rested with her. Failing was not acceptable, determining her worth.

Grandpa visited the farm daily, criticizing the way it was run. Grandpa's fuse was short. It was never good enough in his eyes. It was mom who took the verbal shellacking that sent her into tears.

Knowing retribution was on the way, Ma dreaded seeing her father's 1952 gray Chevy rumbling down the gravel road with a cloud of dust trailing behind. Pulling into the driveway, he'd get out, slamming the car door and come in the house. His angry body language told the story. Ma got him coffee and cream with freshly baked cinnamon coffee cake, hoping to appease him.

Grandpa liked to sling Norwegian slang about my dad at Ma. "Dat lazy bastard! What's wrong with him? Why can't he run a farm?" Grandpa would ask, demeaning both my parents. "Where's the money? Why are you always lending money you can't repay?" The angrier Grandpa got, the more the conversation switched to full Norske swearing, which I couldn't understand.

"I'm sorry, I'm sorry," Ma would say, putting hands up in front of her face, assuming she is to blame. Grandpa verbally pounded her in the ground, grinding shame deeper into her core. Many of her days ended with her feeling like a torn rag doll, battered and tossed about.

Money was often at the center of the discord. Worse yet, Grandpa pitted my mother's farm against her brother's farm, comparing the two, tattling to the other, ginning up infighting, deepening the division and animosity between the families. Grandpa, a sought-after carpenter, was a perfectionist. He knew how to make money in his craft and in rural real estate. He also knew how to run a successful dairy farm. Dad, the oddball of the family, certainly didn't. But neither my mother nor my uncle could meet Grandpa's expectations.

Marrying my dad reflected poor judgment and discernment. Ma was always compensating by minimizing and shifting the conversations so they didn't boomerang into her. She was stuck with the way women were viewed as men's servants. She anchored herself with whatever spark of good she saw in my father. She defended him. "He's a good man doing the best he can. He works hard every day. Leave us alone. Everything is fine."

She felt sorry for him. Her compassionate heart took him under her wing. She hoped Dad saw her sacrifice for him. She wished her love and long-suffering could change his ways. She walked a tightrope between supporting and enabling. Her emotional conundrum was often overruled by her codependency. Divorce was not an option. In the 1950s it was a disgrace to have children and not be married, and her financial prospects, living single with two children, were limited. Ma was trapped. A choice she made.

Dad pushed away the love of his child. Hugs didn't exist, only barriers and verbal grunts. He instilled hurt in my heart the night I innocently went to his bedside wanting to kiss him good night. I told him I loved him. He rolled over, turning away, dismissing me as invisible and inconsequential. Shame surfaced as my face flushed red. Looking back at those times, I now understand that a daughter should not have to beg her father for a relationship or earn love.

My father lived a divided life. His invisible chip on his shoulder and get even attitude was evident. Beyond our walls, an opposite persona prevailed. He could be a man of kindness and generosity, hardworking and honest, good-natured and trustworthy. There was even an occasional appearance in church, on the holidays. In my innocence, I wanted to believe he was a good man. He was my father and I trusted my mother.

At the same time, I was wary around Dad. Much of this uneasy feeling stems from having been violated at home, in the basement near the coal bin, before my second birthday. My body remembers. A part of my brain, the amygdala, recorded the betrayal. My father's malicious outlet—targeting the vulnerable, knowing he'd be unscathed—planted fear in his victim. He took his shot at me while both my sister and mother were gone. If I said anything, he counted on the fact that kids tell lies and stories, so he'd deny everything. I'd be blamed. Whenever I was in the basement and he was there, fear welled up in me. My eyes locked with his on the stairway. I shuddered and ran, feeling trapped, but not understanding why.

My father rarely bathed. He didn't own a toothbrush. We joked about the many tubes of Brylcreem plastered on his head, but never in all the years I knew him did he wash his hair. He wore a baseball cap that exuded grease. He hated the idea of shaving, but did so at my mother's demand. His milk-white, glass coffee mug was off limits to anyone because he thought the cup was cured like a cast-iron skillet and cleaning it would destroy the layers of black coffee built up. Maybe this was symbolic of the dark emotional layers buried in him.

He smoked unfiltered Camel cigarettes. When he thought no one was looking he'd take a butt from his shirt pocket, light it, and inhale a quick drag. If he saw me coming, up the cuff of his shirt the butt would go, only to come back out when I left. I sometimes hung around to see how long he could hold it there and not get a wrist burn. His lower lip bulged with a pinch of chewing tobacco and he'd spit in the cow gutter, wiping the brown drool away with his shirt sleeve. Ma hated this dirty habit. Hiding stuff was common for him, which included his feelings.

Playing solitaire and solving crossword puzzles from the *Chicago Tribune* were two of his favorite pastimes. Occasionally, I beat him at solitaire, but only when Ma wasn't there because cards were against her Baptist beliefs. "God wouldn't like that," she said.

Dad had a zest for learning words. When the newspaper came, his favorite thing in it, besides the puzzles, was news about the Cubs and the ponies, which he used to gamble at the Arlington race track. He enjoyed watching football and boxing. He knew a few magic tricks, juggling, and shook dice to see who could get snake eyes, which made me laugh. It was one of my pleasant memories of being with him.

We all worked on the farm. He taught me how to drive a tractor and handle machinery. In the winter, the milk tank in the milk house that kept the metal cans cool usually had a six-pack of Hamm's beer at the farthest bottom corner so we couldn't reach it. Each time I think of that brand, I remember the bear dancing on a log in water and the trademark phrase, "In the land of sky-blue waters," followed by the fading drum beat and the bear dancing toward the woods with beer in its paws. In the summer, the beer was hidden in the cow's water tank outside the milk house. Inside our home, he had a stash of blackberry brandy that he said was for medicinal purposes. He let me have a sip when Ma wasn't looking. Then he'd dig his fingers in my side, tickling me while on the kitchen floor until it hurt. His rough touch sent a shock wave to my brain that scared me.

After a full day in the hot sun, thrashing hay, and the milking chores done, we piled in the 1950 Chevy for happy hour at Siedles corner tavern near Dorchester. My sister and I sat on the outside step drinking a thick chocolate malt through a straw. When we got to the bottom, we made loud sucking noises that echoed in the stainless-steel cup, and we giggled. Mother stayed in the truck or at home, a reprieve from the fighting, finger-pointing, mean-spirited yelling with rude and cursing language at home. Sex was considered a cuss word. "We just don't talk about things like that in this house," Ma said. Don't ask why, when, how, or where. Querying only brought on the fear of shame, condemnation, exercising poor judgment. "Are you crazy or what?" was my parents' retort, acting as if nothing ever happened and how dare you insinuate it did. Self-doubt rewires the mind. Actions and events are suppressed, silenced, and left unanswered. Because, lingered as the reason.

My upstairs bedroom along the hallway to the attic, facing east toward the barn and silo, was a shelter and hiding place. It was where I ran for cover. The screaming downstairs rose up through the floor heat grate as fire seeks oxygen. I'd crawl into my bed in a fetal position and cover my head with a pillow, hoping to muffle the anger that fueled my fears and insecurity. Escaping the argument provided a layer of safe harbor. For that moment, I wasn't the target. But my mother was, and she was taking the verbal hits.

I was paralyzed by fright that I would be next. Dad intentionally planted fear in me doing a horrific Halloween boogeyman laugh that sent chills through me. I was panic-stricken as he stomped up the stairs, releasing adrenaline till I trembled. Then I would be physically dragged down into the argument.

My sister added her two cents, hollering, "Get down here, right now!" She often instigated fights, was never blistered by any blame, and took sadistic pleasure for being the accelerant. It gave her power and a sense of self-righteous indignation.

Born into this inhospitable place and too young to truly understand what was happening, I was ashamed and squelched. I was an outcast and a dummy. I never comprehended what caused me to feel so odd and unbalanced, not knowing life could be different.

When I was around five years old, my father asked a friend of his to come to the farm and repair some machinery. They were beer-drinking buddies and of the same devious nature, both loner bad boys. Innocent young girls on a farm were fodder for their foul conduct.

My father's buddy's small-engine repair business allowed him to befriend rural families with children. One late afternoon while playing outside, I curiously entered the dim machine shed while dad was in the barn milking cows. The door was partially closed. No one could see in. He was tinkering on some tools when he cornered me against the tool bench, putting his hand down my underwear and fondling me. Running to the house where Ma was making supper, I cried through my tears, "Ma, Frank touched me in my private parts."

Ma had a temper, but nothing like that day. She was outraged. Her beet-red rosacea face extended into her chest as if a pressure cooker was going to blow. She flung open the screen door, stormed out of the house, and stomped into the barn during milking. Her yelling was heard all the way to the house over the loud polka music in the barn. She demanded that my dad remove his buddy Frank from the farm and cut all ties with him. Dad, who had turned a blind eye to the molestation, dismissed Ma. The usual cold division in our household became a gorge. Cold war persisted for days. Dad never said a word to Frank. Frank had his way with my cousins and sister too. She denied anything really happened and told me I was at fault for hanging around him.

The lesson I learned was that abusing the innocent is condoned, even normal. I was not worth protecting. My father's indifference bowled over Ma's moral parenting. She cared and he didn't. The push-pull between them continued. I dared not confront Pa, fearing he'd strike or verbally chastise me. My shame dived underground while I shut down emotionally. I was bewildered. Weren't parents supposed to be the defenders and teachers. It just didn't seem right, but this was our normal.

The true person I was born to be was faced with the disingenuous one they were teaching me to be. I was a farmhand and not a very good one.

Still very young, I was once crushed by a conversation I overheard while sitting alone outside on a well cover underneath the clothesline near the open kitchen window. "We should have had a boy," Dad said. "It would have been better for the farm."

Wow! Now I was the wrong sex, unwanted, and a disappointment. I knew instantly that measuring up was insurmountable and hopeless. I felt as if a forged double-edge knife had sliced a bleeding path through my heart. How could this be my fault? What did I do wrong? Why am I here? Devalued and dismissed, I wanted to disappear.

Assaulting the Innocent

Toodle is a petite, female, mixed-breed cattle dog, almost calico. Her purpose is to herd the cows for milking morning and night. She does her job to perfection, but mostly out of fear.

"Toodle, get the cows!" Dad hollers. Within minutes she has the herd coming up the cow lane from the pasture and into the yard. She is loyal and faithful. She and I are best friends. She knows what I am thinking before I say it. I can tell her everything and she listens.

Toodle births two litters. She hides them in the barn. I sit, watching how she loves and cares for her innocent babies, snuggling in the straw. Their energy radiates pureness. At the slightest whimper, she responds tenderly, comforting and protecting them, giving them the best start in life so they have life skills. She makes sure every puppy gets the individual love and care they need. She licks them clean, keeps them warm and safe. Nurturing is in her nature and shows me what it is to be in a loving family. Her actions are opposite of what I am living. Instinctively, I want what she is giving her babies. Watching each puppy, I see different personalities. Some of the puppies are courageous, exploring away from their mother; others are shy and hover close. It's the brave puppies that catch my eye. They're the survivors. That's what I want to be. A survivor.

With Toodle's first litter, Dad forces me to watch him lump them in a gunny sack and heartlessly sling them against a fence post repeatedly, until the screams end. Toodle sees and hears this from a distance. She is afraid to approach, helpless to protect what she loves most. I feel her pain. My heart breaks while anger and hate take root. This is wrong. They are innocent. I feel guilty for not stopping my father. He buries the gunny sack between the machine shed and crapper. A gray, murky cloud surrounds Toodle. She whines and howls, searching for her puppies. She grieves. I sit with her in the barn, crying and hugging her. She seems to know I understand that we are both trapped victims.

When the second litter is born, Dad puts Toodle inside the barn away from her pups. "Get over here, kid," he snaps as he drags me to where the puppies are sleeping alone in the straw pile.

"Put those puppies in the gunny sack, tie it shut, and bury them," he orders.

"No, not doing that." I have defied him.

He backhands me across the face. "You go bury those dogs and I won't hear another word from you. Don't you ever disobey me again!"

He grabs my hand and forces my fisted fingers around the shovel and stands over me, watching, while I dig the hole to bury the puppies. I hate him and fear one day he'll bury me the same way.

Toodle escapes through a barn window and watches stoically through her grief a second time. She seems to understand it is not my fault and forgives me as I sob, hearing their final screams. She loves me and comforts me.

My father coldly walks away. "Get over it, kid. Life's hard. Buck up," he mutters. The rage he instills in me ignites my determination to be a survivor. Seeing Toodle stay strong through tragedy inspires me to endure and move on. I choose to rise above, as she did.

With a scowl, my father turns, points his finger, and vows, "I better not find out you told anyone about this or you are in big trouble, so shut up."

How could someone be so heartless? The repulsive act heaves up a belligerence in me, like yeast in dough. Anger infiltrates every fiber in my body, tipping me mentally off balance. Worthlessness is already deep-rooted. The indelible marks of unconscious shame are branded, event by event compounding the guilt I feel. I am traumatized by each horrific, unforgiveable event that haunts me into my adulthood.

Toodle was everything that love and respect represent in the scriptures, while home was stained by an oppressive, degrading family culture. I witnessed Toodle's forgiveness, peaceful wisdom and resilience. When her puppies died, she showed me how to accept and climb above oppression. One must move forward to survive. Dwelling steals the present and stalls life. We must live for the living. This is what I saw in her. I didn't then possess her inner strength. But I recognized that I needed what she had. Her tender kindness and sensitivity remain rock solid, serving as a great example to me. She accepted me when my family did not. Being with her grounded me and gave me a sense of belonging.

My Safe Zone

Trying to shake off the horror, burying the live puppies, instinctively, I disappear with Toodle down the cow lane toward the weather-beaten pine tree in the middle of the pasture. It's where we go every day to hide in peace and rebalance our inner selves. We find safety and solitude in nature, and regain our interconnectedness with the universe. It is as far away as I can go for now.

Toodle rests at the base of the tree with her paws crossed, her head down. Her love is pure, patient, and asks nothing in return. Scorekeeping is an unknown to her. We comfort one another; she more than I gives support. She embraces and absorbs my emotional and psychological discord. There was no understanding then of what a therapy dog was, but that's the role she served for me.

Climbing to the highest branch facing the westerly zephyr, I sit there most of the day, gazing out, wondering where life is headed. Envisioning a lifetime of hopelessness and despair, I mindlessly go through the motions, unhappy as depression gains ground. Mistrusting my feelings, I grieve the loss of my innocence, not knowing why. Who am I? My identity lay in the shadows, evaporating in the distance. I had been propelled into a hostile world.

Why did I deserve this? Why didn't I deserve the same kind of care, protection, and acceptance that Toodle gave her puppies? Despite the abuse she got from Dad, she instinctively knew nurturing. What did her mother teach her as a puppy? Contrasting myself to Toodle raised questions of about her understanding of life and how it was different from mine. What grounded her and kept her strong? How did she know to care for her puppies and survive their loss? Love was innate to her but not to me. We were honest, safe, and caring with each other. Toodle demonstrated love to me.

God makes me feel safe. He doesn't judge or criticize me. He doesn't own a scoreboard. I can talk to Him like an imaginary friend. Sometimes He answers, and I hear Him gently whisper. I sense His constant presence. A child of God, I am transparent in His eyes. Today, I vent my anger at God while sitting in the tree. Distraught, frustrated, and unhinged, sobbing uncontrollably, I cry out, "Take me back to heaven. I don't want to live here. Why did you put me here? What did I do wrong? This had to be a mistake. It's not fun.

"I'm not supposed tell, but, God, my daddy made me kill Toodle's puppies by burying them alive while she watched. I heard them crying in the gunnysack. They were scared, and so was I. I now am waking and crying from nightmares, hearing their screams, seeing them underground, gasping. How can Toodle forgive me for that? Would Daddy bury me alive too? I told Daddy no and he yelled at me. He slapped me hard across my face, slamming the shovel into the ground, wrapping my resistant fist around it, making me dig a hole, while he stood over me with arms folded and a laser stare, watching. I didn't want to do it. He told me to 'shut up' and 'buck up' and forget about it. He threatened me, I better not tell anybody or I was in big trouble. You can't tell him I told you. Promise!

"Something else, God. He allowed his friend to play with my privates and never protected me. Ma was really mad. Does that mean he was okay with that man touching me? Another thing, God. I heard him say he would rather have a boy than me. He doesn't want me. I'm not good enough. Please don't tell Daddy I told you.

"There's still more, God. My mommy is always jittery, having panic attacks, ready to spring, and gasping for air trying to keep everybody happy. She chokes on her food at suppertime. She covers up for Daddy, pretending she is happy and everything is hunky-dory in the family. It's not! Nobody is happy.

"Mommy is always crying and yelling when anybody has 'the dirty look'—the head lowered with a cold sideward stare and silent treatment. She lets my sister get away with her teasing, name-calling, and cruel tricks, so my sister thinks it's okay. Then I get beat up worse. My sister's words hurt when she calls me a dummy. She taunts me, saying, 'You're stupid and fat,' 'Get out of my way,' and 'You're pathetic.' I feel like she wishes I were dead every time she stomps out of the room. Sometimes, I do too. God, you are the only one besides Toodle I can talk to and feel safe. I'm scared, God, help me. I want to come home to heaven and live with you. I don't belong on earth.

"In church, the preacher pounds the pulpit, yelling that we are bad people. Sinners, he calls us. He says we are to fear You. Is that true, God? Why am I here, God? I feel so worthless, hopeless, and unwanted. Help me, God!"

My conversation with God is interrupted. In the distance, I hear my father call, "Toodle, Toodle, come!" Fear wells up in me just hearing his voice. It is time to herd the cows. She looks up at me asking if it's okay. Will I be alright?

"It's all right, go home." I am staying. Obediently and fearfully, she scurries up the cow lane to my dad.

There is no one calling for me. I sit in the tree until it's dark. I am curious if anyone cares enough to look for me. Ma finally comes with a flashlight near sundown.

"What are you doing up there?" She's upset. She doesn't understand why I am hiding. There's her disconnect, acting as if everything is normal and it's not.

"I wanted to find out if anyone cares about me." My response makes her sad. But it's the truth.

"Come down and let's walk home together." She holds my hand as we walk up the cow lane. Though I'm angry and crying, I feel a sense of compassion and belonging. I sense her love and empathy. Beneath her shame and fear resides wisdom, a glimmer of nurturing, faith, and common sense about life—many of Toodle's same qualities. Those virtues begin to blend in me.

Ma is always on hyper alert and refereeing the emotionally incessant brushfires. Sometimes the atmosphere parallels a storm cycle. First the long, cold silence, then the drop in barometric pressure as the dark clouds roll in, followed by a dirty look and stare-down that rivets the room. Lightning strikes, igniting an argument. After the minimizing and blame, the clouds clear for a brief truce that gives way for no good reason, and the chaos recycles.

Ma dances between fear and surrender as the go-between who cools the fires that burn inside us. Harmony is nonexistent. Divisiveness is constantly fanned.

Dad's strikes are torturous acts toward the powerless animals. Ma is the opposite. She cares for the animals. But she turns a blind eye, as he bludgeons and bullwhips the cows into submission and when he pours lye on the genitals of stray male dogs while he laughs as they scream, running across the hay field in excruciating pain.

Acts like this are not in my nature. Compassion is. The animals are my teachers. They stand by me. They inspire me with their courage and resilience. Following in Pa's footsteps is out of the question. I gravitate toward the likeness of my mother mirroring the role she lives, acquiring her emotional patterns.

Gaslighting

Sis is a duplication of Pa's behavior. A bully, targeting the powerless and preying on my innocent trust. She takes pleasure in maliciously pulling pranks and following them with beguiling laughter that she knows will crush me.

She usually pounces when no one is looking. My sister's condescending nature strikes me to the core. It's my word against hers, and my parents see her as faultless, which emboldens her. Sis knows she has the hammer over Ma and Pa. They dance to her demands, tipping the scale in her favor. Ma is unable to discipline her out of fear of Pa's reprimands. She shrivels, buttons her lip, and avoids what is morally right. This convoluted pattern matches the one by which she covers up dad's savage behavior.

Sis dares me at the age of five or six to lie down on an old cement foundation barely above ground in the manure yard. Barefoot, innocently trusting, I take the challenge. Out pours an entire swarm of ground bees attacking me. She stands there belly laughing heartlessly as I run away screaming chased by stinging bees. She takes pleasure menacing. She relishes in put-downs, ramming psychological wounds into my soul. I am betrayed. My ability to trust is demolished. Her words and the anger behind them decimate me while her turned-up nose and superior attitude bolster her ego. Her own shame is so ingrown, she doesn't see it in herself. Yet it controls her. She is its prisoner.

Her tantrums that send me away, cowering in fear for cover, cornered in a fetal position, trembling as she towers over me, saying, "Shut up, cry-baby. Get over it, dummy. You're pathetic. Get out of my way, fatty-fatty. You're nothing. You deserve to be alone." Her condescension gouges me. Usually what comes from the mouth is in the heart. Talk like this leads me to believe what I hear. It forms my identity.

The thought of leaving this place is undeniable. Every direction I turn is fraught with discord and dissension. This is not a place I want to be. Safety, the sense of belonging, and love are lacking. My soul cannot thrive here. Suffocating, it will die. This is not who I am. Life should be more than this, and it's up to me to manifest it. Not yet ten years old, I lack the life skills to strike out on my own. I feel like I am handcuffed to the farm.

The old farmhouse has an enclosed three-season porch. From the outside, it looks like a lean-to. It's today's mudroom where the stinky, manure-covered barn clothes hang and that also serves as a pantry. The linoleum is timeworn, exposing the wooden floor. Ma comes home for lunch and Dad is sitting at the kitchen table looking out the window. It's summer. Sis starts taunting me. "Fatty, fatty two-by-four, can't get through the kitchen door. Ha ha ha!"

I can't take it anymore. Malignant rage takes control. I put my head down and charge, striking her in the gut, then pound her with my fists and wrestle her to the floor. I straddle her with my legs around her, my hands on her throat with my thumbs pushing into her trachea as I bang her head up and down. I'm going to kill her. We screech like two tomcats. Her thrashing ruckus finally brings Ma stomping from the kitchen to stop the fight. Her panicking voice like ricocheting shrapnel, "Get off of her," she screams. "What are you doing?" My head is pounding. Adrenaline is roiling through my body. My mother's frantic reaction chisels blame deeper in my core. Coming to my senses, I realize my death grip nearly kills my sister. I'm frightened. What caused me to go ballistic? Self-blame burns through me like a lightening bolt. My conscience tells me, "You cannot do this. It is wrong." I am a bad person. Releasing my hands and lifting myself up, I walk away distraught, sobbing, fearing retaliation, and wondering what would have happened if I killed her? Do they lock kids like me up forever? I figure I have no right to defend myself. I am supposed to take it. Let them walk all over me. Did Ma even notice my pent-up anger and understand my actions before this happened?

My sister pulls herself together, gets off the floor, upbraids, and with a joker's laugh and demonic side glance walks away, mocking me, "Gotcha! Ha! Ha!" Which reignites my fury. But my hands are tied, leaving me no emotional outlet, having to suck it up, again. I'm the scapegoat. She walks away inviolate and shielded.

I've learned it's easier to shut up, be a martyr, and avert an unwarranted reprisal. The message to her daughters is behave yourselves, try to get along, or shame on you. It's how Ma tries to keep peace. It's all she knows to do. Living emotionally and spiritually divided torments her. Torn knowing what is right and conflicted to please others is not who she is. Being conditioned, in her fearful mind, is forced.

The Cover-Up

My mother was raised in a conservative Norwegian home, in a culture where women were taught to be subservient to men. The success of the marriage is on the wife's accepting her husband's dominion. If she doesn't, she is blamed for a failed marriage.

The scriptural verse where wives submit to their husbands was taken literally and out of context. The verse meant equality, respect, and honor; not male dominance and disrespect. Where the man rules the house and provides for the family. The woman is the homemaker. Ma endured the burden of fulfilling the roles of both homemaker and breadwinner.

When Ma first meets my dad, she is pure, innocent, trusting, and sheltered, which makes her an easy target. She has the bluest eyes that are soft and kind. He floods her with charming chivalry. His jokes make her laugh. She trusts him and responds to his attentiveness. He has her believing he's a good man. He is wooing her, and she succumbs to lust. He takes her virginity.

At twenty-seven years old, she is pregnant. He has another wife and a son. Ma's parents hold him responsible to do the honorable thing and marry her. She is beholden to her father. She bends over backward to the relatives in Dad's defense, putting out hostile fires in hopes that everybody will be happy. But Dad screws up all the good she creates. She holds the marriage together and tries to hide the shame from Sis and me. Failure is not in Ma.

Ma is loving and compassionate. She means well. In her heart I believe she is determined to change who Dad is, and at all costs she hangs in the marriage however difficult. She is the glue holding our family together.

Her purpose is raising Christian girls. We learn her value system by watching the way she responds to life that is filled with anguish. Every day she is confronting a home reeking of sarcasm, criticism, accusations, jealousy, arguing, finger-pointing, silent treatment, slamming doors, and yelling. It drains her.

There is no coming together in unity. Rather than helping one another, we are retreating and ducking, it's each person for themselves. We occasionally stick our heads out for an all-clear signal but heated verbal potshot missiles reload to take aim for another go round. Dad rips at anything that is wholesome. If he isn't happy, no one else can be. The same is true for my sister. Together they verbally destroy Ma's good intentions.

Ma is a master at multitasking, baking, canning, never missing a birthday or holiday, inviting relatives over for dinner, volunteering at church.

The homemaker skills I learn at a very early age—baking, cooking, sewing my own clothes—come from Ma as I work beside her. I shadow her as she volunteers with the Ladies Aid in church for the funerals or weddings. My sister wants no part of serving others. It is Ma's quiet support that keeps my flame alive. Hungry, learning new things, and finding the fun of exploring new ideas, meeting new people, helps me socially. I'm like the curious puppy who follows her nose yet doesn't watch where I'm going in a brand-new world, bumping into walls.

Ma keeps the farm afloat, which is always in the red, borrowing money to cover loans, making sure cows are bred on time, cooking for thrashing crews. She is constantly overcompensating, outperforming, trying to be all things to everyone. She works herself into the ground and loses herself for the sake of others. She miscalculates in going to great lengths to make things normal when normal doesn't exist.

Through it all, she lights up with a smile. Yet she is drawn and tired on the inside. Holding a light in her heart is a challenge.

Every day, she's on the brink of a nervous breakdown. During meals, cold silence prevails, causing my mother to suffer panic attacks. Gasping, and hyperventilating, trying to breathe, she flings herself away from the supper table. The feet of her chair skid across the floor.

My body still remembers her fighting for breath. I see the light in her eyes dimming. My dad simply looks away. He keeps eating, with his face in the plate, as if nothing is happening. My sister serves up powerfully painful words. "Why don't you just knock it off? You're spineless," she admonishes Ma. Maybe it is retribution for how she was conceived. She marginalizes Ma's lustful act, twisting the knife while she feels self-righteous.

Our unspoken conversations are meatier than those spoken. My father and sister, their angry eyes glaring in disgust at Ma, appear to me to be shoveling food in their mouths like vultures at a feeding frenzy. The message is "Shut up, keep your head down, and eat your food." If I look up, the first words are, "What are you looking at? Who do you think you are?"

Being emotionally battered takes a toll. Ma's gut twists. There is no recess to down regulate her stress hormones and protect her immune system. She is seeing the doctor for bleeding rectal piles, painful constipation, and bloody diarrhea. Daily, she self-administered enemas and was embarrassed.

My sister mocks her maladies, saying, "Ah, she's on the douche bag again." Self-consciously, Ma dreads the frequent bathroom visits, but her body is breaking and she can't stop it. Sister purposely stands outside the bathroom door, waiting for the moment Ma releases explosive gas and diarrhea, making fun of her bowel movements. "There she blows!" my sister bellows and then belly laughs. Ma cries from pain and the sight of all that blood in the toilet. Mentally paralyzed, instinct tells her where this is leading.

I feel Ma's fear, and my body internalizes her emotional agony.

Ma's Gift

Her fortitude comes from God. Her being begs to be held and runs to the arms of the divine for comfort and safety. It is her refuge and stability through struggle. It's where her smile rises. Despite what she endures, she is keenly aware it is God's grace and mercy sustaining her.

Despite the hostile conditions, every meal begins with prayer. I admire her resilience and have acquired that virtue from her. She carries an inner strength in whatever she does that connects her to a higher power. Faith is her stronghold.

Gospel music gives her soul a voice. It keeps her creativity alive. She has a natural gift of singing and playing music by ear on the piano and the mandolin. My piano lessons are bonding time we share. She plays the left hand, I play the right. We laugh when we nail it. These are the times I feel most connected heart to heart and love being with her. She is beautiful from the inside out. She demonstrates how to redirect and mentally escape reality. I still smile, reflecting on those moments. I hear those old gospel songs she sang and tears wash over me.

My sister's true colors peak with glaring anger and jealousy at seeing our joyful bond. Ma lost control of her at birth. Sis hates sharing. When

I was born, she felt cheated of her fair share, and that is her prevailing theme on most things.

Ma's personal conviction, every morning and evening, is for us to gather in a room off from the dining room where she reads the Bible and prays with her daughters before school. She wants us to love the Bible and God, and to live by God's authority. It is her tool, countering Dad's influence and how he was raised, to enable us to live by faith, with sound values, life skills, and morals, and to make good decisions. She takes a stance in her spiritual life to walk her talk. Committed to raise her family right, she's railroaded all too often, but her faith safeguards against each blow.

She sends us with other churchgoing couples to Sunday school. There's a mix of six in my grade. Mostly farm kids dressed in our Sunday best, sitting on the floor in a circle. The teacher begins with a prayer. "Dear Lord Jesus, as these innocent children listen to your lesson, may they understand they are never alone, knowing the value they have in relation to the world around them. Knowing the light within them upholds them against life's struggles. Thank you, Lord. We are grateful for your love and mercy you provide. In Jesus' name, Amen.

"We are going to start with a song this morning and it's called, 'This Little Light of Mine.' How many know the song and want a candle to hold?"

The children wave their hands. "I do, I do."

"Let's pretend I have the big lit candle that represents God and I tip my candle to light yours."

There are giggles as the children stretch out the candle to the teacher.

She says, "I want you to act this out and be proud of your light. Pretend you are the lit candle that shines in a dark room. Will you let anybody or anything blow out your light?"

All the children shake their heads. "Oh, no."

"Remember, children, God protects the light within you. He put His light and breath in you to shine in the darkness of this world. Wherever you are, God is walking with you and you are in His light. You are meant to be the light for others. Just think, children, how many candles God has in this world."

One child raises his hand and exclaims, "Wow, humongous! God has lots of glowing candles all over the world. Every person born is a child of God."

"Yes, and you are one of them. But God has the big flashlight for all of us to follow if we get lost."

Then we sing and pantomime the lyrics. "This little light of mine, I'm going to let it shine." We all raise the candle in the air. "Don't let Satan blow it out." We shake our heads no. "Hide it under a bushel—no." We try covering the candle with our hands. "This little light of mine, I'm going to let it shine."

Then the teacher asks, "What if your friend's candle isn't lit? What would you do?"

I raise my hand, "I'd give them some of my light."

"Exactly!"

The song seeds in me the courage to take a stand in what I believe and to help others along the way.

"Let's sing one verse of the song 'Jesus Loves Me' and then close in prayer. 'Jesus loves me this I know, for the Bible tells me so. They are weak, but He is strong. Yes, Jesus loves me! Yes, Jesus loves me! Yes, Jesus loves me! The Bible tells me so.'"

This song instills a quiet calm within me, so I feel safe.

"Let's close in prayer. Bow your heads and fold your hands and put a picture of Jesus in your mind.

"Dear Lord Jesus, we are grateful for these children you have blessed us with. We pray that their lights will forever shine as they bravely walk through life remembering today's lesson, never ashamed of their light, knowing you walk beside them granting them the courage to hold their light against the darkness of this world. Should they lose their way, it is you they turn to for guidance. We ask all this in your name. Amen."

Bible stories teach me to put my faith in Jesus and keep my light alive. I learn that all things are possible if we believe. The words come alive in my head, building me up, quieting the chatty critic that tears me down.

"We are to love one another." What does love feel like? The teachings in the church slam up against what is happening at home. Yet they have introduced to me to the idea that another kinder life exists outside the farm and my family. Not all places are like my home and not all people are like my family.

Religion conflicts my thinking. In church I am still pummeled with messages telling me I am a bad person. The preacher pounds the pulpit like it's a revival meeting, yelling we are to fear God and we must repent because we are sinners. The spiritual aspect then was far above my understanding.

Sitting in the pew with Ma, I'm dressed in a pretty plaid skirt with a can-can underskirt and blouse. My hair is combed from the overnight pin-curls and my feet have white ankle socks strapped in shiny black patent-leather shoes that I raised up on the back of the pew, rebelliously shuffling them back and forth to block out the sermon. I already feel downtrodden about myself. I don't need more shame. When I talk to God, I never feel afraid.

I also don't understand what it means to be born again. When the preacher calls for people to come to the front of the church to be saved and baptized, I go because I think it is the right thing to do. But I don't know what I was supposed to feel. I keep hearing I am never alone because God is always beside us with His Spirit. I already knew that. God is like Toodle. The difference is that when I hold Toodle, I talk and she listens. God, although unseen, is everywhere I am, but especially when I am up in the highest branch of the old pine tree closest to heaven, blending with nature. I feel His Holy Spirit wrapping His arms around me and I am safe.

Hope is nurtured through the songs we sing in Sunday school and the Bible verses I memorize that assure me all things are possible and Jesus loves me. It is also in the old pine tree and my life lived through the eyes of a dog.

I dream of being a ballerina. In my bedroom, I seeing myself, dancing freely on stage, floating gracefully to classical music crescendos and diminuendos and belonging to something greater than myself. The vision of a vast stage, magnificent gowns, drums, violins, clarinets, lights, and smoke rolling across the stage fills my senses. I secretly dance in my stocking feet, twirling and gliding along the floor, avoiding the creaky boards by the heat register so Ma doesn't hear me. I am expressing locked-up feelings that cry for release and won't be squelched. It is easier living outside myself than living within myself. It's where I go when life gets difficult. I am reaching for something that makes me happy, but doesn't satisfy the inner joy I crave. In my imagination I find freedom until Ma flings open the bedroom door, slamming it against the wall, hands on her hips, and scolds me. "Stop that! Dancing is a sin. Read your Bible. Get busy!" Smashed again! The whip is cracked. Dreaming is wrong. But tell me I can't and I will tell you I can. Taming me is not in the cards, rebellion is.

Singing! Yes, I will sing! By now, I belt out gospel hymns in the church choir and anywhere in the farm fields far from any criticism. The walks Toodle and I take the down the cow lane to the pasture offer me the liberty to sing at the top of my voice. I enjoy skipping, dancing, and playing with Toodle. She doesn't judge me. Ma can't see me dance. Dad doesn't care.

Coming of Age

The church opens my eyes to the fact that there are people who are kind and trustworthy and treat me with respect. It feels odd but nice and strengthens my intent to leave the farm and find the other side of life.

Becoming a woman compounds added emotional turmoil. My breasts are developing. Pimples erupt. My period begins. I'm eleven years old. What's happening to me?

Ma realizes puberty is blooming. It is time for the bra, girdle, nylons, and "the rags." She equips me with an elastic belt that clipped to old torn sheets used as rags, telling me how to assemble it. Washing the bloody rags is my job. She shows me how to put them between both hands as if they were on a scrub board. Nothing more was said.

The embarrassment my period causes affects my self-image. It reinforces the hiding, shame, and retreating. I'm hypersensitive and hypervigilant. Stress throws my super-system into overdrive.

During many menstrual cycles, blood clots roll out of me the size of a person's fist. I have all I can do during school to prevent blood from showing on my clothes and running down my legs. I wear black skirts to cover the stains.

My body is hemorrhaging. I lie for three days in my bedroom, bleeding, and running to the bathroom downstairs, leaving a trail of blood on the cracked wooden stairs. The toilet fills with large crimson clots, needing two flushes. On the fourth day, I am allowed to lie close to the bathroom. While rushing to it, I faint and fall to the floor. My head barely misses the glass corner of the dining room table. Ma comes to my aid, while my sister remains in the living room, watching TV. Ma rouses her. "Will you get in here and help me pick her up?"

"What's wrong now?" Everything for Sis is an annoyance." She's at it again, wishing I didn't exist. She's not getting the attention.

Ma calls the hospital. My parents carry me to the car, and we drive to the emergency room. The doctors administer three units of blood. More than half the blood in my body drained out. Lying in the hospital bed, I overhear the doctors say to my parents, "If you would have waited any longer, she'd be dead." For a split-second, I think: Well, it'd be better than living here and this could all be over, finally. I can escape this life and be home in Heaven where peace exists. But I guess God has another plan.

The dismissal from Dad and Sis leads me to conclude I am a nuisance. Then false guilt grips me: This is my fault because of the financial hardship I just caused. I've just added to Ma's problems.

There is no diagnosis for what felled me. Back then, stress was not considered part of the medical algorithm. Emotional issues were a hush-hush topic and not dealt with outside the confines of a mental institution.

Blood clots continued through my teen years. I believe my body needed an outlet from the emotional stress and suppression. Bleeding was a way of cleansing and letting down.

The verbal brow-beating was overpowering. When it isn't the words themselves, it's the tone and body language that bear down on me. Change is pushing its way up to the surface. I realize that as long as I live at home, I will never be safe. The only purpose I serve is being the brunt of somebody's prank or doing the heavy lifting of farm chores. There must be more to life than this. The bedrock of an escape plan for freedom is forming. It will take money, which I don't have.

The Strange Disappearance

One day coming home from grade school, Toodle isn't there to greet me.

"Where's Toodle?" I ask Dad. Ma's got her back turned to the kitchen sink as if she couldn't look me in the eye and face me. In her silence she knew what happened.

"Oh, she ran off and got hit by a car," Dad blurted.

I can't believe that. I search for Toodle. If a car hit her, I would see the spot where she died. It was never like her to be on the gravel road. Ma and Dad knowingly lied to me and stripped from me the one life that mattered. Both stole a piece of my heart. In my mind she attacked him and couldn't take it anymore. I understood how she felt.

Disposable, I believe Dad took her out behind the barn, then chained, shot, and buried her in the manure pile. Ruthless and cruel but normal for him. I miss Toodle and our time by the tree. With her gone, I have little reason to stay. She is telling me to find my way out: You can't stay here. Her soul is free of this place. I am holding on until I can escape this prison.

Self-Sufficient

Our farm presented a double-edged sword. Through hard work comes a solid work ethic. The farm holds no future for my personal growth. It's all about back work. It appears that any attempt to intellectually advance myself fuels disparagement. I feel trapped. Freedom is beyond the farm's walls and so are my eyes. Like a duckling readying to fly the nest, a driving force firing from within calls me to stretch my mind, set personal goals, be creative, and thrive.

A woman's employment opportunity is keyholed. We can be book-keepers, teachers, nurses, or housewives barefoot and pregnant. Pregnancy is not in my future, ever. Money and freedom come from the nose to the grindstone and a good education. I must figure out how to put the three together.

Evenings, weekends, and for two summers, I have a job doing child care for two church families. I experience their family cultures, how they respect each other, hug one another, and sincerely say, "I love you." They welcome me as part of their family, giving me a sense of belonging. Their polite caring tone of voice matches their open body language. They build one another up. They willingly offer to help each other. Arguing and yelling are rare. There is no name-calling. It's strange for me. Earning money and being valued feels refreshing. I save the money I earn to buy a car someday and leave the farm.

One family gives me a book by Norman Vincent Peale, *The Power of Positive Thinking*. Aside from the Bible, this is the book that has the greatest influence on my life. The optimism in it, is the catalyst that shifts my thinking to believing in myself. I can see myself being valued and worthy. The book bolsters my self-confidence.

I keep it hidden from Ma. The only acceptable books are the Bible and those for school work. Besides, reading for pleasure means you have time when you should be doing farm chores.

"I can do all things through Christ who strengthens me," is a Bible verse quoted in *The Power of Positive Thinking*. It anchors me. The key is truly believing. I must find a way to believe in myself even though my family doesn't.

I have enough common sense to know I am not making enough money to support myself, so I am not prepared to strike out on my own. But the day is coming where I will leave. My future is in my hands.

Dad's words to me as a child, "Buck up, kid," become my bootstrap. I felt I was the one member of my family most likely to escape. Ma, Dad, and Sis succumbed to the anger and shame. They were imprisoned and permitted their past to take them down. But for me to forge ahead naively ill-prepared for life, to dive head first into an unknown with no forethought of the obstacles would be suicidal. Ma accuses me of being too brave and taking too many risks, of lacking good judgment. Many times, she is right.

Underneath Ma's entrenchment, she encourages me to grow socially, intellectually, and culturally. I appreciate her intelligence and commitment to widening my view of life. Her encouragement is her way of loving me. Her benevolence through adversity is my beacon.

Ma pushes me when I express interest going to Bible camp for a week, being part of the church youth gatherings, joining 4-H, taking music lessons, being a member of the church and school choirs, even entering local beauty contests. I often wonder why she spurs me and not my sister. Is it her way of manifesting in me what she wanted for herself? Maybe, like a mother bird and her first fledging wanting to fly, she supports my courage to leave the nest, to take risks. She sees the survivor in me and fosters those qualities.

It's Cancer

Mother's choking episodes terrified me. I didn't know if she was choking to death before my eyes. I felt her emotional suffocation but feared saying anything. As the severity of her panic attacks increased, my dad and sister refuse to help her. I would grab my mother's shoulders and face her toward me, trying to calm her. I patted her on the back, I wanted her to redirect her focus and release any food trapped in her throat.

"Ma, look at me! Just look at me and slow your breathing. Calm down. Drink some water."

I asked my dad, "Why aren't you helping her?" My words and actions challenged the norm. This was unforgiveable.

Ma conceals the doctor's findings out of shame and fear, which gnawed at her organs. Suffering alone, her mind spiraled out of control. The bleeding piles were diagnosed as inflammatory bowel disease. Her intestines were ulcerated and painful. Her anxiety attacks triggered rectal tenesmus, causing severe bloody diarrhea. Her inner fiber was host to a chain reaction, increasing her embarrassment, shredding her identity and self-worth. She was too young to be incontinent but that's the direction her body was going, and she couldn't stop it.

Dad treats Ma as his property. A woman is to bend over, shut up, and take it, enabling the man to have his way whenever and however he wants it. Dad asserts territorial control and ownership by going up her skirt, ramming his middle finger up her vagina, goosing her from behind, grabbing her rump, twisting her nipple. He laughs as if it was a cute way to behave. Showing us that it is okay to be disrespected and take it. Ma is humiliated. She blushes. I cringe. My body internalizes the scene as if I am being raped all over again by him.

Get Me Out of Here

Book learning is for sissies. Sweat of the brow is the priority. Acquiring a higher education is frowned upon, particularly for a woman. Besides, going beyond high school cost money and the farm operates in the red. Grandpa's words to me at a very early age were, "Women don't need learn to read." But I'm aiming for a four-year degree and bucking their norm. A higher education symbolizes monetary success, a good-paying job, personal freedom, status, and my ride out of here. Paying for it is up to me.

At the end of my sophomore year in high school, I pay $600 cash for my first car and carry all expenses. This is a first step to leaving.

A local restaurant needs waitresses. Working for a dollar an hour after school and until closing on weekends. Earning good tips was step two. Tips were an incentive to provide outstanding customer service, meet the public, and sell items on the menu. Learning how a business operates ignited in me the drive to excel. Working away from home, off the farm, with the public was uplifting.

My teachers categorize me as having an impaired IQ due to my odd, backward, and shy behavior. I am often afraid to ask for help because doing that at home was deemed stupid. I sometimes still see myself as just a stinky farm kid who belongs in the back of the room out of sight. Reading and comprehension are always a challenge. Ma never has time to help me. My English and math grades suffer. Asking my mother for help makes me feel like a nuisance. So I don't bother, and am left alone to figure things out myself, which causes me to stumble, leaving gaps in my education.

The combination of my sister's tantrums and the cranked-up TV made concentrating on my homework nearly impossible. When I ask her to turn down the sound, she slams the newspaper on the glass coffee table, stomps through the dining room, rattling the glassware in the china hutch. Then she kicks the door shut. In the kitchen she bullies Ma. My body recoils. This is my fault.

Sis gets straight "A"s in English and math. It comes easy for her. She can pound out a hundred words a minute from a manual typewriter. I can't do thirty. She rubs my nose in the dirt for being an idiot.

English literature, sentence structure, and grammar stump me. I struggle to write book summaries, which are barely good enough for a passing grade. Understanding the main idea and interpreting the story's meaning go right past me.

But there are a few writers whose words resonate with me. Emerson and Thoreau make me think of the times in the pine tree where the world stops spinning and calm settles my mind. Their writings put me back in nature. They give me vision and purpose.

"The greatest glory in living lies not in never falling, but in rising every time we fall," Emerson wrote. Like the optimism of Norman Vincent Peale, Emerson's advice inspires me to optimistically persevere. It instilled hope.

Emerson also said, "Do not go where the path may lead, go instead where there is no path and leave a trail." That's how I see myself, blazing a trail right off the family farm, striving for a higher education.

Thoreau said, "If one advances confidently in the direction of his dreams, and endeavors to live the life which he has imagined, he will meet with a success unexpected in common hours." For me, this means standing on my own, holding onto my dreams of leaving the farm and going to college. It means keep on keeping on.

These quotations tell me I've been fed lies, and my soul whispers, "You're smarter than this." Staying in remedial classes is not going to get me into college. Good grades will. Stirring in me is a righteous indignation to prove my intelligence, to rise above the remedial group they put me in.

No one was *ever* going to call me a dummy again! Being brainy gets you ahead.

Taking a stand, I set out to convince the high school counselor to let me try taking a higher-level sociology class, and he agrees. The results from my IQ test are above average. I'm not a dummy, just like my soul said.

After locking myself in my bedroom, muffling the downstairs chaos, and studying tenaciously, I become high functioning for the last two years in high school and graduate with a 3.5 grade average.

Outperforming was born, driven by spunk and admittedly selfish ambition. I learned people valued me for my outside accomplishment versus the shame-induced person inside. Admission to college was possible. My plan was working.

The Leech

The second semester of my senior school year, one of my classmates was smitten with me. Galen stalked me in the hallways. Dodging him between classes was impossible. He prowled persistently, lurking at my every turn, stopping me, always in my face. We rode the same school bus. I felt cornered. His overbearing nature sparked fear in me. My reaction was to bolt for safety. He hunted me down. Then one summer evening, he rode his motorcycle to the farm with the intent of asking me for a date. Ma didn't know what he was doing to me in school.

Running upstairs to hide, I told Ma, "I don't want to see him. Get him out of here." I was half way up the staircase when Ma demanded I see him.

"Listen to me, you need to be kind to him," she said. Rather than reply, I realized it would be easier to remain silent and obey my mother who had commanded me into the jaws of a predator. I stood in front of him with my arms crossed.

"Can I take you for a motorcycle ride tonight?" he asked in a jittery voice.

"Yah, I guess it's okay," I replied though my gut said, "No."

Like Ma, I manage to keep an open heart looking for the good in him. After several dates, I gave in, assuming he was honorable and kind.

Galen was raised in a home where he protected his mother from his father, Harold. Doris was a sweet but frail God-fearing woman, married to an abusive, overbearing alcoholic who verbally and physically abused her. She was a housebound woman who was never allowed to drive. She suffered from arthritis, panic attacks, and scoliosis. Fear and tears filled her days. Doris was at this man's mercy, begging for any social contact.

Tending to her vegetable-and-flower garden in the summer gave her peace. It was a way she connected with herself. Companionship came from her three cats, a calico, a gray, and a yellow-striped tom.

She was this man's minion. He was an unkempt bully and a monstrous, burly barbarian with huge, callused hands scratching at cooties in his crotch. He rarely shaved or bathed. His front teeth were missing. He worked as a welder on construction sites. His overalls were covered with grease. He was of German-Jewish descent and carried deep hatred when speaking about Auschwitz, the war, and politics. He detested laughter. He flinched when touched. Any loving expression set off violent outbursts.

In the winter, the house was heated by a single kitchen oil stove.

The bedroom closest to the heat was his. Doris slept upright in a living room recliner. She read her Bible with a small lamp light beside her chair. It brought her peace and inner strength. It's how she endured.

She and her son Galen attended the Missouri Synod Lutheran Church. With Harold's permission, Doris volunteered helping at funerals and weddings. Harold was an atheist. Galen waffled between belief in God and nonbelief.

His father's gruff voice spewed curses from a snus-juiced mouth. His black eyes sliced right through you, staring you down. Evil lived inside him. He always had the final word and made it very clear he was right, using finger-pointing in the face, to put his point across.

He'd pull in the driveway any hour of the day from a job site. Before the house door opened, the cats bolted for safety. The door slammed behind him. Darkness penetrated every nook and cranny of a savage home.

He demanded Galen call him "Father" and bow to him. Reaching for his belt riveted fear. Threatening a whipping was second nature. If his supper was one minute after five o'clock, his bull rage erupted. Doris covered her head with her hands, cowering to protect herself. The black-and-blue marks on her face was his hand stamp. He hit her often.

The supper table mirrored my home. Shut up and eat. Tread lightly or else. Doris managed to say a prayer like Ma for the meal. Dismissing her, hovering disgustingly over his dish like a dog, he dug right in with a fist wrapping the fork, shoveling, and chomping on his food. He ripped off a hunk of fresh homemade bread from his side tobacco-stained teeth. Because his front teeth were missing. He slurped black coffee and beer and used the back of his flannel sleeve to wipe the snot and drool from his nose and mouth.

If an unknown car drove in the yard during supper, he hauled out his loaded slide-action shotgun by the door, cocked it one-handed, and walked outside to the farmhouse stoop to meet whoever had dared to come by. He'd then snarl, "What do ya want?" or "Get the hell out of here." My dad acted much the same way if a salesman drove on the property.

In comparison, this was even more violent than my home, it was also just more of the same in a different household. But I never saw Galen to be like his father. I trusted the side he showed me in the gentle way he protected and cared for his mother. The more attention Galen showed me, the more I liked it. I zeroed in on the good while sifting out his brash boldness. He was charming and convinced me he was a good person. I began to see him more as a life partner. He was a strong male, energetic and gutsy. Aiming to be a self-starter, he signed up for the Naval Reserve. Like me, he was interested in advancing his education. We had a common goal. Like me, he couldn't wait to leave home.

Yet I never connected how his upbringing had imprinted him, how maltreatment was passed down a generation to him. I didn't know what a narcissist Galen was. He drank and had a raw, arrogant mouth. I thought he was more balanced than he actually was. He had lofty goals, an entrepreneurial mindset, and an interest in marketing, but he was attracted to pie-in-the-sky, get-rich-quick proposals, and pyramid schemes. He glommed on to grandiose money scams. Having witnessed how Ma filtered Dad's bad, demoralizing behavior, how she steadfastly overlooked so much and stood by her man, I did the same.

Self-Preservation

Our relationship is intimate and serious. The backseat of his Ford Galaxy rocks during date night and not to the tunes. Tension between our families escalates. Silence be gone! My rebelliousness, intolerance, resentment, defiance, and disrespect grow into intolerance. Deviously, I see Galen as my escape route.

My parents' worst fears are surfacing, that their daughter is promiscuous, like they were. Will this be another pregnancy out of wedlock?

Many nights, at three and four in the morning, sneaking in barefoot, shoes in hand, tiptoeing into a dark farmhouse hoping everyone is asleep. I'm caught. A flashlight blinds me. Ma is waiting at the kitchen table, hyperventilating in a full-blown panic attack. The interrogation and yelling begin. "Sit down! What are you doing until this time of the morning?" "Where have you been?" "What's that black mark on your neck?" "What else have you been doing?" "Look at you, you are a mess!" "Shame on you." "Are you pregnant?" By now it was 4:30 a.m., time for milking. Dad's footsteps reverberate, sending terror through me. He's coming down the stairs. He pours his coffee and walks, letting Ma handle me. He shakes his head in disgust as he sits down at the kitchen table. In the cold silent treatment, his body speaks what his mind and heart feel. I am such a disgusting disappointment. Every nerve in my body tingles feeling the shame rapid-firing at me. How dare I—a wayward, sinful daughter, bad seed—How could I do this to them?

Every encounter like this pushes me into Galen's arms. The longer we date, the more disdain they direct toward him. Mounting her high horse, my sister pits me against my parents, yet again making herself out to be the good girl. "See, she doesn't care about you or what you say. She hates you both. I'd never do that!" Her manipulation spikes an internal rage in me.

Each vitriolic attack is oxygen-welding Galen and me together, bonding us while dividing our families. Shame had us clinging to each other.

Defiantly, Galen and I team up against my parents. Vindictively, I give in to my curiosity to uncover in the attic the chest which has been off limits to me as a child. It's time for me and the world around us to find out. Without rousing suspicion, I make this my secret mission.

Opening the chest reveals a photograph of a military man. It looks like my dad, but from what I was told, he was never in the military. Digging further I come upon my parents' love letters. I also discover Dad has a son and was once married. Dad kept his son's letters. I kneel by the chest and connive how I can use these letters to wreak revenge.

More rummaging reveals that my sister is an "oops" out of wedlock child. There it is, the family disgrace and apparently it happened while Dad was getting a divorce. My mother had an affair with a married man who had a son, and I have a brother I never got to know. Cheated! Betrayed! In the community where everybody knows everybody, this hidden history information could be the stick in the eye. The timing isn't right to play my hand. I know inflicting more pain and embarrassment for Ma is wrong. So is the moral outrage revenge leaves in its wake.

Grief, loneliness, fear, and pain overshadow Ma's life. Along with her failing health as her disease spreads rapidly, she mourns the loss of her parents, a brother, and his wife. The rope's end frays, leaving her little hope to hang onto. Her life source is dimming. An already frayed support system is breaking. With nowhere to turn for help, hopelessness bores a deeper hole in her.

Grandma was her confidante and is now gone. On her own, sick and alone, she dared not talk to other church ladies who might think badly of her. She's always worried what people thought of her. Her life is fractured and emotionally out of control. She compresses everything inside, suffering in silence. Reaching out for help is shameful. Lacking empathy, my father is in denial.

Cut Loose

I am employed after attending a two-year teachers college as a first-grade teacher in Northern Wisconsin and rooming above a honky-tonk bar with two colleagues. Music blares through the floor every night until 2:00 a.m. The jukebox looping Ray Price singing "Please Release Me" irritates me, but it also resonates with me. Thinking about it now, that song fit perfectly. Something dark had a hold of me. It shadowed me like a ball and chain around my ankles. I wanted to be free.

When I was growing up, drinking and smoking were taboo. I was on my own, going honky-tonking with the girls in a redneck country bar called the Highway Eight Saloon. Sneaky, nobody at home would ever know. The girls were out to let their hair down on a Friday night. They showed me how to be footloose and drink hard liquor, unwinding a tight-ass life and letting it rip. We'd strut up to the bar, dressed like floozies in short skirts, low-cut blouses, high heels, upswept hair, overdone makeup, and bangles, teasing the boys with a sassy Marilyn Monroe hip roll.

The smoke drifts in waves across the bar room. The smoke curls rise to the ceiling. Through the haze, on the wall behind the dimly lit pool table are a couple of staring buck deer heads and a bear skin. Every time somebody walks into the place, all the barstools swivel in unison. The guys are checking to see if it is friend or foe or a pickup. Most of them look like they haven't seen a razor or soap in years and crawled out of a hole in the backwoods.

We are eyed head to toe by the lineup of good ole boy drinkers cussing, laughing at their own lewd jokes, bobble-headed over their alcohol, shaking dice, harboring a chunk of Red Man in their cheeks, and seeing who could hit the spittoon for a free beer.

Elbowing our place at the end of the bar, the stools rotate again and all the rednecks simultaneously look our way. Suddenly, I feel like prey. One drunk dude spots me, stumbles off his stool, walking toward me with the "Hey, baby" look. The short hairs on the back of my neck spring straight up. His buddy grabs his manure-splattered overalls and yanks him back down on his stool. "Leave the bitch alone."

We are slamming shots and depth charges. I'm dizzy and slurring my words: "Bartender, I'll have what she's having and make it a double."

Marcia is nursing an Old Fashioned. "Hey Marcia, watch this." I giggle and gulp my cocktail like a bottle of pop, then smash the glass on the bar. "Fill 'er up!"

I am slaphappy drunk. Marcia wants to teach me to polka and schottische. Wobbly, I go on the dance floor with her. Once I have the hang of the steps, we both cut loose to the music. The boys at the bar whistle, stomp, clap, and hoot. The louder the hoots the more risqué I act. I am making a spectacle of myself and way too drunk to care. Here I was noticed.

The music stops and I am spinning. We sit down to have a double shot of straight Scotch. I throw it in the back of my throat, swallow, as it burns going down. I grimace.

"You want a drag off my smoke?" Charlotte asks.

"Sure, why not?" I choke from the smoke, which triggers nausea.

Charlotte and Marcia are watching how much of a fool I am making of myself.

I have no memory of how I got home that night. After staggering up the stairs, I passed out on the floor. When I woke up, I crawled to the bathroom. I kneeled and prayed I wasn't going to die. With my head in the thunder bowl, I vomited and wished I were dead. I lay in a fetal position on the floor between vomits. I vowed I would never drink like that again. Once was enough. After that, just thinking about sloe gin made me sick.

Feeling ashamed for my immoral actions even though my parents or Galen would never know about my drinking and smoking, I knew what I did was sneaky and considered wrong. I got away with it. Telling lies got easier every time I did it. I could sneak by without consequences by never admitting to my actions. The deception and dishonesty eroded away at my faith. Taking me further away from God.

Cultural Conditioning

Since Galen and I both held jobs and had dated for four years, the next logical step, according society's expectations, was marriage. It was part of my to-do list, along with the priority of finishing my education. Creating the American dream was out there. Marriage was fantasized with a *Leave it to Beaver* image. Superficially, we had no clue about what holds a marriage together. For now, it was vitriol and sexual gratification that melded us. Galen proposed and gave me an engagement ring. I say "yes" with one stipulation: I would finish my bachelor's degree in education after we married. He agreed.

"Are you pregnant? Do you have to get married?" was Ma's first response when I showed her the ring. She was imposing her shame on me reliving her experience.

"No, I'm not pregnant. I don't have to get married, but I want to, so I can cut all ties from this farm for good."

"He's Lutheran, not a born-again Christian. The Bible says it is a sin to be yoked to an unbeliever." The knife of guilt twists, with religion as the lever. Bad girl!

"I don't care, I'm doing this my way."

"Well, your dad is not going to be happy with this. Besides we don't have the money to pay for a wedding."

"Don't care what he thinks anymore. We're doing this. We'll pay for our own wedding even if I have to make my own dress and sew it myself."

Dad is milking the cows. He is stooped beside one of the Holsteins with his head shoved into her belly putting the milking machine on the teats. I see him glance up as he notices me coming.

"Hi, Dad, I have something to show you."

His anger builds. The milking rhythm stops. He glares. Fear rolls through me like an avalanche. I hold out my trembling hand, and he sees the diamond ring. Eyes of fire, he shakes his head in disgust. The cows bellow sensing his outrage. He walks past me and cranks up the radio. Mustering the courage, I stick the ring in his face, which gives me the satisfaction of standing in defiance of him.

Tables Turn

Our intention is to use the secret information from the chest in the attic as ammunition against my parents if they oppose our marriage. But I am afraid to betray Ma. "It will only hurt her," I tell Galen. I want to weasel out of revealing the papers I found.

"It's the only way," he says. "And your dad is a jerk. We're doing this whether you like it or not." I am overruled and pushed aside as he takes charge. My opinion doesn't matter to him.

Galen walks in the barn. He goes through the motions of asking my dad's approval for marriage.

I stay hidden in the background, watching over the first line of milking cows, and listening.

My father stands up, rigid and fuming. He walks toward Galen with a pitchfork in his hands. Dad's beady eyes are dark and embittered. He menacingly points his index finger in Galen's face. "You get your ass off this farm. Get the hell out of here. Don't you ever come back here again!"

"We're going to blackmail you. We're getting married whether you like it or not. She's mine now."

That infuriates my dad even more. He points the pitchfork at Galen, poised to impale him.

"Get your ass off this farm *now* before I stick this right through your guts."

Galen stands his ground "We know you have a grown son. You screwed her mother before you were married ending up with an 'oops' baby. We found the picture and the letters to prove it."

My fear and guilt are superseded with satisfaction. It is a liberating moment, knowing I am avenging Dad for all the crap he did to me, each vexatious action that had fed the anger inside me and caused me to fade God out of my life.

Between the two of us, Galen and me, we were going to raise the stakes higher. We planned to tighten the screws by contacting the Bureau of Statistics in Chicago for birth and divorce records. We intended to show the documentation to the church deacons.

"I'll pull the papers in the attic chest and the picture of my half-brother, plus the love letters and the boy's letters."

"Good, that will help. The picture is great proof. If they know we have this, they will back down. This is the last thing your mother wants exposed."

My heart knew this could destroy Ma. She didn't deserve it, but moving forward with our plan took precedence. The joint venture bonded us. Galen and I were malicious partners.

Ma is caught in the crossfire, refereeing between home and Galen's parents, trying to keep peace and minimizing the embarrassment. She wants to support me, but faces the wrath of my father.

Forging ahead, the wedding is conducted military style in the Lutheran Church. Dark energy overshadows the sanctuary. Sitting bitterly in the front aisle pew, hunched over and pulled in with arms and legs crossed, dad scowls and holds his head down. Ma demanded his presence for image purposes. The ceremony draws out the worst in him. His eyes feel like a blowtorch burning through my back and into my soul. My adrenaline kicks in feeling his venom.

The dressings of God are seen, but the heart of God is absent. Turning to the congregation after the vows, I fake the smile of a blissful bride. My husband and I proceed arm in arm down the aisle and rebuff Dad as if he doesn't exist. Hearts are filled with hatred. Acrimony splinters what should have been a joyful celebration. The damage we did to one another that day is reprehensible.

We rent a two-room upstairs apartment in Eau Claire. It will take me six months to finish my bachelor of science degree at the state university.

Carrying eighteen credits, holding three part-time jobs, working split shifts, on alternating days, I'm sleep-deprived and running myself to near collapse. I'm numb to soul's calling.

Just as my degree is accomplished, my plan begins to unravel. Galen's narcissism keeps getting him fired from retail sales jobs. He is pushy, aggressive, often in the customer's face, embellishing the products he pitches. He lies and is caught stealing.

Now I'm the breadwinner, following what Ma did, stepping up, and loading myself with greater responsibility.

Galen refuses to take menial, low-status jobs. They're beneath him. His grandiose idea was being the CEO for a large national car corporation. Getting unemployment checks justifies not working. He stays home drinking beer and watching TV.

Every day after I'm done with work, the conversation is the same.

"What have you done all day?"

"Nothing."

"Why didn't you make dinner or wash the dishes or do the laundry? You can help around here. Do I have to do it all?"

"Not my job. That's woman's work." Followed by, "When will dinner be ready? It's past five o'clock." His father's words resurface. They infuriate me. Berating each other is at the core of our marriage.

Trusting him with the joint checking account is a costly mistake. Galen turns into a controlling miser. My paycheck and the tips I earn are deposited in the joint account. He makes me practically beg him for money to buy groceries or a haircut, just like his mother did.

Verbal abuse spirals. Intimacy ends. Anger consumes us. Screaming matches and projectiles hitting the walls are a daily occurrence. The renter below us bangs on his ceiling, his way of asking us to keep the noise down. The volatile atmosphere that suffocated me on the farm has followed me here.

This is a repeat of my ma's life. How did this happen to me? My life is now a spitting image of hers. It's in me, controlling me, but submerged in my subconscious. The same is true for Galen. All the strong qualities I thought I saw in Galen were fallacies. Many of them matched my dad's. Like Ma, I denied the bad, pretending they were good qualities for the sake of self-preservation.

The comparison astounds me, falling for the same kind of man as Ma. I blame this on my own disobedience and rebellion. I kick myself, disrespect myself, for poor judgment, compounding the shame that shrouds me. My self-criticism runs amok in my head.

I must have been delusional, running away to find freedom and love. I have sacrificed myself as Ma did, and I am suffering the consequences. The farm is my shadow and my prison with every step taken. It's an unseen enemy, glued to me. It was all I knew then. I didn't escape.

God is nowhere to be felt. I am spiritually lost, reeling, never having time for God. Strife drowns out my soul's calling. Luckily, the scripture Ma planted in me is deep-rooted and remains my lifeline. Ma was wise that way, but she can't save me anymore. I now must save myself.

This time, there is no tree to run to or woods to walk in or dog to pet and hold. Venting comes via riding my bicycle to and from work, when I can burn off the oppressiveness of this marriage through physical exertion.

Education and work offer the only stability that rights me. I am determined not to let anyone mess me up. Headstrong, operating without anyone's help, building walls of isolation for self-preservation in a code-pendent relationship, my husband and I are islands in a sea of lost dreams.

Believing there is freedom in escaping into marriage was perfunctory. Stifled, I am living with a freeloader. Looking back at the mental prison that confines my parents and sister shocks me. But my new life is the same. My marriage is going down the tubes. I must rally and rise above it.

Sometime in the future the time will come when breaking free means a course correction. I vacillate between a very uncomfortable situation to one of being alone, adding insecurity and emotional discomfort. I will tough this out until the time comes when I can't. Then I will blaze a trail and take risks for personal growth. It won't be easy. It beats withering away.

Why be foolish enough to expose myself, face the scorn, the finger pointing, and the "I told you so" by admitting to my parents the marriage failed? It's my secret. I won't give my parents and sister the platform for ridicule, stark judgment, and malicious laughter to reduce me to ash. My survival demands tenacious determination and an insatiable will to put distance between what's ahead and my prior poor judgment while toughing it out to save face.

The Snowy Owl—God's Messenger

I can imagine Ma is sitting nervously, alone with her doctor, when he recommends removal of her rectum and the lower part of her large intestines. She has been sucker punched, Ma has cancer. She feels broken and shattered and believes all hope is stripped from her. As her mind races, knowing life is short, she draws inward, bearing the full weight in her heart, hoping no one will find out. She is consumed, laser-focused, as her mind races worrying about cancer.

At home, we ask how things went with the doctor. "Fine, everything is all right."

She is scheduled for surgery, and we learn its cancer. The disease is racing through her body, chewing her apart. Her physical and psychological pain escalates. Her modesty is compromised with the use of a stoma bag. Her femininity and identity are destroyed.

We are sworn to secrecy. Any discussion about her cancer to relatives or the church is off limits. The family lives another lie. Cancer is added to the other family skeletons, all submerged in denial and shame. Instead of pulling together for support, shame divides telling us to run to our corners, coping and suffering alone in silence, hidden, isolated, and emotionally paralyzed.

Ma's hope is anchored to the power of prayer and her faith. They are her strongholds. Through her suffering, she lives her testimony, for others to see the love of God in her, while being obedient to God's will. I see God's light in her. It's a gift she gave me and will sustain me.

Through her eyes and heart, her anguish and pain go deep inside me. In a house of islands, she is emotionally alone, bracing herself under cancer's weight. Dismissed by my father and sister, she and I sit together during the night hours in the dimly lit kitchen when sleep escapes her. Holding her, as she cries, I wipe her eyes and give her the comfort, compassionate support, and love she desperately needs. I wish I could change this for her and take the cancer away, but it's out of our control. Life's curveball isn't kind. God has a plan, but one I don't yet understand. She doesn't deserve her life to be stolen; she doesn't deserve the oppression she endures.

Her mind runs rampant. She is frightened about the future of the farm and her own demise. Her face is wet from tears. Sobbing, she asks, "How much time do I have before I die? What do I do with the life I have?" Her strength is diminishing, her body breaking from the inside out.

Daily, Dad notices the unusual appearance under Ma's bedroom window of the white owl sitting on the fence post behind the house. We don't understand the owl's rare presence. We hear its eerie hooting through the night.

Cancer's blow is deadly. Ma is dying. Yet the closer death's door approaches, the stronger her faith grows. Cancer is just another challenge that expands her faith. She faces cancer's sting of reality head-on, sustained by the words of Romans 14:8: "Whether we live or die, we are the Lord's." She humbles herself in full surrender, trusting completely her life and soul to God. Mental demons took her down into what evolved to be a full-blown disease. She lifts up her sorrow and grief, and hands it to God. The promise and gift for believers is eternal life in Heaven. Faith's resilience stabilizes her. One day she will be at peace.

My peace as a child was the pine tree. Ma sat at the piano, passionately singing and praising God. Seared in my brain is the vision of her there singing old-time gospel music of the Baptist hymnal. Transcendence replaces oppression. Sitting now on the sofa of the living room listening and watching her, I learn the value of having true faith in God. I hear the melody and words, "When peace like a river attends my way, when sorrows like sea billows roll; whatever my lot, thou hast taught me to say, 'It is well, it is well with my soul.'" In her dying days, Ma is luminous as God shines his light on her. Her blue eyes radiate love. Faith is her fortress. Faith grounds her. Faith is never a dress rehearsal. Faith is real. Ma's music gives voice to both the pain and gratitude inside her.

She is feeling the presence of angels gather around the piano, and a sightless hand of Christ on her shoulders reassures her. Heaven is waiting to receive her. Peace washes over her.

When she walks away from the piano, strengthened, she bears witness for me. Though she doesn't know what is happening in my marriage and life struggles, the words she sang teach me to grin and bear whatever the cost. Her belief in Christ's suffering the cross is small to her flesh. My test is living what she believed.

Reflecting on the mess of my marriage, I realize that she showed me life is hard and has painful hurdles. Life even with the best intentions may fall apart, and for me, it did. The lesson she drilled home was that strong faith will carry us through the worst of times. Maybe God used her to teach me how to go forward in life. I would come to trust that.

For the rest of the family it was the eerie calm before the storm. Ma held us together. Without her, the farm overwhelmed Pa. He couldn't do it alone. A decision was made to sell the farm. Ma always put others ahead of herself. Her final act of love was to buy my dad a house near my sister. Ma made sure he would never be homeless when she was gone. She knew that shortly after she was gone my sister would marry a farmer, and Dad could be cared for and watched over the rest of his life.

The death call comes. Ma is in the Marshfield hospital on her death bed. We drive to the hospital. The family gathers. Ma asks to speak with me alone. I stand beside her bed. She holds my hand one last time, looks me in the eye, and says, "I love you." Her final words were, "Always be kind to others and be of a pure heart. Please, try to get along with your sister."

She clung to God as a child clings to a mother's hand. God reached down and took her hand that day, long before her time. Her soul was free, cleansed, and forgiven. Her internal conflict ended. Faith carried her to the other side. Gone was the errie hoot of the snowy white owl. She was buried next to her parents. Her headstone read, "Whether we live or die, we are the Lord's."

Her work on earth was finished. She lived long enough to see me married and living independently. Although I developed poor life skills, Ma's wisdom instilled in me spiritual tools. Passing down spiritual behaviors is her legacy. Knowing her earthly presence was gone left me feeling empty and alone. Life was up to me. I was on my own. No support from my sister or father existed. Sis had Dad all to herself, while I was disenfranchised from the family. As hard as Ma tried pulling us together, the shame broke us apart. But Ma, through her spiritual transcendence, was home and at peace.

Rising Beyond

Waitressing was the financial bridge that supported me for nearly four years, but advancing myself through this job didn't seem possible. I needed to expand my work beyond earning tips. The purpose of the four-year degree was to position myself for greater opportunities, and that's what stirred inside me.

Cold turkey, stepping into selling straight commission life insurance was a frightening step. Initially, it didn't prove to be the best decision. All the money I earned was dependent upon my ability to sell and succeed interacting with the public. But I saw this as an opportunity, and the potential to make substantial money was the basis of my choice. It was difficult for me to introduce myself as someone who mattered, because inside I didn't feel like I did. But, it was reason to begin believing in myself.

While employed selling life insurance, a great income opportunity came to me in pharmaceutical sales. My college degree, experience as a teacher, sales and waitress experience, and work ethic from the farm were the foundation for a home run. The interview process was extensive. I appeared well-groomed, in a smartly tailored, tan business suit that made for a good first impression. Having a hunger attitude to succeed, portraying an air of confidence, an amiable personality, and willingness to take direction were paramount.

"Why do you want this job?" the regional sales manager asked during the final interview.

Sitting upright, looking him directly in the eyes, my feet firmly planted, respectfully leaning forward with open body and hand gestures, I replied, "Well, sir, I'm tired of working for less than $10,000 a year when I have a four-year degree and the ability to learn and work hard. I'm smart and I want this job. I promise I won't disappoint you, sir." If there was a tinge of desperation in my voice, it didn't matter.

With pursed lips he sat back, contemplatively silent, mulling my answer. He then sprung up from his chair, grabbed his coat, and said, with no frills, "Let's go to lunch and talk."

My shoulders tightened. Here I was, a country bumpkin flown on the company dime to Chicago being transported in a limo with the big boss to an upscale restaurant. I was totally out of my element and blown away by being given the royal treatment, respect, and lavish accoutrements. What is proper protocol here? Ma gave us lessons of etiquette, sophistication, and how to be a lady. This is where it would come into play.

The regional manager observed my manners and how I conducted myself in public. He sensed my tenacity and drive to succeed, though he didn't understand what was driving me. He was all about the bottom line and exceeding quotas.

Playing into his hand, I presented myself as having common sense, intelligence and poise, as well as being congenial, gracious, and worldly enough and malleable to adapt.

When lunch finished, he said quite simply: "Congratulations you're hired. Your district manager will be in contact with you to arrange your training and needed paperwork."

Appearing confident and calm, but underneath paddling like a giddy duck, ready to flap my wings, quack, and fly, I told myself: "Yes, nailed it, I can do this!" All my hard work striving for a good education was worth the struggle.

Smiling in humble gratitude, I confidently extended my hand. "Thank you, sir. I promise I will do my very best for you and the company. Thank you so much for this second chance."

Corporate was required to include minorities. Women and people of color hired were the 5 percent minority. Then reality struck. I was over my head. The learning curve was steep. All the medical terminology and working with doctors, nurses, hospital administrators, and medical equipment were mind-blowing. Keeping my promise to not be a disappointment lit a fire under me, scrambling to succeed at all costs. I can't screw this up.

Having a substantially greater income affords us the means to buy a house. Realizing my income alone could cover all the living expenses rubs Galen wrong. He feels he is losing control, which threatens his male ego. Division and jealousy increase between us to the point where I am considering a divorce.

Leaving for work, I give Galen my ultimatum. "You have a choice: Get a job and contribute or you can leave. You're not needed here."

"Why? What's wrong with the way it is? I don't have to work now since you have good job."

"Everything! So you think I'm your meal ticket?"

"Yup, pretty much!" He is slouching in the sofa, legs crossed, slovenly sucking on his beer bottle, arrogantly flicking the ashes of his cigarette, blowing smoke curls.

"You're disgusting. You're dead weight around here, you freeloader. I thought you were going to be a life partner. Boy, was I wrong. You're worthless. I'm bending over backward, carrying the entire load to make ends meet, trying to be the good wife, and that means nothing to you. You manipulate the government system, taking money that others deserve when you are fully capable."

Dismissal, cold silence, isolation, and riveting suppressed anger run amok in the house. When he's not there, he's hanging out in the bar drinking.

Faith becomes my companion. Being an island in my marriage and the fear of living alone for the first time ratchets up havoc in my mind. Asking myself, can I really handle living alone?

To the Rescue

It's my last sales call of the day. The pharmacist and I end our conversation about his wife's cat. She loves the cat, he hates cats. He's compelled to go home and shoot the cat after work. Taken back by his harshness, I say, "I'll take him home." Sight unseen.

The cat's name is Brandy, a handsome three-year-old Siamese male who is living in a divided home. There is no remorse on the pharmacist's part, and his wife doesn't know his cruel intentions.

"Here, take the damn cat."

Brandy is afraid, pacing around in the car. He yowls all the way home. I comfort him, "It's okay, Brandy. I will take care of you."

Galen hates cats, too, even though his mother found comfort having them around.

Unfortunately, Brandy has left one anger-filled divided house for another. He sparks jealousy in Galen. Sharing isn't a quality he has, being an only child.

We are barely in the house when the arguing starts. Galen and I are in each other's faces, yelling and finger-pointing. Brandy frees himself from my arms and bolts into another room.

"What the hell are you doing bringing a cat home? You never asked me about that."

"I don't need your permission. Who do you think you are that you can boss me around when you can't even get off your dead ass and find a job?"

I find Brandy cowering and shaking in a corner. His water, food dish, litter box, and bed are set up for him. Sitting with him on the floor, loving him, I reassure him he is safe with me and this is his forever home. He curls in my lap and purrs. We are bonding.

Brandy perches himself on the back of the sofa by the picture window in the sun, waiting for me to return home from a day's work. As I walk through the front door, he runs to me like a happy dog, winding and rubbing himself around my legs in affection. He struts around with head and tail held high. I pick him up and snuggle him around my neck, scratching his ears while he purrs.

The relationship between Brandy and Galen grew testy. He'd claw, bite, and hiss when Galen tried to grab him. Reaching my limit from the daily arguing, divorce seemed the obvious answer. Caring what others thought of me or how the church viewed my getting a divorce didn't matter. Taking charge and striking out on my own was what counted. Placing myself above faith and God where faith was a will-call prayer during desperate times, and then I'd dismiss Him when the storms subsided. I revert back to my old nature of I don't need anybody's help but my own.

The marriage had lasted nine years. Relatives knew nothing about the tempest in the marriage. That's the way I wanted it. My plan was to be out of town when the divorce papers were served on Valentine's Day. I gave "irreconcilable differences" as the reason for divorce. Galen had a month to pack up and leave. It took more than a year to resolve the dissolution of our marriage. The year was pure hell.

Brandy took the brunt of the emotional turmoil. Stressed-out and fearful every time Galen showed up, he'd isolate himself as far away from the conflict as possible. Periodically, he was treated for kidney infections. Marking on the basement baseboard became common. He yowled and vomited from pain and anxiety. He lost his appetite and became increasingly guarded and edgy. Through the constant strife, we clung to one another. Every night I fell asleep with him wrapped around my head. Brandy was my comfort and calm while he took the brunt of hostility.

Pa Kicks the Bucket

Dad's ankles were surgically fused because of chronic pain from osteoarthritis. I wheeled him to the car after he was discharged from Marshfield Hospital with thirty-eight prescriptions, each pill compensating for another's side effects. Learning he had a heart condition was a new finding.

It had been seven years since Ma's passing. He missed her as he sat alone in the house she bought him. Despite daily visits from my sister and brother-in-law, it wasn't the same for him. Studying the Bible and prayer comforted him in his solitude. This was Ma's gift to him. Faith grew in him as he aged. Only God knew how much.

It was 5:00 p.m. when I brought him into his house. The mood was melancholy and empty. The far-right end of the sofa was Pa's groove. Between the living room and the kitchen was the dining room. On the kitchen table sat all his drugs.

"I'm not doing that anymore," he said pointing defiantly to his medications. There was an unsaid, underlying, determined message. His decision seemed final. I didn't then understand how final. He asked me, "Can you please stay for a while?"

An invisible wall rose, as my hands went up in defense. I took a step backward. "No, I have to get back home." He was saddened by my response. Rejection and dismissal work both ways.

At 11:00 p.m. my phone rang. It was my brother-in-law calling to tell me Dad died from a heart attack. They found him slumped over in the sofa. I was surprised, but not really. A feeling of relief came over me. Any future obligations were gone.

My father had lost hope and a will to live. To this day, a question hangs in me if his decision was an act of suicide, willing himself to die, or did I break his heart when I told him, no. He carried the unconscious toxic transgenerational DNA of shame to the grave.

He died, believing my marriage lasted. The marriage was a temporary bridge to escape.

What was so important for me to hear from him: "I love you, I'm sorry?" It didn't matter. My animosity had blocked hearing him out. Forgiveness didn't exist within me, and I felt justified, further distancing myself from my sister and finding my own path.

During the funeral service and internment, I shed no tears for him. He taught me to buck up, so I did. Turning tail, wearing invisible blinders, I checked him off. He was one less thing to think about.

Dad was dead and the divorce was settled.

On that day of final court proceedings, Brandy trotted joyfully to the door, tail held high, meowing, when I walked into my house.

"Well, now it's just the two of us and we have to make it," I said, picking him up and nuzzling him.

The words had barely escaped my mouth, when, feeling the heavenly hands tapping my shoulders, I heard the words, "We're here for you. You'll never be alone." Smiling and cradling Brandy, I realized it was like having an ace in my back pocket with an angel on my shoulder. Was it Ma or God watching over me? Maybe both.

God's love surrounded me, patiently waiting for me to open my heart. Gently leaning into the spiritual aspect of myself and partially trusting my intuition, I was reminded of Ma's deep faith and the safety she felt seated at the piano, surrounded by heavenly hosts. A sense of strength, peace, and comfort infiltrated my being. I tasted calm and hope.

We two became three, now having Spirit walking beside us. Together, God and Brandy's love kept me upright and grounded in sync with my willingness to accept the love offered. But it was on my terms.

Having grasped that my free will and life choices put me here, I knew that moving forward was solely dependent upon me. I would be wasting time grinding over the divorce and Dad's death. Grieving was a nuisance. Get over it and move on. There was money to be made. Driven to excel, my career was my top priority. It was where I found an identity.

But evil lurks.

"What are you doing in my house, much less my bedroom? You're dead."

It was several months after the divorce, another sightless hand grabbed my shoulders and spun me around. No heavenly presence with this one. It was combative. A murky darkness consumed the room. Dad came to mind. Brandy was on the bed backing up, growling, and hissing. Dad was after me, trying to corner me. Enraged and terrified, I swung my arms and fists to get him off from me. Screaming, I had a flashback of him violating me. "Don't touch me. Get out! You're not wanted here. You've done enough damage in my life."

Brandy bolted off the bed, airborne, and ran screeching into the hall-way. Chastised, Pa's hunched spirit disappeared, raising my subconscious, now knowing that spirits walk among us, crossing from the other side of the veil. Or didn't Pa's soul cross over?

The Medium Appears

Like clockwork, every Monday through Friday at 7:00 a.m., I have breakfast at the local family restaurant in a booth parallel to the parking lot and highway, facing the doorway. There I gather my thoughts and go over my sales progress and account goals for the day. It is a Wednesday in June, an ordinary summer morning as I wait my turn to order.

The welcoming aroma wafts across the restaurant, fresh-brewed coffee, sizzling bacon, and pancakes. The hustle of the place hums, silverware clinking, phone ringing, coffee cups clanking, dirty dishes being bused from the empty tables, cooks belting out, "Order up!"

I overhear the rowdy regulars at the counter, many of whom I had waited on when I worked there, good-naturedly harassing the waitresses about their short skirts and nice legs. The guys bantering about politics and spreading local gossip. From the other side of the restaurant come audible snippets of business deals and the stock market. A married couple is snapping about his adultery and their divorce. I tune in and out of the conversations, all the while immersed in my work.

There stands Rita cheerfully holding the bottomless pot of coffee, filling my cup on the fly, like a hummingbird. She asks for my order, but rarely writes it down. She already knows it.

"Two poached eggs on a dry English muffin and coffee. Thank you."

"It'll be right up."

I put my work aside and peruse the *Wall Street Journal*, and checking to see how the company stock was doing that day.

Suddenly, an unfamiliar woman stands by my booth. She simply appeared. I didn't notice her walk in nor did I hear the bells jingle on the door. She stands about five feet five inches. Her ethnicity appears to be Filipino. Her hair is jet black, cut short and styled so the ends roll under by her ears. Bangs sweep across her forehead. She's wearing dark-rimmed glasses. I guess her age to be fifty. Her energy is strong and grounded, her temperament unshakeable. She's hefty and unwavering. Her formidable presence throws me off guard.

"Can I help you? Would you like to sit and have coffee? What is your name?" No response.

Obviously, purpose is in her presence. Without a hint of hesitation, she gets right to the point. She asks me my name and I tell her. She sits down across from me and leans forward, elbows perched on the table and one hand folded over the other. She makes direct eye contact.

I brace for what is coming next. I scan her, quickly trying to calm myself. Despite the air she projects, I see compassion, respect, and spirituality, woven with tough love. I never met or saw this woman before, and I am in her sights. I look beyond her person, reading deeper into her, trying to figure out whether she is to be feared or respected. Is this some kind of trick or is she being honest? Holding my composure, I restrain myself and wait politely for her to speak.

"I have a message from your parents."

"Yah, right! My parents are dead."

"I know that."

How can she know this? What else does she know and how? Is this another secret the family withheld? Now it was my turn to shoot questions.

"Where do you live and how do you know this?" No reply. I ask her name. No reply.

Ruffled and befuddled that she is not offering any information, I concede to her. Control is hers.

Is this a malicious prank? Because across my life, I got used to being the pawn for another person's pleasure.

It feels eerie and creepy. Is this my mother reincarnated? Did her time in Heaven teach her to take charge and she has come back to show me? This is jarring my mind.

The woman provides their names.

Okay, you got that one right, good guess lady. "What is my father's middle name?" Surely she doesn't know that.

"Mark."

What the hell! How does she know? Where does this woman come from? Flabbergasted, I flop back in the booth. She has my undivided attention.

"What's your message?"

"Your parents want you to know how much they love you. Love exists beyond the physical body."

I am dumbfounded. My hands lie limp in my lap. My strength drains and my breath leaves. My spiritual core unravels. Why now? What is its importance? What does this mean for my future?

Breakfast arrives, and Rita asks, "Are you all right? You're white as a ghost."

"Feel like I'm sitting with one," I reply sheepishly.

Rita gives me a cynical side glance, questioning if I lost my marbles.

The woman gets up and walks right past Rita. I'm tempted to follow her out to discover where she came from. I watch her pass through the first set of double doors, but the bells' jingle is silent. She disappears, but I never see her pass through the second door.

"What are you looking at?"

"The Filipino woman who was just sitting with me."

Rita laughs, looking at me like I am weird. "You better eat your breakfast."

For me, she was real. The moment taught me that communication travels across the veil. Heaven is real and the soul goes on. Was this the reason?

Tailspin

According to scripture and Christian upbringing, the strike against me is being labeled an adulteress, damaged goods because I am divorced. This cements another layer of shame added to my mantel. Was the divorce really my fault? Rationalizing, I maintain unfaithfulness was not my failure. Giving it my all until it was impossible. I was working myself into the ground, being the martyr, like Ma. Yet it didn't matter. Divorced and choosing between letting Galen take me down or leave. I have been running to save myself where Ma died trying. I am responsible for my actions.

Others, my sister most of all, judge me, looking down their noses for my choices. Shame's mind-games spins me dizzy. Sleep escapes me, as my mind runs helter-skelter.

Ma's scripture reading replays in my head: "Be ye not unequally yoked together."

"See, you didn't obey me," Ma said. "You sinned against God."

I am even more confused. She was the one who pushed me to be nice to Galen. How does that make sense?

The pressure-packed stress of the divorce ended. Incoming was the letdown. The divorce felt like a death. I buried my grief for the sake of my survival. Denial came easier than facing reality.

Solo, having accomplished the dreamed-of freedom, I asked, "What do I do with my independence? Where do I turn?" Being in a state of fight or flight, dizzy, my mind was spinning. I found it hard to concentrate and focus each day. Confusion and disruption drained my energy. Lifting a fork to my mouth was like pumping iron twice my weight. Past emotions that had been bandaged rose to a conscious level, summoning nauseous fear in my core. This was shame's opportunity to rule over me being alone in my mind. I asked myself, what was the truth versus lies?

The road ahead resembles being caught in the vortex of a sandstorm, spun out of control by centrifugal force, thrown to the outer edges, stumbling with no direction, boundaries, protection, or purpose, and nowhere to turn.

I was lost. I craved to be held and comforted. But I knew if I wanted to subsist, it was up to me, and me alone. Being soothed had to wait. I had to be strong, all the time, on constant alert, dismissing all emotions. Life is hard, like Dad said. He wasn't kidding.

I bucked the urge to surrender to mental defeat. It took fortitude to offset the war within. I needed the courage to get up and step out of my box. I had to acquire street smarts. This is where the school of hard knocks rears its head.

Ma gave me spiritual tools, but my lukewarm relationship with God was benched. Shame snickered as it swindled me. God watched and waited while my free will played out, taking a swing at life. Off this fledgling goes, skipping down the yellow brick road, like Dorothy in the *Wizard of Oz*, embarking on a fantasy life of exploration, quick fixes, and adventure in the material world, believing there was the perfect fit to satisfy my longings that churned but could not be identified.

And still needing to test my independence, I kept fist-punching away. I heard Ma's voice. "You be careful. You're too brave for your own good."

I'm sure, as a child, there were times Ma feared what I'd do next, adding to her angst. "Where is that kid now? What's she up to?" I was a daredevil.

At just over thirty years old, my life was a revolving door of dead-end relationships and erosion of my faith. I just didn't know what to do with myself to take up the slack being alone in a quiet house other than bringing chaos into my life. Floundering, I got involved in risky behaviors searching for the highs to numb emotional pain. Some nights, I ended up sitting uncomfortably alone, nursing a soda, at the end of a loud, smoke-filled honky-tonk tavern, watching people trying to hook up. Or I tried imitating other women, carousing, dancing to gain attention, nervously engaging in meaningless conversations as foreplay, signaling sexual come-ons, prowling, and hunting men with a look that said, "Bring it on, baby." Feeling like a whore, I figured I deserved no better. Bereft of reality, I was smaller than ever.

Completely out of my element, I was naïve of the risk of being raped. I plead guilty to being in a bar and disrespecting everything moral Ma taught. Scoring and giving myself up, engaging in one-night stands compounded the self-loathing anger, self-inflicted degradation, and disrespect I brought upon myself. "Just love me" was my craving. But I pushed away any possibility to know love by simply using sex recreationally, deluding myself that this would lead to be being accepted and belonging. Teasing men on, while blaming them for what they did to me, I pretended they were the predators, not me. They recognized my desperation and vulnerability. They took advantage of me, and I let them. When they were done, they'd throw me away, like my dad did when he coldly turned his back on me.

The heartache and shame drilled deeper, bringing emptiness, rejection, and even more isolation upon myself. Every encounter caused my faith to fade. Dissatisfaction, despair, and discontent drew me deeper into depression. I detested myself for the string of disappointments.

Hopelessly pounding walls, I interrogated myself: "Why can't I find a decent partner? What do people see in me that I don't? What's wrong with me? What attracts me to these men? Am I wearing a target on my forehead?" It felt like I was.

Self-preservation and self-destruction collided. My humanity was clutching outward for transient satisfaction versus inward for a peaceful soul. I was sinful and I saw Ma's image scolding and waving her index finger at me while I hid my face.

I drag my disheveled self home from these escapades. Brandy, waiting on the back of the couch by the window, joyfully greets me. He winds himself around my legs and meows, stopping to preen himself. Later he lay on my pillow, his warm body nestled on my head, purring me to sleep. Many nights are tearful and painfully remorseful. Brandy's love is unconditional, and unrecognizable to me. He knows no judgment. It contrasts my understanding of what love is.

Ma's piano sits against the north wall of my living room. I imagine her playing chords and us singing together. Time stood still during those childhood sessions. Her spirit was beside me, quieting shame's bullhorn in my head, making me feel safe.

As this period in my life fizzles, a positive shift begins to take place. The few outside friends I had encouraged me to network with new groups of people who shared like interests. What interests? I hadn't developed any. So everything is new. I start developing an agenda of personal growth, engaging in outdoor activities and cultural events, setting goals, and striving to achieve my full potential. Motivating myself to get out of the gutter and gain direction is a sign of faith working to combat the enemy. Leaving behind the frantic pursuit of men adds substance to my life. Breathing substance into my free will and opening up to trust, I am regaining self-confidence and learning my life has oxygen again.

Competing in bicycle races, racquetball games, tennis tournaments, and 10Ks, sailing, skiing downhill and cross-country, and exercising to exhaustion grants a reprieve from depression. I tackle anything challenging, performance-related, and adventurous.

Within those activities is the underlying motive for being involved and the hope of sparking a higher-caliber relationship. I take up attending the opera, symphonies, and plays, hoping to meet a person of means, intelligence, and success, thinking maybe I can meet somebody really nice if I am socially well-rounded. Keeping the body and mind distracted and in constant motion anesthetizes the enemy within.

Taking Flight

A pilot's license is my next adventure. The idea originated after having dated a businessman who owned a low-wing, single-engine plane. Flying to Aspen, Colorado, he lets me have the controls and teaches me a few things about flight operations. The feeling is powerful. It gives me a sense of self-reliance, confidence, independence, and being in control, rising above and gaining a new outlook of the world around me, stirring my soul, and launching new introspection. Seeing myself separate from the conventional homemaker role, I am busting through another macho barrier. This is the era of Sandra Day O'Connor, the first woman to be a Supreme Court justice. It is the time when the high court overturns state laws designating a husband "head and master" with unilateral control of property owned jointly with his wife. I think if a man can fly a plane, so can I. No man is going to dominate me.

My workaholic nature affords the time and income to fly. I am winning sales awards, exceeding expectations, outperforming my peers in a business on an upswing. Work is my laser focus. Work offers a personal payoff. Work grounds me and feeds my self-esteem and gives me value. The company recognizes me for my intelligence and customer relations.

I'm belonging and contributing to something greater than myself. Here, the expectation is conforming to competencies, yet, functioning independently away from the corporate cubicle. Every day is purpose-filled and creating a framework in my life. The face I wear is that of a positive, strong, up-and-coming, successful businesswoman. Corporate is unaware of my personal life's dark side, and the darker it becomes, the better my sales numbers. I am running away from myself, driven to succeed and gain value in achieving goals.

Paradoxically, my talent is building business relations when I can't build personal relationships. Doing business with the medical elite is a rush. It medicates me. Clients trust my intent. If I have faith and trust that my motives in expressing care and concern of others are for the right reasons, the financial rewards come. The philosophy sets me apart from other pharmaceutical salespeople who approach the doctors with dollar signs in their eyes and pen in hand.

My cockiness is noticed walking into the flight base operations for my flight lessons. I'm looking slim and sassy in a tight-fitting, blue-denim, zip-down jumpsuit, taking a stand for women's equality against the good ole boys' code.

An older, cranky, eccentric, divorced Italian man latches onto me. He's got unruly, wiry, salt-and-pepper curly hair, dark wide-set bug eyes behind thick rimless glasses slipping down his nose. He carries a slight paunch, hunched, and wears a worn, tweed blazer, a white, tucked-in, oxford, cotton button-down, open-neck white shirt, open at the collar over a white T-shirt, jeans, and tattered dress shoes. He's a freelance photographer and stringer for *Time* magazine, *National Geographic*, and the *Chicago Tribune*. Beyond his scruffy surface, I detect sadness is sensed in him, much like what's hidden inside of me, and a reason to be attracted. He invites me for coffee.

He rolls different from other men in my world. Aloof and self-contained, he's an introvert who has no interest in sex or alcohol. He hates being touched, and recoils if you enter his personal space, but he's also open to companionship and support. With a complex reverence about him, Al is a mysteriously complicated man.

Since he's thirteen years older than I, he is more of a father figure than the usual friend. His deliberate movements are slow and measured. He has what is missing, but unidentifiable, in me. Intrigued, I want to learn more about him. As we sit talking over coffee, he draws me in by his wise inward-looking manners. I listen intently to what he says about his Ojibwa photo essay project, which consumes and transcends him. He tells me of the Native American people, who are holding onto their belief in the Great Spirit, even as the clash of capitalism with the way of life crushes them. Al's spiritual conviction for their Indian culture captivates me. He aspires to have his exhibit used for teaching at the International Center for Photography in New York City. Not only for purposes of technique, but also to open a window on human suffering, and to have White Anglo-Saxon Protestant America see the poor with compassion, respect, and an appreciation of their lives and values.

Al believes that photojournalism requires truth, honesty, and objectivity in its commitment to serving the public with the highest ethical standards. To walk the talk is his core belief. This certainly collides, philosophically and spiritually, with my divided life. Here, we are opposites.

I am awed by his courage in leaving a nine-to-five, working for little pay, risking safety, and leaving behind his former lifestyle while pursuing his passion as an artist. The thing he needs, money, is what he hates. His life's mission conflicts with sustaining a livelihood. He strides to his own beat because society's superficial drum numbs his soul and mind. His clustered body language expresses rejection and loneliness. Life has been hard on Al. His facial lines show anger is deeply rooted in him. He has bonded with those who suffered internally.

Al opens his portfolio. Every portrait strikes me as deeply emotional. As his essay unfolds, he comes alive from within. My heart is touched. I feel a mystical tenderness and compassion for the oppressed. His lens is as an advocate for the downtrodden, showing their plight to the world. He is driven to stand up for the underdog because it is so much of who he's become and what he's captured in others. He hopes to change people's hearts.

His images preached empathy and matters of the heart, driving home the need to care for others less fortunate. They speak the words of the muted and demand they have a voice. In mirroring his wounded inner child, Al's work expresses a range of emotions from rejection, loneliness, struggle, and irony to beauty, joy, love, and dignity. Every photograph bears a message, announcing a piece of himself, aiming to awaken the observer from within. His work surfaces similar patterns out of my subconscious.

I look, listen, and learn where affluent white Americans turned a blind eye. He captures dramatic truths as he forges ahead on his soul path with a fire burning deep within, proving a purpose greater than himself. This is where he finds his own identity and value. It is no coincidence, the timing in which he arrives in my life. Al is pointing out the value of purpose and a spiritually guided path. It's all new to me, and lays the groundwork for me to do self-analysis and cross over into a life of purpose versus one of ego.

He's reached a place in his spiritual life I don't understand. As a self-made artist, he's insulted at my having called his work a job. From my limited perspective, I unintentionally devalued his accomplishments. "You just don't get it," he snapped. "You are so thick-headed and self-righteous." He considers me a cheap materialist fraud and accuses me of being the greedy capitalist. This jolts my mind, which makes me broaden my viewpoint. His isn't for love of money or outpacing the other guy, as it is mine. "Empty, purposeless, hypocrites" is what he calls them, hostile toward organized religion and the workaday world. "Self-righteous bastards!"

Taken aback, I think how can this be my fault? It's what I know to do.

The comforts of home and a good job are my limited impression of security. He's fighting against the material world to have a legacy, which butts up against my belief system. I hear a wake-up call to reconsider looking inward, using a new lens. I am enthralled. This is a man of internal substance who is jarring my unconsciousness.

A small deerskin pouch and leather lace around his neck rouses my curiosity. When I reach to touch it gently, he flinches. The medicine bag's contents are sacred to him, designed for his soul's calling. My touch meant contamination. He tells me he was given sweet grass as a holy form of healing and purification, but declined to explain it further because of its personal nature. A metaphysical world, which allows one to transcend one's self and senses, shines its light through to me. His soul dances between the material and the spiritual worlds.

Sorrow, compassion, and admiration for Al are in my heart. I agree to partner with him, helping him achieve his dreams. Hearing in my mind Ma's words about kindness, I offer him the couch in my home. There he sleeps in his street clothes and rarely bathes. Staying and working from the city is financially easier than his crude log cabin isolated in the backwoods of Hawkins, Wisconsin.

Al is not fond of cats. His edgy static energy along with his anger and resentment trigger Brandy's fight-or-flight response. He positions himself near an escape route when Al is around. Looking back, Brandy echoes Al's edginess by being ready to spring at the slightest motion.

Al was extremely serious. He seldom cracked a smile around me. When he did, it was a guarded angry and sarcastic cynicism. Pursed lips or a scowl were common.

Through his tough exterior rose an extreme tenderness, which he expressed to me one morning. He was sitting hunched over with his elbows resting on his knees. His hands masked the tears running down his face, "What's wrong?" I asked.

"My dog Cassi, I miss her so much. She went everywhere with me. I'm alone. She loved me for me. She kept me warm and watched out for me. She died last year."

The "me against the world" was a familiar refrain and my heart felt his pain. Being so fortunate to have Brandy gave me a sense of appreciation of unconditional love and not being alone.

Depression was in Al, as it was in me. Al's fix, like mine, was work. He exchanged hatred for compassion. He transformed adversity into dramatic black and white images. Here was where we agreed, both of us striving, on different paths, but compelled to rise above our condition. For me, that meant not understanding the push-pull force heaving inside.

Shock Waves

Dressed in my business suit and high heels, I stand in Al's ill-lit, dilapidated cabin lacking amenities or electricity. Clothes, dishes, garbage, paper, and cobwebs are strewn across the room. Mice run along the counters. A damp chill hangs in the air. There is a breeze between the logs.

Yet this is where science, art, and the sacred sanctuary comingle, breathing life to his images. Al finds his peace and safe harbor here. Once again, I am uncomfortable and out of my element as he opens my mind to observe and learn. The risk of being alone with him, off the grid, never crosses my mind. I am honored that he felt safe enough to bring me into his inner sanctum.

We are so much alike, yet so different. With our personal lives a shamble, our work medicates us. As some people pray before embarking on something sacred, Al performs a purification ritual, acquired from the Ojibwa, before he begins developing the film from his camera. He demands absolute silence. He lights the braid of sweet grass from the burning candle to smudge any negative energy and clear the cabin, then proceeds to sacramentally fan above and below himself. He asks the same of me. My traditional Baptist upbringing is tested. It makes me superstitious.

I feel the room's mystical presence while trying to be open-minded and resist it as demonic.

I watch with admiration his ability and courage to dive passionately inward, trusting his soul to guide his images, grounding himself while shutting out any noise, even the voices in his head. Zeroing in on his work is a mesmerizing feat to see and feel firsthand. His life testifies the importance of following the soul's calling, impressing upon me actions I needed in my life.

Silently absorbed in his work in the recesses of his darkroom, he lets me watch him work and teaches me about camera formats, the value of lighting, and the technical aspects and tricks to develop dramatic black-and-white photographs. He stresses the qualities of having a good eye and finding balance when using light with an eagle feather, fanning technique to seize the raw essence of the portrait. I witness time stand still. The sharing of his art creates oneness between us.

Sheet after sheet of photographic paper is wasted until each image had the perfect emotional essence. This isn't work, it is a labor of love that drives him, breaking all boundaries as his creativity expands his life force. His images are soul-driven. He has a God-given gift.

I being like a wide-eyed child experiencing life from a brand new angle. Symbolically, like a gardener, he sprinkles seeds in my subconscious; good seeds which in time will sprout and grow. What is my gift, I wonder?

We travel to Arizona onto the Navajo reservation and meet the tribal elders and the spiritual healer. They greet me but quickly dismiss me. They distance me from the circle of fire. I must stay in the background. Only the men encompass the fire. Shame sweeps over me. I step back respectfully, twisting their meaning and feeling unworthy to stand with the men. I didn't understand why I couldn't be an equal. It hadn't registered with me that my world is what they rejected. Its grounds for contaminating their sacred union.

In their presence, Al is transformed. The dark veil lifts, revealing a relaxed, shared open heart and oneness. They trust him, and it is mutual. He moves prayerfully toward the circle with his head down, unpretentious and transparent. They appreciate his truth and his shared suffering through his photography. He has learned to walk in their footsteps with empathy.

Being exposed to another culture where oneness is real lessens my triviality as my consciousness is spiritually enlightened.

Native Americans have a deep respect for nature, believing the Great Spirit of Earth is in every part of Creation. Their culture identifies with power animals serving as spirit guides in this world. They believe the Creator assigned one power animal to walk with us through life since Creation, sacrificing themselves for our existence. The eagle was Al's. The eagle in Native American culture is sacred. It represents a visionary messenger to the divine and symbolizes honesty, truth, freedom, and courage, qualities that parallel Al's work.

The simplicity of their way reflects a universal balance of peace and harmony. This is what my soul longed to have. Mother Earth is their sacred existence and a spiritual gift loaned to them. It is not owned. They are the stewards. They offer gratitude to their Great Spirit. For me it is God. Traditional religion with its rituals and man-made dogma were an intrusion to their culture. Religious dogma separated their souls' connection to the earth and universe, nullifying the metaphysical forms, stealing the soul and their moral values.

Al told me during the trip that the Navajo elders invited him into their sweat lodge for spiritual rebirth and healing of mind, body, and soul. Something my conscious mind was not attuned to absorb, but my subconscious sponged it up. He was vague about the ceremony, explaining only that old life patterns were shed. He was changed from the inside, or born again, with a variation of the heart's desires or change of heart. In rising as a reincarnated soul, he was directed down his life's spiritual path, purposely serving the greater good. The gifted eagle feather symbolized a symbol of high honor a cherished bond and a powerful reminder of his inner metamorphosis. The tribe elders accepted him as family. He found healing and gratitude, a gift freely given by the tribe. In return, they received a voice, where a Divine Source flowed through his images.

He graciously gave me two braids of holy sweet grass that had been blessed by the Navajo medicine man. A sacred presence of the medicine man vibrated, when I touched the blessed braids. The medicine man's energy came through. The powerful intent of his being caused me to visualize myself as a speck of a greater cosmos, which is unlike a supreme being, controlling and owning the world. It shifted my perspective to an interdependence and oneness in creation.

In receiving the sweet grass, an unsayable energy stirred my heart, moving me to tears. Al's love was of a kind unrecognizable, gentle, and genuine. The sacred sweet grass spoke the words he couldn't say of how much my being with him meant. The braids would ward off evil from me and my home. A cherished visible reminder, the blessed sweet grass now rests atop of my living room TV, acting as the central protection and purification in my home. I am humbled that one would care so much for me.

Our relationship lasted three years until it ended in an all-out screaming brawl over life's philosophical differences. As I was about to boot him out my door, the shame in him berated me. Pointing his finger, he said, "You're just like the rest of the WASPs—artificial. You and your corporate bullshit! False empty pursuits! One day you will understand what it means to have purpose in life. You don't get it. You're too self-centered and oblivious to focus on what's important around you." He slammed the door behind him. He called me out my moral misalignment.

I felt face-slapped, side-railed, cheap, foolish, and ashamed. How could this be my fault? I was living the way society expected and what I considered normal.

He had my missing pieces, but they were unidentifiable and intangible. Having a cause to fight for was never in my upbringing. A cause meant everything to Al. It was his soul essence to exist. He lived from the heart. Apparently mine was from the head.

But a cause doesn't pay bills. I was tempted to chalk the relationship up as another failure. Yet it wasn't, many soul lessons evolved from it. Al instilled in me the balance of taking up a cause to protect all that is worth protecting. His work recorded reality that lit my way to look inward. Teaching me to walk in another's shoes and drop the judgment. Indirectly, he awakened that healing from ill patterns is possible. Life has a promising other side. Al was my spiritual mentor who taught me to have passion and seek truth in living out life for the greater good. He triggered questions, which led to self-examination. He was instrumental in shifting my egotistical and materialistic patterns to a framework for placing more value on the intangible.

He led me to take up the camera and see the world through a new lens, helping me connect with reality. Photography brought nature back into my life. A hobby became my passion, nurturing my creativity and raising my desire to find peace. The art and science of photography satisfied my anxious critical mind. Creating images gave me permission to look inside and feel safe. Like playing gospel on the piano, photography gave the child in me a voice and the courage to take a step forward toward the light. For that I am grateful to the late Alfred Charles Bonanno who taught me the value of having passion and purpose. His unique and dramatic black-and-white photography is known and respected world-wide. His work is exhibited and used for teaching at the International Center of Photography. Al and Studs Terkel shared many intellectual and historic conversations, which connected Al to the renowned writer and Chicago radio host's network of artists, celebrities, and movers and shakers.

The Invisible Copilot

My flight training was near completion. There were a few more flight procedures to learn and practice before taking the flight test for a VFR license. On this day, the instructor was teaching me how to stall an airplane and recover from a full spin, which is the physical concept of Bernoulli.

The angle and speed of the wing's airfoil to the wind is the fine line lifting the plane because of higher pressure over the wing and lower pressure under it. As that angle steepens, drag increases and the plane stops flying. The plane's dynamic is out of balance. One must keep the wings straight and level for the plane to fly. This mirrored another principle in life that I was subliminally learning about imbalance, spiritual resistance, control, and breaking free of the things dragging me down. Headwinds are inevitable; it's the route and approach into and through them that matters.

Bob frequently reminded me, "Whatever happened before getting in the plane, stays outside the airplane. Here you fly the plane, or you die. Focus!"

With the preflight procedure complete and the flight plan filed, we are taxiing to runway 22. Sitting on the tarmac, we wait for air traffic control to give us air clearance.

"Tower, this is Cessna Whiskey Tango 1380, ready for takeoff," we announce to the flight control tower.

"Check air traffic if anyone is on approach," Bob instructs me. I scan to see if anyone is entering the flight pattern even though no one else is on the radio.

"Ah, Cessna Whisky Tango1380, this is the tower, you are cleared for takeoff." We did a final run-up, checking that all systems of the airplane engine were operational, then took off flying out of the traffic pattern and into the practice area.

"Take it to three thousand feet," Bob says. I pull back on the stick and hold the right rudder, leveling out as I scan the instrument panel and traffic. Bob talks me through setting up the configuration for power-on and power-off stalls. The remainder of the flight lesson is putting the plane in a full spin. He then assigns me to go out and practice this solo.

The following day flying solo, to practice the procedure, my gut-instinct tells me to climb to four thousand feet. I configure the plane into a full stall, but didn't expect a full spin. The aircraft is now wing over wing and spinning like a corkscrew, winding toward the ground. I am trying to breathe and not freeze. My mind blanks. I am numb, trying to remember yesterday's procedure, what to do first. But the plane is already committing to a spin. I am facing death as life races through my mind. The distance between the earth and the plane grows closer. Calm sweeps over me and everything is in slow motion. I am peaceful and ready to accept death.

Then the shame speaks as I begin to think: Who cares if I am alive or dead? Life lacks purpose. Just going through the motions of living. What difference does it make? Nobody will miss me. Maybe Brandy?

My thoughts are interrupted. "Let go of the controls and cut power," I hear His inner voice say. "No! Grip it harder," says the other voice. Then I hear Him again, in disbelief. "Let go of the controls and cut the power!" The copilot seat is empty. Or is it? Where did that come from?

I let go of the stick, resisting the counterintuitive urge to pull up, trusting the plane will level itself, and countering with right rudder, pressing with all my strength to the floor, countering the P-factor, long enough to be able to pull the elevator back into a climb. The plane levels out at one thousand feet.

Faith's angel was in the plane that day, riding copilot. It was not my day to die. It was a deciding moment: stay in control doing it my way or save my life by letting go. Which was it going to be? This was a time to stay calm under fire. There was a reason I was alive. I just had to figure out the clues. Even with a near-death experience, the true depth didn't register its spiritual lesson. The signs to change life's course were there. At the time, it was not obvious to me.

I land the airplane, get out soaking wet, from stress sweat. I tether the plane and walk to the flight station. As if stepping out of a nightmare, I look back at the plane in disbelief, double-checking if somebody was actually sitting in there. Empty!

I was hell-bent to finish my VFR license, which meant climbing back in the plane and flying again. Quitting was not an option. This taught me to live in the moment and pay attention to reality. It was a wake-up call, but for what reason and who? Why am I supposed to live?

Here We Go Again

I am closing my flight plan and chatting across the counter with Fred, the flight inspector, when Burt, the airport manager, aggressively elbows in. He struts forward, wide-legged, hands on hips, and aggressively braced, rocking side to side with a puffed-out chest and a bulging belly draped over his belt, looking at me as his next meal. Creepy!

Suspicious of his domineering approach, I stand my ground and wait for his next move.

"Hi, I'm Burt, I run the airport here." Flaunting his status, he acts like the big boss throwing his weight around. He's got thinning red hair, blue eyes, fair freckled skin, a full scruffy beard, and a hairy chest that protrudes through a blue, open-collared dress shirt. He's just full of himself!

Fred sneers, half-turned away, with his head down. He watches the exchange progress, then casually slips away. I hadn't noticed on my way in from the plane that the two of them were huddled in a conversation. Learning later, Burt was monitoring me on the FBO radio during my flight lessons.

He and I stand facing one another as I give him a crisp, "Hello." Skeptical of his advances, leaning my elbow against the countertop and crossing one ankle over the other, I go eye to eye with him, wondering what he wants. He seems clean, nicely dressed, and responsible. At least he had a full-time job, unlike my ex-husband. He struts around like a rotund peacock offering his "Hey Baby" look as he whips his tongue around his lips like a snake. Very boyish, brash and immature, he's trying to convey a sexual come-on. It's more than a little repulsive at first glance. I should have gone with my gut reaction, but at that moment Ma's "be kind" phrase shot through my head.

"Ya wanna have coffee sometime?"

"Thanks, not today. Some other time. I've gotta get back to work."

"Sure, you name it."

"I'll see."

Despite having brushed him aside, two days later I say I'll meet him after work for happy hour. I find him sitting slouched over the restaurant bar drinking a beer. The bartender brings me coffee.

"So you like flying airplanes? What else do you like to do?"

We are definitely opposites. My silent sports versus his roaring motor toys. Competitive athlete versus couch potato. Drinker versus teetotaler. Health nut versus food junkie. Introspective idealist versus unrestrained materialist. But there was common ground. Photography and flying.

I share with him my upcoming photo safari to Kenya. By this time my cultural and travel interests, and emotional and spiritual growth are more mature than just a few years ago. My photography skills are greater too. The freedom, creativity, and self-sustaining independence are enjoyable.

Al had taught me much about the technical and the creative eye in photography, and more so about the spirituality and compassion that he poured into his images. Those qualities left a mark and were growing in me. He awakened an inner peace, whereby my curious mind delved into searching and exploring to find purpose. The philosophical contrast between Al and Burt was stark, yet a similar dark undertone acted as a magnet. Again withholding judgment, I set out to see the good, and dismiss his faults.

It is the third date. He has invited me to visit his parents for their weekly Sunday dinner. I recall my mother's dinner after church and feasting on her wonderful roast beef and gravy, cooked carrots, mashed potatoes, and fresh baked bread. Dessert was homemade sponge cake with fresh-picked strawberries from our garden and whipped cream. Ma had skimmed the cream out of the milk can in the morning from last night's milking. So I welcome the invitation. It sounds pleasant. Burt calls his parents to let them know he's bringing a guest to dinner.

"They're very excited to meet you and happy learning I found someone in my life."

I think it's odd to assume this was to be a relationship. But I dismiss the remark. Friendship was more on my mind. Upon our arrival Burt's stepfather opens the door, nods, and walks zombie-like to the living room. There's no invitation to me to step inside, and Burt brazenly pushes his way in, dismissing his mother. Still respectfully standing at the door, I'm wondering when the welcome was coming.

John, the stepfather, is a frail, gray-haired, hunched-over man with dull eyes, He's puffing his pipe, and defers to Burt's mother, Darlene. A broad, rough-faced woman, she shuffles side to side from the kitchen as she approaches. A cigarette droops from her lips. She's wearing an apron over purple baggy sweat pants, white bunny slippers, and a man's cotton plaid shirt hanging over it all. It's a tense moment when she takes a wide-legged stance and hands on hips, suspiciously sizes me up, deciding if I meet with her approval. It's apparent that she rules the roost. I nearly bolt and run, but instead opt to hold my ground, which she interprets as a threat. Fight or flight dangles in the air.

Two obese, blonde golden retrievers limp and waddle over to greet me.

"What are their names?" I'm being polite.

"This one is Ginger and the other is Cinnamon," Darlene said judging my reaction. I gently pet them both. Darlene finally invites me to sit down in their living room. The dogs follow, sniffing me. After sitting with the dogs, Darlene grabs my earlobe like a toddler, marches me into the upstairs spare bedroom, and sits me down on the end of the double guest bed. I have a feeling that a scolding is coming and not a clue why.

"Are your parents alive?" she asks, blowing the smoke from a newly lit cigarette in my face. I see her hands and face tremble.

"No, my mother passed away when I was twenty-two. My father passed away seven years later."

"Good, I'm so glad your parents are dead. Now I don't have to compete with relatives for Christmas."

The doorbell sounds a few minutes after the noon hour when Burt's brother and wife stepped in late.

"Why the hell can't you people be on time for Sunday dinner?" she grouses. I didn't see that coming.

"Church let out late and Polly had to visit her mother. We came as soon as we could."

Polly's mother was a photojournalist for a St. Paul newspaper, whose retirement business is photographing weddings.

"You're late. Don't you have any respect for your own mother? Sit down and let's eat."

"Let's say grace!" the brother trumpets.

Shot down. "No, there's no God! That born-again stuff is a bunch of malarkey. Why waste your words? Eat!"

Excusing Darlene's remark, Polly tactfully redirects the conversation to the weddings her mother photographed over the weekend.

Doesn't work! Darlene has it in for the daughter-in-law. Polly comes from old money. That rubs wrong in this family. The mood at the table is a familiar one from the farm days. Head down and shut up.

Now I'm targeted. "Where do *you* work?" Darlene wants to know. Being cordial is not in her nature, unless it can be riddled with anger and sarcasm.

"Medical sales."

"Huh, so you make good money?"

"I am able to support my . . ."

Rudely interrupting, Darlene barks at John. "Go get my cigarettes and light one for me."

John hops up like a bullwhip struck him. "Yes, Darlene." He is her whipping boy. She likes controlling him and everyone else. This woman is a bona fide battle-axe.

An hour later, Burt has fulfilled his weekly Sunday dinner obligation, and we leave.

My only comment in the car is, "Well, that was interesting. Is she always like that?"

"Pretty much!" The remark holds raw history. He makes no attempt to apologize for her abrasive behavior though his bitter resentment is obvious. After a pregnant pause, the subject changes to my Africa trip. I tell him I am excited I'll be traveling with and meeting five other men, camping on the Serengeti, and photographing animals in their own natural habitat for three weeks.

Burt is quick to offer me the use of his telephoto lens. I own my equipment, but I hear the "be kind" voice of Ma, which switches on my inability to say no. My gut fires a warning shot. What just happened? His offer feels conditional, there's strings coming my way.

Another Eye-Opener

Similar to the ways of Native Americans, unity and harmony are the basis of the Maasai social structure, knitting them together with a common purpose. They believe disorder breeds destruction. They gain wisdom from the animals. They are a humble and peaceful nomadic people who live in balance with the nature. From childhood, they are nurtured with respect and responsibility, knowing they belong and are a valuable part of the tribe's overall existence. They learn that everyone contributes to the good of the whole. That's a huge difference from my upbringing.

Traveling the dirt roads of Kenya, we encounter the Maasai children running nearly naked alongside our vehicle, singing and laughing while selling their vibrantly colored, handmade beaded wares for a few shillings. Our guide stops, hands swarm through the window waving their creations. These kids, who speak a combination of Swahili and their tribe's Maa language, know how to sell and aren't bashful.

At first, my money-oriented mind sees poverty and oppression as I look down on them thinking, "These poor people." But it isn't how they see life. They run with purpose, a joyous soul, and an ethereal richness bubbling from within, harnessing peace and freedom. They're spiritual interconnectedness enlightens my disconnectedness to the universe. Materialism blurs my lens. Questioning my value system, I wonder who is the richer between the two. I'm the poor one as they open my mind to see life through a new lens.

When it comes to the spiritual power of animals, as with American Indians, the Maasai cattle are sacred and believed to be a gift from God. They are life-giving. The Maasai see themselves as the custodians of all cows on earth, nurturing life. They possess nothing, waste little, and use only what is necessary to exist. What a sharp contrast with our culture; we are wasteful, live to own, control, hoard, exert power over, and possess goods to prove our worth, which supposedly gives us bragging rights.

God demonstrates to me humility through the camera's lens during my three weeks on the Serengeti. I hear His voice, telling me, "Look at this and this and this." I photograph a pair of four-month-old cheetah cubs nestling with their mother, camouflaged in the brush where the land's threat of lions, ready to kill them, reeks. Mom tenderly licks them and keeps watch. They are safe amid danger.

"Look here." The topi, gazelle, and impala gracefully mill around, grazing in the sun. Unexpectedly, blasting from the brush, the mother cheetah runs full tilt chasing down a young gazelle she singles out. Life is hard here, yet life has its own rhythm of coexistence in a vicious land of eat or be eaten. Hunger and reproduction drive the animals' survival. Staying alive means pressing on. Standing still is death. Harmony is survival within a lion pride or hyena pack. An unspoken order exists. The animals show me how life is to be lived through peaceful coexistence versus internal chaos. Each has a place in order to survive. Each is an integral unit of something greater versus the supreme human being.

Our guide knows the animals' daily patterns, so we sit back awed by the Serengeti's quiet, beautiful, breathtaking vastness as he drives, searching out a pride of lions and a herd of elephants. In every direction I point the lens, the camera snaps a snippet of a new perspective that God injects into my subconscious. Dawning on me is how insignificant I am in the greater scheme of the universe. I am not in control and He is. I had it all backward. Concluding how disconnected I am in comparison to the animals interdependent and interconnected balance between humanity, nature, and the other animals is telling. Until one's feet touch the vast Serengeti earth and eyes look in all directions, words are insufficient.

We visit a Maasai village. I immediately feel a respectful hierarchical order in the tribe. Unlike my Navajo experience, they welcome and accept me. I see firsthand, all working in concert, like a beehive, for the survival of the tribe. No slackers, only busy hands.

A pregnant thirteen-year-old girl walks over to me. She wears a yellow garment knotted at her right shoulder and she touches my red shirt. Her touch rekindled in my mind the energy of the sweet grass. Flowing from her is a divine light. We both smile. I am uncertain why she picked me, but she did. Our hearts tether us. It feels safe, not dark and heavy, but pure.

Yellow means hospitable. Red is the main color of the Maasai culture which means bravery, strength, and unity in the incredible challenges the Maasai people face each day. Red is the sacred symbol of cows' blood, and the times the tribe comes together to celebrate.

Words aren't necessary as our eyes meet. Taking off my bright red shirt, I offer it to her. She wraps it diagonally so the knot crosses over her heart. She is angel-like and luminous. She has soft eyes and a pure white smile that complements her dark rich skin. I feel the love coming from her heart and soul. She knows no pretention or preconceived motive. She is honest and peacefully grounded. My lesson is that life is lived united, from the heart, not through materialism, prejudice, or division.

Respecting her privacy, I point to my camera, smiling. She nods yes and gifts me her portrait. She stands with dignity and strength, looking directly into the lens, while gracefully holding a beaded necklace that she made. I honor her with a gentle wave, respectful bow and hands over my heart.

Leaving the village a gentle wave as my wet eyes convey how special it is meeting her and how she moves my heart. Love doesn't need words, only an open and willing heart.

Was it coincidence? No. My small-mindedness didn't realize how significant our connection is. While we are worlds apart, the shirt connected us spiritually. She may never realize how she opened my heart that day and made a difference. But I believe God did.

From that day forward, when entering my office, my eyes rise and I gaze toward the angelic white aura radiating around her head that my camera captured. It is an unseen aura in her presence, but I feel it. She is with me, and I thank her.

It is the last day. In the misty morning stillness at the base of Mount Kilimanjaro, I step out of my tent and I am blessed. I see elephants and giraffes peacefully grazing in one direction, and zebras off to my right. I am standing alone, quietly in the freshness of a cool, magnificent sunrise, drinking in the panoramic beauty that softens a thirsty heart. What a beautiful world you have made, God! If this is what Heaven is like, I want to be there, awake in my dream! I am learning to hear His whisper that speaks harmony to my heart. It is a voice that silences the critic. For once, I feel at home. It is like none other. I feel safe, one with nature, balanced and peaceful, and my soul is fed. "Peace like a river attendeth my way," the words of the gospel song "It Is Well With My Soul," pair perfectly with the serenity of this scenic sanctuary.

My soul wakens a smidgen more. The eyes of my heart are clearing. I am stepping into a world greater than mine, longing to stay, and soaking in more of Africa. This is what Al was driving home to me: Find your light within, follow it, and move beyond yourself, out of love for others.

Africa shifted my perspective. My heart and mind is in the process of waking to change. A sense of calm, humility, and gratitude washes over me. My dream is ending as I peer out the window of the plane, the Statue of Liberty beneath us. Back to a society where the dollar means everything, noise, confusion, unrest, and chaos are the norm. Africa sacredly teaches me how skewed my value system is. Harmony among animals and tribes is survival of all. Infighting leads to extinction.

The Roller Coaster

Africa's peace and tranquility rapidly fade. The rat race, chasing the dollar, succumbing to other people's demands take over. The roar in my head returns. So do the heavy-heartedness and inner longing. Loneliness rears up, knowing how the Maasai depend upon community and family, living a life of an interdependence while I live isolated from family.

Africa roots in me a craving. *Maybe, just maybe, a peaceful coexistence is possible.* I hope one day to live a balanced, harmonious, purpose-filled life, shared with a partner.

I give Burt a call. "Hi, I want to return your lens."

"Great, you can bring it to my office and drop it off."

He invites me to go skiing and snowmobiling with him and his friends. I am blindly trusting. He appears normal and fun-loving. We laugh at his silly attention-getting antics. Our conversations are friendly and have smidgens of substance. Most are superficial.

On the sixth date, he whips out an engagement ring. "I love you. I promise to satisfy your every need." I am gullible. Fulfilling my every need is unrealistic. But these are words I longed to hear. Trusting, I cave, but first learn from my first marriage to ask more questions about beliefs, money, and kids. Then he reminds me this is the year that the state of Wisconsin enacted the marital law statute. It goes right over my head. So What? Why was that brought up? Strange. I dismiss it.

There would be no kids is one stipulation. He was diagnosed with early stage type 2 diabetes. The doctors advised him to take charge of his life, lose weight, and exercise or he will be a prime candidate for a heart attack and surgery. He scoffs at the doctors. So I choose to carry this cross for him.

Regarding money, we agree on a joint checking account and I give him control, never thinking twice about it since he managed the airport budget. I believe he is responsible.

The subject of faith and religion is met with sharp discourse. His comment is snarky. "God does not exist. God isn't real. Religion is a con and takes your money. The Bible is malarkey. Bunch of holier than thou hypocrites."

I bite my lip and offer no comment. Ma taught us to believe in God, have faith, and follow His teachings, even when we fail. My beliefs and learning patterns rise to a mindful level. There are wide moral differences between us. But the eternal optimist in me is out to win. I am bullheaded and it's full steam ahead.

Fred, the flight inspector, and his wife are of the Baha'i faith, which strives for world peace and three oneness principles: God, religion, and humanity. They source their writings from Bahá'u'lláh, the Promised One, not from the Bible. Their worshipping of a human prophet versus the Holy Spirit of Christ causes me to question where my faith stands and what my beliefs mean. Asking myself how Ma felt about remarrying outside a Bible-based church summons guilt and shame.

My chest tightens hearing the scripture repeat in my mind, "Thou shalt not have any other Gods before me." My throat thickens. Nausea takes hold. Was God being denied and betrayed by me? Is this a cult? Ma isn't here to ask.

They explained that under their faith we'd be married by the justice of the peace with Fred and his wife the witnesses. I concede, caving to others expectations and a learned behavior.

God was not invited. That doesn't feel right. I am conflicted, but go along to get along, finding it hard to say no and afraid to disappoint people.

The day his mother learns of our marriage, Darlene herds me upstairs for another heart to heart. This is her boy. In no uncertain terms, she protects him, as a bear sow protects her cub, and extends her claws taking a swipe at me. She is going to make damn sure she drives her point home. Inhaling a long drag off the cig and blowing it all in my face.

"Listen to me, that boy has been through enough in his life and he doesn't need some bitch messing it up any more than it already is. The last one about destroyed him, by breaking the engagement." That should have been my clue, but no, I am determined now more than ever after accepting her challenge.

"The way that boy grew up as an abused child is unspeakable. He watched his father rape and shoot at me. He sexually molested and verbally berated him. Slapped him repeatedly across the head. He hasn't been right since and his attitude about life sucks. Traumatized." She jostled my subconscious, but I lacked the cognizant to see similar trauma in me.

"But I can help him change. I know he's not perfect, but I can support him."

"Good luck, sister, I know better, I'm his mother! He will suck you dry and move on to the next sucker. He's a user. Watch out, you've been warned. Mark my words, this marriage won't last six years."

Her point was crystal clear as her eyes narrowed. Yet, brushing aside her remarks, I want to believe only the good. Hell or high water, I'd prove her wrong. Game on, lady! It was a pattern rooted in me. When told I can't do something, I rise up to prove them wrong and never consider the repercussions.

Reality strikes shortly after we were married. The beast in Burt is exposed. Depression, repressed anger, and hopelessness move in. Brandy hisses, spits, and growls at Burt. In a fit, Burt launches Brandy off the couch, an eye-opener for me. This has been Brandy's home for more than six years. Attacking an innocent animal is intolerable.

"You leave my kitty alone."

"Damn cat stares at me. Get rid of the thing. He bites and scratches me."

I hold my tongue and let it ride. Burt tells me he did a background check on me. Oh, that did it.

"What the hell! Why would you do that? Sneaking behind my back."

Brandy is startled by my sharp tone. Stressed and anxiety ridden, he bolts into my bedroom for safety, yowling in terror, urinating on the baseboards.

Similarities of Burt's childhood to mine become noticeable. Our family environments were both the vulnerable versus the beast. Each relationship cries of the same behaviors and outcomes. I am beginning to see old trends being repeated in this marriage. What have I done? Burt was along for the ride. Same as before, my role is being the glue and breadwinner, holding us together, again. I am thinking how my marriage mirrors Ma's. Disheartened, I deny my actions; it couldn't fail. But this marriage is a rubber stamp of the last, only worse. How did I get sucked in again?

Africa keeps coming to mind, where everyone from young to old contributes to the tribe's existence. Order, respect, and leadership are understood both in the tribe and with the animals, too, knitting them into one unit. Division and infighting don't exist. In our house it is the opposite. Chaos, leeching, discord, and self-destruction alienate and isolate us. Right from the beginning, harmony and peace clashed.

When it is just Brandy and me in the house, calm resurfaces. Peace is possible in this home. But as long as he is here, there is only contempt. Brandy's love and devotion pair with the Africa animals. But the edginess Burt creates causes a hostile disconnectedness.

I run to my piano. God wraps his arms around me, grounding me, as I play and sing gospel songs. Ma was gone, but God was there, filling my emotional emptiness. My faith is deepened, as the music quiets the voices of shame. The songs are the soul's cries.

Snapped back to reality, I see Brandy lying spread-eagled, upside down by the glass front door in the sun. Safe and contented, purring with the music, he resembles the cheetah cubs relaxing in the shade of the shrubs.

The sound track from *Out of Africa* loops, transporting me back onto the Serengeti. It is programming my mind and speaking to my being. I don't understand why or what causes my soul to cry. Being overtaken by the wondrous handiwork of God's creation was humbling. But I am haunted by the prospect of living in dissonance, rather than a peaceful life.

Each advancing year we are married compounds the rolling heat in my belly, a lump in my throat, and a tight neck. We ricochet off each other, bickering and hailing personal attacks. We are experts at delivering verbal blows and berating each other. The interests I enjoy—piano, bicycling, and even now photography—he hates.

Burt's despondency ratchets up every time he's encouraged to exercise and lose weight. He is determined to self-destruct, voraciously using food and alcohol as his medicants. When that doesn't satisfy his unethical and out-of-control monetary practices, such as buying loud, luxurious motor toys, put us in bankruptcy. For him, it's *the one with the most toys wins* without regard to how to pay for them. He has a knack for conning the banks into giving him loans without my approval. He doesn't care; the more grandiose, the better.

We are two people living in quiet desperation, lonely and imprisoned by our own doing. He drives my friends away with his condescending behavior.

Brandy dies during our marriage. Missing his quiet presence was deafening. I leaned spiritually into Brandy's unconditional love that asked nothing of me. He graciously gave comfort and stability through the upheavals. Often, he was taken for granted, and I feel ashamed for doing so.

The shame that brought us together takes raucous pleasure tearing us apart. How could life go so wrong? What was love? Rummaging through the kitchen junk drawer, I find a snapshot of me, sparkly eyed, youthful, and smiling, before the marriage. Who is that person in the shattered hand mirror with dull eyes, a sad heart, and a loss of identity? My friends are gone. I have to sell my piano to help with loan payments. Next to go are my 35mm Nikons and medium-format cameras, ending my photography, snuffing out what gives me joy.

Faith had roots and Burt hated my faith aspect, scoffing at me because it gnawed at him. He took every opportunity to degrade and tear me down. He didn't see any reason to change his life, only to increase his self-annihilation, taking me with him as peripheral damage.

I was committed to not quit on him. Life mattered. In fact, when he had sextuple heart bypass surgery, my efforts amped up, for his sake, as a caregiver, reaching deeper into myself to do the heavy emotional lift in support of him. Still, he had no desire or purpose to change his life. He was dead set on dying before retirement age. Hopelessness and depression snowballed.

He'd push me farther away. He didn't want to be helped and my efforts were futile. I am resuscitating a flatliner. I didn't want to die and he did. Confronted, I had to make some serious life choices. Emotionally suffocating and frightened, I had to change and rise above. *Save yourself,* the inner voice screamed.

Reaching for faith, remembering that when Ma went through unbelievable struggle, her faith grew by leaps and bounds. I go to church to find community and spiritual support. I invite Burt to come, trusting he'd find God and latch onto faith. I realize Ma was right. God needed to be at the core of our marriage and wasn't. I am shocked, he came along, and hopeful his life could change. It didn't. Shame owned his soul from birth. He lacked the spiritual nurturing Ma gave me. He grabbed for stuff and I grabbed faith.

Ten years into our marriage he demands we get a dog. In my mind, owning a dog is out of the question. Time for me was sparse, and Burt wasn't responsible. When the shine wears off, the dog is disposable, like everything else in his life, a throw-away. The chores would fall on my shoulders and his parents for once agree with me.

He is insistent. "I want a golden retriever like Cinnamon and Ginger."

I reluctantly give in. "Okay, I'll see if there is a breeder who has a litter, but I'm not promising we will get one."

Asking around and visiting with a veterinarian who owned golden retrievers, I ask if he knew of anyone who had a litter.

"Yes, an older woman just left here. Her name is Flo. Her golden will have a litter in May. You can call her. Here's her phone number."

I call Flo. "Your vet said your dog is having a litter of puppies in May. We are interested in buying a puppy from you."

"You need to meet my qualifications to own one of my dogs," she says sternly.

It never occurred to me that owning a dog had stipulations. The farm had strays.

"Will you put me on your list of buyers, please?"

Gruffly, Flo agreed. "Yes."

"What are your stipulations?"

"If you are to get one of my puppies, you will take the pup to doggie kindergarten and obedience classes, and you will work with me learning to track with her. The pups go home at week seven."

I agree, thinking this would make Burt happy. But I am clueless about formal dog training, or what I was getting myself into. Regardless, we were getting a dog.

The puppies were born May 2, 1996. There were nine in the litter. Singled out, one pup catches my eye sitting at a distance in the fenced-in country backyard. They are four weeks old. Sitting on the ground cross-legged, I wait for the puppies to come to me. The others swarm me, nipping, and pawing for attention. But the one I spotted held her ground, keeping her distance, analyzing me. She trots with her tail held high and I sense her confidence. Even at a distance, her eyes lock on me, as if she is making up her mind about me. She trots some more and watches me. When the litter goes off to play, she comes and sits by me, getting a better feel of who I am. Harmony exists here. She has been lovingly handled, with respect and gentleness. Her environment imprinted a balance of peace, unity, safety, and security—the opposite of mine.

She has all the right stuff. She is confident, independent, even-tempered, resilient, self-assured, grounded, joyful, and authentic while retaining an innocence.

Two weeks later, Burt backs out from seeing the puppies. Sitting with the litter, the same little female bides her time, watching from a distance, while the other puppies want to be picked. When they scamper off to play, she chooses me. She was special and my guarded heart opened and crumbled, falling in love with her. Touching her held powers like the sweet grass braids, Holy! In another week, this puppy was coming home with me.

On week seven, after completing the paperwork, I am holding her. Burt distances himself. A peaceful calm washes over me. A tremendous sense of responsibility rises in me. I clutch her little, light, golden body to my heart. Her call name is Sadie, which means princess and beauty, inspired by her soft angelic face. The sweet fragrance of puppy breath is divine. An innocent new life with a clean slate is in my arms, ready to face a big world.

After a quick lick on my chin, she buries her face in my chest. Here for the first time, I feel the oneness I sought. Is this what love feels like? Then I want more.

On the way home, Burt's cold war tactics permeate the vehicle. His red face goes green with jealousy, seeing the joy she brings me. He just can't stand it, competing for attention. It pushes too many of his buttons. His wish has backfired.

At home, a glowing bundle of golden fur bats a tiny, toy, stuffed yellow duck around, flipping it in the air, catlike pouncing, and trying to kill the squeaker with her needle teeth. I smile. She has restored the twinkle in my eyes. It's something I hadn't felt in a long time.

I am playing with her on the floor, enamored. Burt isn't. It drives him nuts seeing us happy and bonding. If he wasn't happy, nobody was supposed to be happy—a common pattern of the men in my life, beginning with my dad.

Sadie senses the darkness inside Burt and attempts to comfort him by crawling up in his lap. He slouches stone-faced, glued to the TV. Instantly, he kicks her across the living room floor. The poor puppy rolls and yelps. Was this why he wanted a dog? Was this a pattern, beating and bullying innocence around?

What have I done? The pup was meant for his happiness.

Rescuing her, my mom instinct explodes and I growl. "Don't you dare hurt her. She's done nothing to you." Sadie cringes, then piddles from the unexpected hostility. Love was seeded in her, not anger, a feeling unfamiliar to her. Unknowingly, this is the onset of Sadie's fear period that leaves a lifelong imprint.

From then on, Sadie and I are knitted together. No one will ever hurt her. She becomes mine.

Who's Training Whom?

As Sadie's caregiver and trainer, it's beyond my comprehension what it is to care for a dog and provide training.

Naming her causes a contentious upheaval. Having a papered dog versus a stray held pretentious requirements. One of Flo's stipulations is having her kennel name lead on the formal AKC registration. Not according to Burt's parents, their two dog names took precedence.

Uneducated about proper protocol, I am in their gunsights. Flo lost and his parents won. Flo is incensed at me. It's my fault. Not a great way to start training with her. She's got an algorithm of training goals established for Sadie's life which she expects me to fulfill, beginning with puppy kindergarten, obedience, tracking, and competition obedience. All this is foreign to me, but I am pressed under Flo's thumb to comply. Her allegiance to a particular trainer determines the training methods she expects me to follow. This is overwhelming for a first-time dog owner. Not only do I feel awkward, I have no sense of where to begin with Sadie's training. The poor dog got stuck with me.

Flo is a strict heavy-set masculinely dressed retired elementary school teacher and my tracking instructor. She gets me out in her eighty-acre farm field. Her standards are lofty. Compliance is a must. This means time away from Burt and increased time with Sadie. Going through the motions, doing what I am told, *Yes ma'am.*

I'm marching like a soldier, but bumbling my way through dog training classes, dropping treats with bad timing. I mimic Flo. I'm disciplined. I practice every day. I'm surprised Sadie learns anything because dog training takes concentration and coordination, something I didn't have.

That fall, Sadie's mother dies unexpectedly. Flo asks me to enter Sadie in the conformation specialty held in Minneapolis. Clueless to the purpose of conformation, I can't grasp its importance and meaning for Flo. Sadie is my companion dog, not a dog to put on display.

Flo's high aspirations pigeon-holed Sadie, placing the breeding burden on her because of her champion lineage. Breeding Sadie was never my intention. Accelerating Sadie's obedience, tracking, and now conformation titles has served to achieve Flo's goals. Now she tightens the noose, forcing me to agree to her wishes.

The week prior to the dog show, Flo grooms Sadie's feet to look genetically tight and manicured. She trims Sadie's ears to proper angulation and her beautiful feathered tail proportionately to her body.

In the obedience training center, we practice gaiting Sadie around in the ring, the stacking to show her bone angulation. I'm all thumbs in this foreign language. I don't understand stacking from standing or gaiting from pacing, and my eye then for a dog's angles and movement isn't developed. But Flo has a sharp eye for a dog's assembly. In a compromise to my ineptness, Flo settles on having Sadie, who is structurally balanced, walk into a natural stance.

In the show arena, excitement, applause, and high energy prevail. All different breeds are vying for first place. Professional handlers bustle urgently to line up their prize dogs outside the rings. Handlers, with plump cheeks that look like squirrels', have combs and brushes stuffed in their clothing, ready to nervously primp. They double-check their left numbered armband is rubber-banded and facing out for the judge to see. This is the Miss America pageant for dogs.

Sadie and I stand in line according to our number among twenty-four female golden retriever puppies, waiting to enter the ring. Flo coaches me.

"Remember, watch the judge, and if she nods, you've been selected." I promise to do my best.

The stakes are high. Only one dog wins. That, I didn't know. I'm now too nervous to move, so I simply stand still and observe. Sadie looks up. *What are we doing here?* I look back at her thinking the same thing. We are so out of our element.

I'm armed with liver chunks packed in my bra and ready to bait. I'm brightly dressed as a peacock in a flowing long skirt, heels, and sweater. The others are dressed conservatively in tailored suits and flats. My inexperience is laughable. Clumsy and clown-like, I imitate how others are gaited and stacked, acting like I know what I'm doing. I've been thrown into the competitive dog world, chasing ribbons, and this is baptism by fire.

Wow! The judge nodded. Sadie places sixth. That's all Flo needed; Sadie is breed material. Flo and I were not yet on the same page, but accepting that first ribbon is where the road to many more begins. The epiphany and sense of identity and accomplishment alter my perspective of owning a dog and give me purpose—and an obsession. Competing in the dog world parallels the personal benefits of my corporate world like achievement, value, and self-worth. One nourishes the other.

Sadie becomes my vehicle to satisfy my selfish ambition, with me lacking regard for her feelings or purpose. Immersing myself into training allows me to deny the underlying depression.

Sadie's spay throws a contentious wrench between Flo and me. She was my dog and puppies were never a consideration for her. When Sadie left the litter and came home with me, it never crossed my mind that she looked to me as the mother figure in her life. I didn't have a clue about pack leadership or dogs' social order. My human understanding for Sadie was referenced from the farm where dogs do what they want. So it didn't sink in why she mistrusted me.

Dog packs are hierarchical. The leader makes the decision for the entire pack to follow. The remainder of the pack establishes the rank and file order with all having a position in the pack that supports harmony and survival working together. The young learn respect from the elders through appropriate body language and healthy play styles that demonstrate self-control. Rogue behavior draws swift correction to fall in line from the alpha. All of this is an unknown to me. Besides, my human foundation is one of division and chaos. We are opposites.

I am still uncoordinated during her obedience training, and I have no understanding of correct timing, rewards, and corrections. As my first dog to train, she was messed up and got the brunt for my mindlessness, inconsistencies, and passive-aggressive behavior. And still, she picked me. I'm a dumb-dumb when it comes to customizing training to fit the dog's temperament. Sadie learns in spite of me. She received the right nurturing from birth, *before* I got her.

"Come on, Sadie, let's go play." Set free and out from under the umbrella of an oppressive home life, running with Sadie out through the back yard gate, I cherish the privacy and peaceful separation in our early morning and evening hikes in the woods as we explore nature together. Sadie freely romps off-leash, sniffing and checking out her world. We wade through the rushing, crystal-clear Otter Creek. The birds chirp. We catch a misty glimpse of a silhouetted doe and her fawn. Sadie puts a bead on rabbit, for fun. Here we are one without expectations. A glaring contrast to a quarrelsome house.

Burt rarely attends Sadie's obedience classes. When she's met at home with his verbal guerilla tactics, she slinks off with tucked tail and low body into a corner, where she wraps herself, curled, nose to tail, and watches the mayhem. This is *not* how a pack should function for its existence. No one was in charge. The tangled chaos was unsustainable. We weren't pack leaders, and that frustrated Sadie. Somebody needed to lead, so she did.

Outside, Sadie lowers her head and gives me a piercing stare that could spit fire. Dismissing her actions, besides being clueless in reading her body language, I think she is playing the chicken game. Wrong, she comes charging around from behind and leaps on my back, trying to take me down like prey. "What the heck are you doing?"

She's less than a year old, but her dominance jars in me to step up and be a leader. But what does it mean to be a pack leader?

Sadie is an exceptionally bright dog. She's savvy to emotions, grounded, gracious, forgiving, patient, and steadfast. She is built solid from the inside out. Over my dog-training years, I would learn the importance of meeting dogs at their level. For now, Sadie lowers her expectations of me. She accepts my rinky-dink leadership and recognizes a greater need to open a wounded heart. Training is an all-consuming positive distraction, the reverse of dealing with another failing marriage. Sadie provides the emotional support.

The stick that broke the camel's back, with Flo, was when I decide to change dog trainers. Ballistic is an understatement. Impatient after many months of obedience, Sadie still is not heeling. Hastily and feeling Flo's pressure to get Sadie's first obedience title completed, I assume all obedience trainers are the same. Wrong again. Their methods and approach to training vary greatly. Sadie was receiving food-based rewards and positive praise. Flo detested the physical force and screaming used on the dogs by the other trainer. She felt Sadie was being put in harm's way. How bad could this be? Catching ribbon fever, stubbornly, I opposed her and impulsively forged ahead.

After a cooling-off period, I consider how Flo had the training skills Sadie needed and I didn't. We set aside our differences, moving Sadie's tracking skills forward. Sadie's accomplishments begin to roll in, one after the other. In April 1997 at eleven months old, Sadie titled for the American Kennel Club Tracking Dog. Not satisfied, Flo expects me to advance her titles to achieve Tracking Dog Excellence. Because of Flo's advancing age, she was physically unable to continue our joint training and referred me to Doug, a good friend of hers who is retired from the army where he trained dogs to track and works for the Clark County police department. Seven months later, Sadie earns Tracking Dog Excellent, TDX.

The routine training and competition seduce me. I am constantly pushing to achieve the next higher title, Champion Tracker. Sadie was a smart partner who feeds my ego.

Doug's wife held the Canine Good Citizen test at his training center. Doug asks me to bring Sadie. She passes her CGC and is registered with a therapy dog organization. I never really thought much about the CGC except as another ribbon to hang on the wall.

Sadie goes everywhere I go. She is my constant companion during training, our walks, at home in my office, and traveling my sales route. She rides to work with me every day, often stretched out in the back seat asleep. Burt couldn't hurt her there.

Finishing the sales call of the day in the Mauston hospital, we wander into the attached nursing home and over to the nurses' station. Sadie is wearing her red therapy bandana.

"Would the residents like a dog visit?"

The nurses beamed and came around the front of the desk to ooh and ahh and pet Sadie. She wiggled with joy and gave them her paw, and very gently pushed her golden body against theirs, offering a doggie hug.

"Absolutely, come with me to our sun room."

The residents' faces lit up, heads raised, their hearts opened like the petals of a flower bud in the morning sunlight. Life and love warmed the room. The mood shifted from depression to hope. Sadie was in her wheelhouse doing what she was born to do, open hearts. Standing back in amazement, I watch her discerningly work the room, knowing which ones need comforting, teaching me where my values should be. And where love lives.

A woman in a specialized wheelchair surrounded with four nurses came into the room. Her head was slumped into her chest. Debbie was in a severe car accident that left her living as a quadriplegic and nonverbal. Sadie saw her coming. She jerked the leash from my hand and beelined directly beside her chair. I tried to catch her and maintain obedience. But her golden head already lay on the lady's lap. Her cold black nose nudged and she gently licked her hand several times. Debbie's hand twitched and met Sadie's head, feeling fur and sparking a memory. Sadie unlocked the soul trapped inside a diminished body. Out of the depths of Debbie's soul, a squeal of joy echoed across the room. She lifted her head slightly, smiling inside and out. Powerful love from a dog. The nurses wept. In that moment hopelessness became hope.

"This was the first sound we have heard from her in years."

Innate and nurturing as a caring mother, Sadie comforted Debbie until her energy faded. This was what mattered to Sadie, not empty ribbons.

On a later visit, Debbie was in hospice. Sadie instinctively and urgently led the way to her room. Sadie quietly sitting by her bedside, observing and dialing into her. Ears perked, head cocked, wheels turning, Sadie listened to Debbie's labored breathing. Half raised from a sit, looking at me, with her paw on the edge of the bed, she was asking permission to lie next to her for reassurance. The nurses stood around the bed, admiring Sadie's respectfully quiet interaction. Sadie understood what Debbie needed. Making eye contact with the nurses told me it was okay to lay a towel on Debbie's bed, and I lifted Sadie into it. Sadie lay quietly, back to back, sharing warmth and comfort. Sadie synchronized her breathing, being one with Debbie. We were witnessing the beauty of unconditional love in action. God's being was present. Tears rolled from Debbie's eyes, as they did from all in the room. Sadie's healing effect was God-sent. Her gentle, calming presence, sensing a person's emotional condition and giving unconditional love as a remedy, was her life's purpose. This was her calling.

Debbie died shortly after our visit. I believe Sadie knew. Service for the sake of others made Sadie glow. Serving and healing were never conditional. She met life with an open heart, great passion, and graceful wisdom. She taught me a powerful lesson about healing and having purpose.

Still, I only applied it to others and didn't apply it to myself. My priority remained focused in the material world of winning ribbons, providing customer service, and surpassing corporate quotas to earn good money. The selflessness that Sadie demonstrated didn't strike me as important enough to change my priorities. It didn't put food on the table. I was hungry to find a life purpose, and when it was placed at my feet, I overlooked it as menial.

Sadie drew compassionately closer to me as the emotional distance widened between Burt and me. When I was working in my office, engrossed, she put her head on my lap, raising her golden eyebrows, focusing her soft dark eyes, staring into mine, telling me, "I am here for you." She sensed what my heart lacked. Work filled the gap inside me. As evening crept into morning, she'd nudge my elbow with her cold wet nose, interrupting my typing, reminding me that it was time to stop. It was bedtime. We fell asleep, holding one another, while Burt lay loudly snoring with his back to me, in rejection and bitter resentment.

The more the division, discord, jealousy, and indignant indifference mounted between Burt and me, the more it pushed me toward being entrenched in Sadie's training and accomplishments,

My relationship with Sadie was off-kilter. An emotional barrier existed. She was cautious around me, cowering and shrunken. We loved one another, but, she did understand that. I was protecting her at all cost. Trust was compromised. Again, I didn't understand why she couldn't trust me. I didn't see what she saw. My lack of awareness raised more questions, which led to more self-analysis.

The exhilaration of the ribbon chase and training challenges drove a hunger to learn and excel, and I dived deeper into dog training. Sadie reluctantly obeyed, because I asked her, not because she loved performing. It was stressful and conflicted with her service aspirations. My ego-centric mind and her soul-driven heart were clashing.

Starting with the new obedience trainer for purposes of finishing her Companion Dog Excellence, CDX, title was a shocker. Flo was right. The trainer was harsh, loud, and bossy. "Get that dog into heel!" "Here give me the leash." She jerked it out of my hand. Sadie resisted her bully tactics. No rewards for Sadie. Do it or get slammed. Dispassionate commands, demanding disrespect, she treated Sadie like an object. Finally, when the trainer said, "Exercise finished." Sadie bolted from the training room and escaped down the hallway. She'd had it with this circus.

"Go get the damn dog," she yells.

I echo her harsh tone, buying into her bullying, thinking this was leadership. "You get over here right now, don't you do that to me, bad dog! What do you think you're doing?"

I stomped down the hallway after Sadie, cornered her and grabbed her collar, yanked it forcefully, dragging her back into the training room. She planted her feet like a stubborn mule. I was forcing her to comply. We blocked all doorways. Resentfully, she gave me that fire-eyed glare that reminded me of my sister's dirty-look at the supper table when we were growing up. It was clear to Sadie that I did not understand her and how dogs need to be treated. This was not leadership but disrespect. My anger compromised the trust between us once again. Every time she looked at me, she looked through and beyond me, making me shrink. Shame fired back.

She had an uncanny ability to know my needs. She recognized my struggling heart, looking for an opening. Wisdom was hers to teach me about discovering and choosing self-love over self-deprecation. At times, her belligerence was meant to copy mine, hoping I'd see myself through her actions. The potshots of anger aimed at her were a product of dissension in the household. She was a target in the heat of the moment. Anger was so deeply layered, it created invisible walls and a melancholic heart that I couldn't recognize.

Our getaway from home is walking along the country bike trail, together in nature relieving stress. She forgives me, looking up at me with her sweet smile, inquisitive gaze, quiet *woof*, and the double meaning asking if she can carry something for me. Often it is her tracking item, a glove from her first tracking competition. True friendship required no words. Just being together was all that was necessary.

Sitting or walking quietly, surrounded in stillness, is one of many humble gifts she taught me. Sadie was a tangible expression of God's love to reach out and touch, supporting me when I distanced Him. She was by my side, supporting, and counterbalancing the shame within. Loyal and forgiving to a fault. Her heart was always open and mine was shut.

The warring at home was stressful. Everything about coming back after work was a drag, with the exception of seeing Sadie. She waited at the door, always greeting me with her toy duck and wiggles, spinning in circles of joy. Sadie made me feel special, like her queen. She filled my heart and made me smile. To her, I was somebody. To Burt, I was the nemesis.

In summer's early morning light through my bedroom window, I watched Sadie in wonder. Her favorite spot in the backyard was under an old oak tree, sitting quietly as she raised her jet-black nose, twitching. She breathed the fragrances in the air and gazed at the clear blue sky watching birds until they disappeared. Her ears rotated as she listened to the birds singing. This was her moment of oneness with the universe. I felt nature's spirit running through her and flowing into me, alerting my dark heart to pay attention. *Do as I do, reconnect with yourself.* Something I found difficult.

Her calm conveyed the need to be still, breathe, listen, slow down, and be present. She cherished life. By her example, she wanted me to *just be*. She knew that if I paused long enough, I could hear my heart speak as my mind stopped spinning.

A depth within her that reached beyond herself. It was pure, honest, and life-giving. She drew me inside myself, stirring up an unfamiliarly warm feeling. It was programmed in me from birth, and my heart wanted more.

Normally, a very docile and unassuming dog, Sadie was a tigress in disguise. We are walking through a county park, when a scraggly, unkempt staggering man approaches me. His energy is dark and foreboding. Sensing harm, Sadie comes to my side, curling her lip upward, growling at this person, fending him off. Her guttural growl and the showing of teeth drive the man away. I didn't expect this behavior from her. She held her ground and led by example. She didn't take crap from anyone. That's what I admired about her. The life lesson for me is to stand up and defend myself.

The Disrupter Arrives

Sadie has been with me for three years. I've learned positives and negatives about dog training and trainers. She's taught me quite a few things about dogs. But one dog does not make an expert. I remain naïve and inexperienced about the inner workings of a dog pack, its hierarchy, what makes them fearful or safe, and why the first weeks of life can impact the rest of their lives. I'd never considered a dog's emotional makeup or how the environment helped them thrive, or just survive. I figured all dogs were the same, male or female in temperament, and should be treated alike. Many other things about dogs never caused me to question.

"How many years between dogs is a good gauge for another dog?" I asked my friends.

"Three years is good" was my answer. Their advice was to get the opposite sex. I pondered the idea over the winter and decided to get a male puppy in spring. Corporate was realigning my territory, increasing travel. Sadie would be home alone. The divorce was impending, Burt just didn't know it yet.

Life held many in-betweens. Squeezing in Sadie's obedience training and tracking was tricky. The increased time and responsibility of adding a puppy to the fray never crossed my mind. I'd wing it, figuring it out as I go, piling more on myself without having made a plan. Justifying Sadie had a playmate. This was my rationale. I guess I envisioned getting a puppy could fill my hollowness and fix my life. I imagined the joyful energy that would lift the elephant in the room.

I'm not sure why I leaned toward getting a show dog. It just came to me, a male golden retriever. The worldwide web opened an entire world about pedigrees and health clearances, about which had before never entered my mind to ask. The construct of pedigrees was meaningless. I didn't know one dog from another. Following a trail of breeders, I clicked on the name of a top national breed champion, Ramala Surfurr. It sounded strong and masculine like a lion. The breeder was in the business for more than thirty years and lived in southern Wisconsin. Feeling compelled, I called about an upcoming litter.

"I'm wondering if you have a litter available this spring. I'm hoping to find a male show puppy."

"Yes, I have a litter due on March 2," Ellen replied.

"Are they sold?"

"No not yet. Would you like your name on a list?"

"Absolutely, I am looking for a male of show quality."

"When they are four weeks old you can come and visit."

"Perfect, I have a meeting in Chicago. On my way back, I will stop to see the pups."

Burt was furious. "What the hell are you doing getting another dog? I don't want the dog in this house. I better not see you coming home with one."

"Or what?" I thrust back, sarcastically. "You and your folks can stay out of my decision. It is none of your business or theirs this time. It's my dog and a companion for Sadie. Besides, he is going to be a male show dog." Oooh! Two things he and his folks despised, male and show dog.

On March 2 the litter of two puppies were born, both male. I didn't know the importance of having multiple litter mates, teaching body language, rank, bite inhibition, and play styles within a pack. The puppy's mother wasn't there. It didn't feel right. I was not aware then how this was a major factor affecting his future. Later I learned that research reinforces the view that undesirable social behaviors like fearfulness and anxiety are more likely when premature separation from the mother occurs.

Ellen greets me at the door, invited me in, and introduced me to her husband. He's a nice quiet man. Ellen runs the show in this house.

"The puppies are downstairs. Would you like to go down now and see them?"

Giddy, I am so excited, I can hardly wait. She flips on the light switch, leading down a dark staircase. At the bottom, the two male puppies are huddled alone under a heat lamp in a whelping box with newspaper on the floor. They are just under four weeks old, barely weaned and eyes just opened. What bothers me is their isolation that feels like cold abandonment.

Slowly and calmly, I sit down beside the box to see which puppy comes to me.

"One puppy has a crooked tail and isn't show quality. The other one is." Without hesitation the show pup zeroes in on me and hightails it, wobbling eagerly for me to pick him up and hold him. He is the pushier one. I am overcome with the idea of finding a puppy. I don't recognize his strong will and dominance, only his exuberance. He's the show puppy. What else is important to know? This one grabbed my attention, penetrating my heart. Yes, this is the one. We are meant for each other. He seems to need me as much as I need him, though I didn't know why.

My heart is sad for the pup with the deformed tail. I relate to what it's like to not be good enough, to be defective, to be denied love, to know loneliness and rejection.

Ellen catches my hesitation. "A couple in Michigan will be taking the other pup." I'm relieved. It's settled. I've found my boy. I put him back in the box. Waiting two weeks will take an eternity. But I'm overjoyed.

We turn off the lights and walk upstairs. Ellen brings out Surfurr's national record accomplishments in the show world, which include claiming show dog hall of fame status and repeated best in show plus designated the number two golden in the United States. Impressive. And all beyond my comprehension. On our way to my car, Ellen briefly introduces me to

Laney, the female, noting she had a cortisone shot. Why? That nagged at me for just a bit before I dismissed its importance.

During the next two weeks, the breeder socialized the puppies to children and toys, but not other puppies, to learn play styles and bite inhibition. With their mother gone, this was a time with no leadership, no body language lessons, no idea of harmony or unity, no give and take, no boundaries, and no nurturing. Where Sadie got everything, Saxon got next to nothing.

A clear-minded person, which I was not, should have walked away from this.

"Another dog, now! You must be crazy."

He was forty-six days old when I picked him up. The breeder whisked me in, sat me down, filled out registration papers, and had me write a check. No emotion, it's all business.

I was coached by my dog friends to ask about health guarantees and temperament, but sheepishly I let the latter slide, feeling intimidated to ask, but I did ask about the health portion.

Ellen bristled. "I've been doing this for more than thirty years. I don't need to provide a guarantee." Her words and tone shamed me, and shut me right down from asking about temperament testing.

"It doesn't matter, I will love him until his last breath."

"Don't let him play with your older dog. Keep them separate."

Wait. That's why I got him. Odd she said that. Well, she knows dogs, so I better abide by it.

The instant we see one another again, his little butt wiggles uncontrollably and his tail just about wags off his body. *You're back!* He spins in circles and prances with delight toward me, a same joy felt with Sadie. He takes the toy, stuffed yellow duck from my hand, parades around, his eyes glued to me, strutting his stuff with a sweet smile and a cute puppy bark. Funny boy. My continuous giggles amp his prance. Quite the showman, and a heart of gold filled with pure unblemished love. This is who he is. Stunning, witty and smart, he comes to me at the sound of my encouraging hand clap. "Pup, pup, pup!"

Scooping him and the ducky into my arms I hold him, softly saying, "Hi, sweetie, I'll call you Saxon," Amberac Saxon Surfin Safari. He is mine to have and hold, for better or worse.

He's put in a puppy kennel, with warm blankets, his yellow ducky, the section of his whelping blanket, and a Kong with treats for the four-hour ride home. The whelping blanket smelled of his mother and brother, which made him feel safe. Everything in his world for a while would be unfamiliar. His next associations and experiences will form his life's foundation.

He's vulnerable. The strange smells, the movement of the vehicle, the separation from his brother cause him to briefly whimper and bark. Soon he falls asleep to the sound of classical music playing in the car. I stop every hour to potty him. I praise him and treat him for a job well done. Each stop, he quickly relaxes, knowing he was safe.

At home, I put Sadie in the backyard. But Saxon's security is immediately fractured when I open the door from the garage to the house. Standing wide, chest thrusted, hands on hips, glaring dark-eyed and red-faced, veins bulging, posturing to attack, Burt blocks our entrance. He waves his index finger in my face and yells.

"I told you not to get that dog. I don't want anything to do with it. You need to bring it back. Get it out of here." He sweeps his arms in the air.

Bristling, my heart racing, tightening my hold on Saxon, sending fear through him, my own feelings of rejection and displacement blast to the surface.

"The puppy is staying and you're the one that's going. So, put a sock in your pie hole." Defiantly, I barge past Burt. "Back off and get out of my way. This is my house. You're lucky to have lived in it this long. The street is right through that door. Use it if you don't like it here. I don't need you." I point to the street. I won't tolerate his overbearing condescension and control.

Traumatized, Saxon climbs and claws and wraps his stiff frightened body around my neck, clinging desperately for safety while screeching in fear.

Burt, sticking his tongue out, shaking his head, roiling with anger like a snorting bull, displaying his sour contempt, grabs a beer, and all three hundred pounds of him slam on the sofa. The TV cranked loud.

Saxon is on the floor with his ducky trotting after me down the hallway to my bedroom. Sniffing and exploring, he smells Burt's side of the bed. His ears go flat, his body retracts, and he comes running to me. When he finds his kennel on my side of the bed, his little tail swishes happily and he shyly wiggles. Oops! What did he just smell? Cautiously, he smells the blanket. A dog! Jumping and barking with excitement, he spins in circles.

Saxon is acclimated to where his kennel, water, and food dish are located. It's potty time. I carry him outside to meet Sadie.

Saxon does his business first, then scampers to Sadie. He is uncertain how to act with her. Sadie stands tall. Her ears perked. Her tail wags slowly while her clear, bright eyes look directly at Saxon, telling him with her body that she is the boss. She is gentle but firm, preventing him from jumping in her face as she stands straight and tall. Saxon gleefully runs to her and starts playing. Cautiously, he stays low, submissively, and softly licks her mouth. He respects her. His experience with Sadie is positive. This is his first lesson with a new dog and pack leadership, boundaries, and respect.

In softness, yet grounded demeanor, Sadie's smile tells me she is happy that Saxon is here. For her, it, too, is as if Saxon is a lost friend. This was the right decision for Sadie. She has a companion to share her life, my gift to her.

I walk in the house, while they continue to play outside. I know Sadie is not a threat to Saxon. It was the neighbor dogs I forgot about. Sadie knew how to cope. To her, the incessant barking and fence-fighting had become white noise. But they weren't to Saxon.

Inside, Burt has refueled his hatred about Saxon. Being distracted, we get embroiled, fighting and yelling, and then we hear what sounds like a vicious dogfight. We run outside to find Saxon trying to crawl under the wooden fence after the vicious dogs. Sadie comes to the rescue, pulling him back by the neck. Fear shoots through me. I realize I could have lost him through carelessness. But my angry reaction targeted my dogs.

Shame's second nature spills out from me, acting like Ma when the last straw snapped. My dogs bear its brunt. I grab them both. Saxon gets the worst scruffing. He feels my anger. My verbal and physical outrage imprinted Saxon's fear. A bad start, forming a negative association to strange dogs.

His world became more confusing and uncertain during the two weeks I stayed home to potty train him. He is escorted out every thirty minutes, and every thirty minutes, the neighbor dogs reinforce his fear, lunging and attacking the fence. Short of moving or have the neighbors leave, there is no escaping the situation. My scolding and yelling at the neighbor's dogs are constant. Saxon accumulates the collateral damage, assuming he is in the wrong. The combination of a harsh correction and yelling makes him wary of whom to trust. In the midst of peeing, he freezes and is in a fight-or-flight decision.

He watches Sadie as she bolts toward the fence. She seems to be the leader. Saxon follows, charging behind her, barking and showing his teeth, fighting versus fleeing. His adrenaline is flowing. It penetrates every cell in his body that is beyond its internal threshold. He doesn't understand how to normalize, so adverse aggression kicks in. The seeds of anger are planted. It is who he is becoming.

Saxon's first six weeks of life left him ill-prepared compared to Sadie's. Saxon didn't understand what to do with his fear emotions. He lacked impulse control. He only understood the instinctual fight or flight. So his reaction to strange dogs was to strike out. Aggression is a survival instinct in dogs and used when threatened. Saxon was still too young to know how to use his aggression correctly. He lacked boundaries and a pack leader.

Inside, on the living room floor, Saxon and I are playing with his stuffed yellow ducky. He pounces, growls, and shakes it, killing the squeaker as I tease him with it. He retrieves a small soccer ball, which enhances his chase drive. He attacks the blue food cube, trying to figure out how to get the treats to roll out of the box by batting it with his paws. Then, for no reason, he stops and sits front facing at Burt's feet, giving Burt direct eye contact, looking deep inside him, wondering why he is so angry or what's wrong. Saxon wants to be accepted and loved. Belonging is natural.

Burt turns away from him as my dad turned away from me. Saxon comes to me rejected. It's hard to crack a heart of stone. This is a freeze-frame moment for me, seeing such wisdom and insight coming through a puppy. Saxon is triggering old memories.

Often, I wonder if something inside Burt conceals a wound that Saxon, in piercing the pain Burt harbors, has intuitively identified. One thing is certain, Saxon is a threat to him. He offers what Burt can't—love. It's something Burt aches to have, but doesn't know how to give or receive. The same is true for me, and it's something neither of us understands.

The sting of puppyhood strikes home for me. My winged approach to having another dog is crumbling. Saxon's upbringing is secondary to Sadie's last obedience training. Finishing Sadie's CDX title hangs in the balance.

On top of that, corporate realignment pulls me farther from home, with less time to give Saxon. It is a time where socialization to other dogs, sounds, places, and people is vital. This is Saxon's fear period, around eight weeks, and still after raising Sadie, I haven't grasped its grave importance.

Burt dispassionately is giving basic care to the dogs, while I traveled. The dogs distance themselves from him, keeping to their corners to hide after he targeted them, maliciously throwing objects, kicking them, swatting them with newspapers, and spewing foul language, just because he could. He hates Saxon's presence.

They were surviving, like I was, but not thriving. Joy comes when I walk through the door and they come running to me, delighted, each bringing a toy stuffed in their mouth. Burt is jealous seeing their delight. The suffocating darkness rolls in like a chilling, damp fog that penetrates to one's core as cold silence and icy stares squash these happy greetings. Their cheerfulness nurtures me.

Sadie's CDX title is accomplished. Saxon is four months old, a time to start dog school. While there are trainers who offer puppy kindergarten, Sadie's obedience trainer doesn't believe in puppy kindergarten and she refuses to make that introduction to other puppies.

It's because of the friendship and loyalty I developed with Sue who substitutes for the trainer that I feel obligated to stay. Her intimidation blocks Saxon from getting the socialization he needs.

Suffering shame and betrayal by returning to Sadie's first trainer whose methods were food rewards and praise, I buckled and opted to stay here with this aversive trainer. Belonging and being accepted takes precedence over

Saxon's needs. His socialization is impaired from my decision. By putting a conditional friendship above Saxon's needs, I have done him a disservice.

Saxon's first class is basic obedience (called a "puppy class"). It's supposed to double for his kindergarten class. The trainer hates puppies, yet she breeds. Both Sue and the trainer find no value having kindergarten. They yell, using physical force, which is projected with anger. It is the farm all over again.

Burt agrees to come along to Saxon's classes. When we arrive in the training center, I look cautiously through the doorway to see how many puppies are there. I count just two but then twenty-four other owners who have big dogs, different-looking dogs, old dogs, dogs from a pound. They are restless, barking, unruly, and aggressive. This is Saxon's moment to make positive associations. He is pulling, anxious to play, trying to go nose to nose. The trainer is yelling above the barking and chaos. I jerk the leash back sending a shot of fear through it. Saxon cringes and his positive happy attitude dissolves into fear. The hope of Saxon having a positive interaction with new dogs disintegrates. He's with aggressive, unfriendly dogs like the neighbor dogs, when all he wants is to greet his classmates. Shot down again.

Chaos and confusion build in him as he's forced to suppress his enthusiasm. With a twisted angry face, stamping her feet, the trainer hollers, "Keep your dogs away from the other dogs!" She dramatically pans the room, pointing at all of us. Again, Saxon has encountered another wrathful experience as layer by layer his roots of life are forming.

Keeping our distance is nearly impossible in a packed room, sitting elbow to elbow. The dogs are scrunched under our folding chairs. Saxon is normally curious, and this would have been his chance to socialize. The yelling heightens his fear. The aggressive dogs target him. The tetchy training center reeks of hostility and intimidation.

Across the eight weeks he learns the basics of sit-down-stay, heel, and come as he realizes a reward follows compliance. During that time, he and Sadie get obedience training twice a day before each of their meals. I make training fun for Saxon. He is a quick study and wants to please. He places third in the class's completion. But two things come from the course: basic obedience skills and a negative association with dogs in an angry environment. That environment was the most influential aspect of the experience—and the most detrimental.

Sadie is Saxon's stronghold. He needs a pack leader as Sadie demanded of me. Leadership never occurs to me, so the chaos continues. It is my ignorance and improper life patterns causing Saxon's behavior problems, although I still don't realize it.

At six months old, Saxon is in the same training center, enrolled in conformation classes. The negative associations are in him. The instructor is teaching us to properly stack our dogs as if in a show ring. Saxon and I are next to the last dog in line to stand for exam and have the instructor exam him. I'm chatting with the lady behind me when I glance down at Saxon. Stiff-legged, forward, and head down with direct stare at the dog in front. Gasping and popping the lead, he understands my fearful reaction. Half-grown and built strong, he's ready to take on any dog in sight. He misreads the dogs' stacking as aggressive posturing. Without warning, using nature's element of surprise, he bursts into rage, snapping, snarling, baring his teeth, and rising up on his back feet, lunging, and attacking the shepherd in front of me. The dog reminds him of the neighbor dog. Saxon red-zones. The dog did not provoke Saxon. It doesn't matter to Saxon. That dog's very presence is enough of a threat.

Before I can react, Saxon rips a gash in the shepherd's neck and face, drawing blood and barely missing the dog's eye. I freeze. I have no idea why this happened.

The shepherd is a pointed show dog. I scold and shame Saxon in front of everyone as I apologize to the handler, offering to pay the vet bills. She is upset, but gracious. This incident extends beyond the vet bill because her dog would now be off the show circuit for months. My anger in the midst of all the other dogs knits more aggression in Saxon concerning strange dogs.

The instructor scolds me. "Don't allow him to look at other dogs while working the ring." So every time eye contact is made during the entire class, my hypervigilance and fixation redirects his focus. Each time we walk in, a shockwave rolls across the room at the sight of our entry. Dogs and handlers are on alert. The unspoken shame roars. *There's that dangerous killer dog again. I'm smeared* with humiliation.

Saxon is confused. He can't understand the other dogs' body language. He is trying but everything is wrong. Pleasing, praise, and finding the right way to behave usually are met with a harsh correction. His confidence is crushed. I'm seeing my puppy becoming a wild animal, emotionally spiraling downward, pressing down his anger. When self-restraint is impossible, full-blown feral rage, lunging, and attacking the dogs in class with the slightest glance from another propel him to an angry release, which also draws the most attention. I could relate to the times he redlined. It's like when I nearly killed my sister because I felt forced to compress my shame and anger. I aimed to be pleasing to the point of perfection, but never feeling accepted or belonging left me empty, unwanted, unloved, and never good enough. Saxon and I are mirrors of each other, blamed and shamed.

Tension hovers in the classroom. The class's opinion of us suggests we are the enemy and outcasts. We are pushed away from the group. "You will have to work from the other side of the room and not around these dogs." All eyes fearfully focus on Saxon's unpredictable temper. My body acquires muscle memory, ready to spring at the slightest notion of his outbursts. We react to one another. We feed our fear.

Distance doesn't matter. Saxon's direct eye contact increases, taking aim at the other dogs in class. We aren't welcome. How did this happen? How do I fix this? I don't know where to turn. But I'm aware I need help in solving my dog's aggression.

The trainer blames his poor genetics. I know they are stellar and don't accept her explanation. But I am counting on her help. I will trust her ability and am willing to follow her instructions. She's the dog trainer and should know.

Very little in Saxon's world was fun or happy. Oppression and survival grounded him in his world as they did in mine. Survival is what drove us both. The negative environment and poor programming braided us closer. We would use adversity to our advantage.

Course Correction

My life reaches a fork in the road when Saxon is eight months old. Burt continues his downward spiral of self-destruction, stagnation, and financial ruin. My career and overcoming Saxon's aggression overshadow the desire to rescue a draining marriage. It's irreparable and the hope of changing Burt is futile. I'm a go-getter tethered to a deadhead. Secretly I am searching for a divorce attorney.

Saxon's behavior puts Sadie in the shadows. Pursuing her Champion Tracker title ceases while my focus is on Saxon. The blessing of being involved with tracking is learning other training venues like the hunt test competition. It's led me to look into whether this could be an opportunity for Saxon and Sadie.

Sadie's intermediate obedience training taught her the trained retrieve (force-fetch), which is foundational to retrieving birds. But an obedience dumbbell is not a bird. Saxon needs the same training.

In mid-September, Saxon is enrolled in the intermediate classes, with the same trainer, and I hope she has the expertise to roll back Saxon's swelling aggression and help him develop skills for hunting. I worry that controlling his hostility is becoming futile.

Both the trainer and her assistant Sue compete in hunt tests. Sue brings her dog Jordie to obedience class. Outside of class, she is training Jordie for the Junior Hunter title and the Golden Retriever Working Certificate.

"Since you are involved in hunting, can we work with you to learn the hunt test skills to qualify for a Junior Hunter title?"

With scrunched faced and pursed lips, Sue holds off in silence before responding. "Sadie is no problem, but Saxon is. He stays on a long rope."

That is a yes. We get a break.

Sue describes the test setup for me to visualize what skills the dogs need to pass the test. "The Junior Hunter has one dog at the test line at a time. That dog is considered the working dog to be tested. Each dog is brought to the test line on lead and walked off the line with the lead attached only after testing. According to the rules, the dogs are supposed to retrieve one bird at a time, then wait for the second one to be thrown so they can mark the fall and retrieve. The distance of each mark is about one hundred yards. They do this both on land and water and must pass four tests to be titled."

Right away, it rattles me thinking about Saxon bringing back the bird, off-lead and disobeying coming into heel and delivering to hand. I know that behind the holding blind, the next dog is waiting his turn, so having Saxon on lead to and from the test line doesn't worry me. But he has yet to respond to a one-time command off-lead.

The underlying goal is for Saxon to become a normal, happy dog. My not understanding the workings within a balanced pack keeps Saxon at a disadvantage. His emotional life is a reflection of mine. How do I help Saxon find a normal when an emotional imbalance exists in me? It's my internal imbalances I don't recognize.

I'm thinking if I can reverse his aggression by forming new behaviors using hunt training and through retrieving birds, he can be normal and happy. Faith has led me to believe transforming him into a working dog is possible. What I didn't foresee is my lack of vision to grasp how steep the learning curve is.

"Nothing is free" is a concept of leadership and a paradigm shift from the use of force. It surfaces in one of his classes, and I tailor my own ideas to fit Saxon. Having him respond to the one-time command yields compliance the first time.

No longer multiple commands of sit, sit, sit, and he sits on the fourth command. Sit means now. Otherwise he'll tune me out as I nag. The other requirement he learns is to focus on my face, asking approval, and he earns everything from petting, attention, playing, treats to special spaces in the house, and earning his food by waiting at doors and sitting. He is rewarded for his compliance using the Premack principle, that is, more probable behaviors reinforce less probable behavior. Compliance brings reward.

Resource guarding is a learned behavior that Saxon never acquired. That's because I taught him to trade one item for a higher-value item, like a meat treat. I often take a toy from him, then give it back, which gains his trust. When he finishes his food, he sits and waits for Sadie to finish before he gets permission to lick her dish.

A balanced training approach is my method. It primarily is based upon positive rewards but countered with a correction for noncompliance. The correction means withholding a treat or denying him his favorite toy for playing tug. He loves the problem solving and being praised when he nails it. Our sessions are short and frequent, usually before he eats. Our communication becomes intuitive and he quickly understands. It's as if he sees my thoughts before I do. Very smart boy!

He is above average in intelligence and aptitude. His quick progress energizes me. With the right guidance and methods, Saxon can overcome his aggression. We are doing so well and we are happy.

Then our momentum hits a wall. During his obedience class, Saxon detects a challenging stare from a black Lab. Saxon growls back, as his stare locks with the Lab's. Their growls escalate and the trainer snaps, taking matters into her own hands. She flips Saxon over on his back, body-slamming him down in front of the entire class, pinning him to the floor with her full body weight while beating his head with an empty plastic pop bottle. "Bad dog! Bad dog! NO! NO! NO!" she berates him, brandishing her own gnarly facial expression. Traumatized, poor Saxon yelps and recoils. I'm shocked and appalled. I wonder what other detrimental associations Saxon makes to the strange dogs and whether this is helping him.

The trainer makes Saxon an example. She shames him and me in front the class, making both of us feel small and worthless as her sanctimonious authority reinforces her power.

She's in my face, yelling, "Keep Saxon away from the dogs."

After that, in each class, he is hit. Still, I believe the trainer is experienced handling aggression, so I stay with it. Saxon's behavior is getting worse. His outbursts form a pattern of targeting other dogs. He is acting out the offensive human posture lorded over him. Aggression breeds aggression. Confusion screws into his fiber. He just doesn't know what to do with his fury. Baffled about what is right, he reacts out of fear to survive. He models what he learns, just as I did.

Saxon and I go for leash walks. Seeing a strange dog at a distance fires up fear in me. He hears my slight gasp and smells the fright in my breath, feeding his reactivity and igniting his aggression.

Our daily walks in the woods with Sadie are done before dawn and after dusk. It's a time of feeling safe, so I let them run free off-leash to burn off pent-up energy. There's a palpable calm when the three of us are together.

Deliberately, I begin to question. Is the anger at home and in his classes affecting Saxon's health? Burt's hatred is our enemy. Coming to class, Saxon's hackles rise and the low guttural growl rumbles in the back of his throat. Many of the other dogs react similarly to the same environment. Is Saxon's aggression a result of charged energy in the room? Would he have the issues if he was in a calm environment?

If he emitted warning signals, they were so subtle, inconsistent, and buried within him that I missed them. Saxon's explosive ire was unpredictable. He loved people but not strange dogs. He literally ravaged a couple of his classmates. We are isolated from the others, yet still allowed to train. He has become a product of his environment where his being is pelted with ill will at every turn. He can't help himself. His outbursts are infectious and poisonous to the other dogs. As his welcome wears thin, my optimism wanes. In a hostile environment, my hope of rebuilding positive associations is fragile.

More questions. Was this all his fault, maybe not? I believe he wanted to be a good dog. That possibility spurred a turning point. I had to find reasons for the problem and solve it.

In the fifth class, Saxon gets pounded again. It's volcanic. The trainer and I face off. Her stiff body leans into my personal space. She's finger pointing and screaming.

"You need to kill that dog! He's no good! You will never change the aggression. It is in his genes. He will ruin you financially. Get rid of him! He is not worth the bother! He is a huge liability! He is not welcome in here!"

The anger in me rears up, boiling to the surface. I remember incidents of being made to feel worthless and unwanted. That's enough! Tolerating her abuse or disrespect is over. She's a fraud and doesn't know diddly about aggression. She only makes it worse. The chance of reversing Saxon's aggression here is nil.

The handlers and their dogs recoiled, freezing in silence. Bug-eyed, they await my next move. My evilness roused, I stand up. My jaws clench. I put Saxon behind me for his protection and walk directly at her with determination, disdain, and anger. After trusting this person, I am now awash with a sense of betrayal. My steely-eyed stare is locked, and I start spewing fire at the dog trainer. It's a face-off.

"Get out of my face, you bitch. I'll train Saxon myself. You traumatized him. You can take your anger and put it where the sun doesn't shine. You never intended to help us. You played us." Saxon and I turn tail.

We never looked back. She deserved my wrath in front of her clients. She had shamed Saxon and me enough. She had also generated in me a feisty grit to prove her wrong. I'd find a way, however long it took to overcome Saxon's aggression.

"Why would you change your life for Saxon?" Sue wants to know as we talk on the phone. "It is just not worth doing. You can't use him for anything. He is not worth having for a show dog. You can't put him with other competition dogs. You can't let him breed. Just get another dog and get rid of him."

Her remark elevates my rage. Dogs aren't disposal objects. That's it. Saxon is my cause, and I am unwavering in my fight for him. I'll do whatever it takes, even if it means changing my life to save his. I feel for Saxon what compassionate humans feel about their troubled or deformed child. Do you just throw away a child or do you help them succeed to whatever level they can attain, by supporting, loving, and guiding them? Besides, is this Saxon's fault, or is it genetics? Is it possible that his aggression spans generations? That question gnaws at me. Yet, I don't see the same trait in myself.

Now Sadie and Saxon are my family. We need one another, because we were all we had.

Goals! Goals! Goals! They are pounded into me by corporate. Close every sale and push no matter the cost. Make it happen. Find a way. It's your job to figure it out. It's about winning and clawing through adversity. In childhood, rising above hardship was a self-taught survival mechanism. It is ingrained from emotional maltreatment, and woven in me. I've transferred this mindset to performance dog training. Corporate fostered the drive and I use it to help Saxon succeed.

Reprogramming Saxon and chasing ribbons for self-respect are my intentions. Performance and accomplishment provide self-worth. I am tenaciously driven to succeed. Lying down is out of the question. Winning will energize and define me.

Hunt 'em Up

A few weeks before Saxon's first pheasant hunt, Sue and I meet in an open field where she had a couple of caged pigeons. We wing-shackle one of the birds to see Saxon's prey drive. The bird runs and Saxon pounces and pins the bird with his front paws, flipping it in the air. Standing, looking at me and then the bird, he is not sure how to pick it up. A mouth full of feathers feels strange.

Sadie's reaction is more reserved. Both Saxon and Sadie have a soft-mouthed approach holding the bird gently in their mouth. They need to be taught how to pick up a downed bird, retrieve, and deliver to hand.

Once the dogs have developed the consistency in picking up pigeons, we expose them to hen pheasants. We meet at Zwickey's pheasant farm to show my dogs an actual hunt and hear gunshot from a distance. Listening from far away is the first step to preventing a gun-shy dog. Sue is hunting with Jordie, her golden retriever.

The hunt comes on a glorious, palette fall day. The air is cool and damp against an azure sky. Looking over the rolling farmland lifts the oppression from home.

Saxon and Sadie are waiting excitedly in the car kennels for the pheasants to be caught. Saxon sees the birds running and flying in their pens. He comes alive, uprooting his kennel pad, digging, barely containing his eagerness to chase the cackling birds. I let him out and he goes running to and fro, jumping outside of the bird pen, panting, and barking. He stops and checks in with me, smiling, then returns to the chase, tail whipping wildly. His body does a rapid S-curve move. His guard is down and his heart open. It's a wonderful contrast to the training center and home. His adrenaline is racing for all the right reasons this time. He is safe and in his wheelhouse. This is who he is.

Saxon watches Dean net the pheasants in the pen and put them in a small wire cage. Every time he swings the net, there's the pounding rush of pheasants' wings. They fly to the top netting, covering the pen. Roosters cackle and scatter. Saxon is amped. The caught birds are in a cage on a four-wheeler, headed out to the field. Saxon is kenneled as we follow a four-wheeler to where the hunt will start. Dean explains to me how he'll set the pheasants in the field.

"I dizzy the birds by spinning their heads in a circle. Then I tuck their heads under one wing as if they are sleeping. They're nestled in a tuft of grass, so they think they are hiding when they wake up."

He speeds off into the field and hides a bird in the tall grass. Saxon is panting, barking, spinning, and digging in his kennel. He's anxious to hunt. Here he comes alive, kindling the light within.

Sadie is first to hunt. Dean gets his gun. Sadie bolts from her kennel.

"Hunt 'em up! Find the bird!" Sadie's nose is keen. She instinctively understands quartering the wind and finding a scent cone. She's on it. The bird flushes high enough for a clean shot. "Fetch it up." She prances with a lilt through the tall grass. "Here."

Sadie snatches the bird, holding it softly in her mouth, releasing it to me. Having earned praise for her work, she is prancing and smiling beside me. We make a good team. It's a happy time out here. Dean speeds out again, setting another bird for Saxon as we walk back to the truck.

Saxon is out of his kennel with a long line attached to his collar, not another strange dog in sight. He is jumping and lunging with joy. He is so birdie. "Saxon, Hunt 'em up! Find the bird!" Bounding like he has leaf springs attached to all fours, quartering between the gunner and me, he feels the wind in his face. His ears perk with his nose held high. He's in a full tilt run. His golden tail rotates like a windmill spinning in the wind. Hitting bird scent, he skids, his head pops up. Then nose in the grass, butt skyward, tail whipping side to side, he's on it. Get ready. He goes straight up like a fox and pounces, pushing his paws under the bird, flushing. The bird tries to escape and Saxon pins the pheasant between his paws. He nuzzles the bird, trying to gently hold it in his mouth. The bird struggles, then flies. It is shot and falls to the ground. Saxon marks where it fell and grabs it in his mouth. He prances with pride back to me as if it is the greatest prize he could give me.

What a great day being together, assured of finding a direction and purpose for us because, out here, we are one. The oppression is replaced with a sense of who we really are, and there is joy filling our soul. Hunting isn't the solution to reversing Saxon's aggression, but we're moving in a positive direction, shaping new behaviors. It is who he becomes as much who I become.

Repression's cloud hovers as we head for home. All our free spiritedness folds in and dissipates with the prospect of facing Burt and the vicious neighbor dogs. We turn solemn, tight-lipped, heading into the cold, quiet world of desperation, anger, and survival.

Saxon's legs quiver. He's limping. Diarrhea is a frequent reaction to the vicious verbal brawls between Burt and me. Our safety is threatened by being held hostage in our own emotional prison. The dogs shut down, freezing, shivering with fear. Something buried in me is astir. Images of my childhood surface. The dogs are mirroring me on a physical and emotional level. They are showing me how unhealthy this way of life is and how desperately change is needed.

Can't Stand No More

It's midnight. I'm home, exhausted from an eighteen-hour travel workday. Sadie joyously runs to greet me. Saxon is right behind, scurrying to find a toy, full of wiggles, dog talk, and joy for me. Burt is slumped in bed watching TV. He then announces happily, "I quit my job today." He is so proud of his decision.

"You what!"

"I quit my job today. I thought you would support me."

"We never discussed this," I fire back. "How dare you make major financial decisions without me, yet again! We're barely making payments and collection agencies are harassing us. You're the one that wanted a thirty-four-foot sailboat for a charter business. We agreed that it'd take both our incomes to make the business viable. Now you are reneging."

The real reason comes out. The county board is after him for misappropriating county funds. He quit to avoid being convicted and sent to jail. On top of that, he was caught fondling the restaurant manager in public. That is the final straw.

"You worthless piece of crap. Why do I even bother to support you and care about you when you have the balls to cheat on me? Pretty gutsy to do it where you work. You repulse me. You do everything to drag me in the gutter with you."

My poor dogs! Sadie is lying in a somber heap, trying to avoid the arguing. Her ears are down, her face on her paws. Saxon bolts into my office seeking safety, and hides under my desk, panting and yawning.

Burt held out for ten years knowing I'd take the martyr role for him. He played a full-blown victim, claiming he was destitute, disabled, and unable to work because of a bad heart and diabetes, then added cancer for good measure. He didn't have cancer, but it made him sound more desperate when he tried to take me to court and, under Wisconsin marital law, I was supposed to pay him at the ten-year mark.

In an effort to save the marriage, I suggested counseling, but he is singing the same old tune: "I don't have a problem and don't need to talk to anybody."

Burt's anger targets the dogs. He stomps on the joy the dogs give me. He detests Saxon's presence. Saxon's body shows the rejection. Ears flattened, eyes dropped in sadness, cringing and trembling, and he watches Burt from my office.

The hostility is unsustainable. Burt senses a divorce is forthcoming and threatens me. "I will have your pension. Take Sadie and you will owe me alimony for the rest of my life."

Red-zoning, red-faced, blood-pressure spiked, I clench fists and want to rip his face off. I slam my fist into the wall, restraining my compulsion to kill him, because he isn't worth going to jail over.

"You don't deserve a penny! Furthermore, Sadie is staying with me. You can get your ass out of this house. It was mine at the beginning. All you brought to this marriage and to this house is your emotional baggage, fat ass, and debt. You are running us into bankruptcy so fast I can't keep up and you don't care. We will settle this in court."

How do I turn to God and faith when all I want to do is take control on my own and survive? I am pouring hope into myself and others, not God. I'm isolated. God never crosses my mind. Years of failed relationships have eroded my faith. I presume holding onto myself and the dogs is all that matters. I quickly learn that the legal system is ruthless. It's not about right and wrong, but about who can win, who has the money to pay. Morals and decency be gone.

"You are out of my house the end of the month, so get packing. I just will not put up with you anymore. I'm done. Find someone else to leech off."

Divorce weasels its way into every fiber of my life like a drop of food coloring in water. Though Burt is out of the house, strife invades through email, phone calls, legal meetings, and court appearances. Blocking the stress from the dogs is insurmountable. It's me, brush-blocking to provide a calm in the house.

Burt's mother gets involved, suggesting blackmail. I can have Sadie, but only for a large sum of money. I'm infuriated. Sadie is not going to be a bargaining tool. I stay strong. Burt's blackmail scheme fails. But the divorce drags on.

Being one in nature with my dogs provides the grounding I need to quell the daily turbulence. They are my safe place during the emotional storms. As we walk and play together, an indescribable sense of Divinity encases us. They are carefree, sniffing, and wandering at leisure, and I'm still burdening myself with guilt, assuming blame for the disservice done to Saxon. Sadie is balanced enough to divert the hostility, yet continues to feel second-class and dismissed. Shame gets passed along to my dogs.

Each month, Saxon's fear-aggression magnifies, each month no solutions.

Near dusk, we three are walking in the woods. There's a frontage road near the area along the railroad tracks. We are almost to my vehicle when a panel truck drives up and parks on the road. A man flings open the side panel doors and pouring out of his truck come five dogs, a Rottweiler, German shepherd, malamute, Doberman, and mixed breed. The dogs spot us and charge directly for us. Saxon doesn't see them coming. A terrifying bolt razors through me. I know Saxon will fight to the death and be killed. I grab him, race to my van, and shove him in his kennel a split-second before the pack attacks the back of the van. Saxon is riled, clawing, snapping his teeth, and barking. I try to get Sadie and she doesn't let me. We are exposed to the pack. I'm thinking for certain they will kill her when she surprises me by taking charge. She spins around, facing off the entire pack, head and front shoulders low to the ground, ears flat on her head, fire-eyes, and teeth gnashing, issuing a low guttural growl, and standing her ground. The pack freezes. The alpha bitch rises, setting boundaries and saving our lives. The pack backs off as their owner breathlessly catches up and apologizes. I'm proud and grateful for Sadie's courage and leadership. But angrily, I speak my mind, letting him know the damage that was nearly inflicted and how negligent he was not to notice others in the area.

The Injured Lab

Saxon's breeder would rather kill a dog, to uphold her reputation, than believe what I suspect about her breeding. Money, it's always about money with this breeder.

"After you euthanize Saxon, you can get another puppy from me," she proffers. There it is again: Dispose of the dog. The attitude of "it's just a dog" infuriates me. That is not going to happen. I will find an answer for Saxon.

Neutered, he's stripped of his identity and desire to play and mount Sadie. Despair and depression are invading. Sadie tries to pull him out of his doldrums by bringing a toy and encouraging him to play tug and tag. Nothing. She is left standing motionless when he lies down. Her pleading eyes meet mine. *Please do something. Help him! You're supposed to be the pack leader and you are not.* Her thoughts reflect the words and feelings I said to my dad when Ma was choking. I'm ashamed for Saxon's emotional state and helpless to change it. I trusted professionals and it did no good. Neutering didn't extinguish the aggression. It had him and was in him.

Our late afternoon romps in the woods are the highlight of each day. Saxon springs out of my van, spinning with exuberance, knowing he's free to run like a normal dog. He and Sadie are running full tilt, high-jumping logs and brush when their rejoicing turns to terror. Saxon sights a couple walking their Labrador. He targets the dog, charging full speed. His fear-aggression supersedes his ability to obey. Nothing is stopping him. Just the sight of another dog triggers his anger.

The middle-aged couple is minding their own business, slowly leash-walking their senior chocolate Lab along a trail. Saxon ambushes them, aiming directly at the dog. An ingrained sound of terror courses through me when I see the flash of my dog's gnashing canine teeth and hear his dog's guttural growl and vicious snapping bark. Another attack is coming. He's in red-zone rage.

"SAXON, COME, COME, COME!" Nothing. The Lab never projected any threat, but to Saxon, it didn't matter. A strange dog was reason to fight.

I run to catch him, but he has already T-boned the Lab, snap-rolling the dog off his feet. Saxon's primal kill instinct goes feral. He is on top of the old Lab and has it by the neck, in a death grip, shaking and squeezing the life out of the dog. The Lab screeches in pain and yelps for help. The man and woman are kicking at Saxon and screaming, "No, no, no, get away!"

Catching up with Saxon, I tackle and barrel-roll him off the Lab, clenching his collar to leash him. Grabbing the scruff of his neck, I hoist his front feet off the ground, and eye to eye scold him. "No, bad dog. Down and stay." Aggression spills over him like a shroud of darkness. His deep-rooted role-modeling is acted upon toward other dogs.

Fear, anger, and adrenaline spill from each of us. Sadie keeps her distance quietly and stays calm. I put Saxon in the van. I snatch a towel to wrap and apply pressure to the Lab's neck wounds. The incident sickens me. Covering my face with my bloody hands, I apologize. "I am so sorry; I will meet you at your vet's office and cover any expenses." The owners carry the Lab to their car and they're on their way to the vet.

At the vet's office, I'm asked, "Is the rabies vaccination current?"

"Yes." I reply. Saxon was about to be quarantined and possibly put down.

This time, the dog recovered from the head and neck puncture wounds. But Saxon changed that Lab's life forever. He was traumatized and never the same. Paying the bill was a small price, considering what could have happened. My gut told me there would be a next time. And then what?

The trainer's voice shoots through my head. "You need to kill that dog. He's a liability." I block it out of my mind. In my heart, Saxon is innocent. I love him and he feels it. I believe in him and am determined never to quit. There must be an answer. I will find it. Losing or quitting on Saxon amounts to an unforgiveable personal failure. How to help him is at this point beyond my knowing, yet I trust an answer will emerge.

One thing I do know: Keeping him isolated isn't a solution. Though Sadie is his stability, we must find other balanced dogs for him so that he can thrive and outgrow his aggression. I am dialed into Saxon, and he shows me how we share emotions, behaviors, and upbringings. We were both damaged and confused souls because of the environment we were raised in. Aggression blocked his natural talents.

Any physical attack on Saxon is like impaling him. Righteous indignation rises in me. I want to spit in people's faces for denouncing Saxon. A persistent thought races through my brain. *I'll show you you're wrong, and one day you will eat your words.*

Maintaining a can-do attitude, changing to a positive environment in field work gives Saxon purpose, building his confidence. It provides a sense of accomplishment for me, and I foresee a finely tuned team.

When his environment felt safe, his gentleness shined through. Eileen, an older retired woman, worked part-time at a local convenience store and often came out to pet my dogs. She admired Saxon. Saxon turned inside out for her, shyly smiling and wiggling in his kennel anxious to be petted. He became the innocent parading puppy in his whelping box. Eileen coochy-cooed with him. He grabbed his toy with a slight *Woof-woof* and melted. Saxon delighted Eileen and filled her day with glee. She nicknamed him "Old Softy." The clown in him gleamed when I opened his kennel door, and he came out to greet his friend. He poured out all his love and compassion spilled as he sat straight up on his haunches with a gentle bark, asking for a treat. Then he leaned over and hugged her.

Saxon and I stop by Eileen's apartment one afternoon for a visit during our leash walk. Her five-year-old granddaughter is there. I'm careful and trusting but keeping an eye on Saxon as the angelic young girl slowly approaches him. She is gentle, unafraid, and quiet with him, as if she intuitively knows what Saxon needs. She lies down on the floor napping while Saxon spoons next to her. I never saw that coming. What a blessing to witness the peace and calm the two of them share as Eileen and I chat over coffee. My hope mounts as Saxon's life grows stronger. These are the times he reinforces my belief in him. My optimism soars when he demonstrates such gentle, unconditional love. He has a heart of gold and a godlike presence. He stirs in me a spark of hope, where only darkness lived.

Working long hours fill my days, but I rush home to exercise the dogs and fortify their obedience training. I remain hypervigilant, knowing every off-leash walk is risky. Saxon needs the exercise to calm his anxiety and counterbalance his aggression. The end of the day is always the best part of our time together, a special space to cherish. At night, when we go to sleep and it is just the three of us snuggling, we create a cozy pack. We have peace, privacy, and unity. The dogs wrap their bodies around me, supporting each other, sharing a sense of safety and security. We anchor one another, becoming one. They fulfill their purpose through their outpouring of love to me. Home is a snug shelter now. All barriers are down and we're safe to be ourselves. This is the way life is supposed to be, building one another up in harmony and love.

Most of the time, their best efforts go unnoticed, because of my preoccupation with work and the divorce. Too often, I have to learn to live in an altered state of reality because it's what I know is needed to persevere.

My decompression time is teaming up with Sue after work or on weekends. She and I are granted permission by local farmers to train our dogs on their land. This is Saxon's chance to work in a new situation around Jordie. Hunting has redirected his focus on finding birds instead of fighting with dogs. This is when he receives praise. As long as he obeys his commands and is a good dog, we'll continue to train together through the fall and winter. Sue brings dead, frozen training birds. Saxon is attached to a long line for safety around Jordie and Sadie. We set out in the field with the dogs. The setup is for one person to hold the dog's collar and the other person stands one hundred yards out, while the dog waits to hear the *Quack! Quack! Quack!* The gunshot report, and the bird is hailed high in the air to mark the fall. The dog runs the distance and retrieves to hand.

Anyone watching would roll with laughter at us donned in our winter camo parkas, orange sheepskin-lined caps with earflaps, pockets loaded with the trailing stink of dead pheasants, in our knee-high muck boots as we trudge through the snowy fields, practicing for the hunt tests in spring. We're packing a loaded 209 starter pistol and a duck call. Nothing stops us. We laugh at each other, bemoaning ourselves. "What man would want women like us?" Then we giggle again. Well, whatever it is, it must be in the eye of the beholder! Ha! We were having a good time. And so were the dogs.

A Raucous Rebound

Out here in the field with Saxon and Sadie, our place of sacred solitude, away from the malicious berating, angry yelling, and cold silence, we treasure our oneness. We trust one another. Our protective shields vanish, creative innocence emerges, and our hearts feel safe to love freely, offering a vulnerability and openness to be ourselves. It's a chance for me to discover pure love, without condition or interference, where tippy-toeing around an eggshell environment is cast to the wind. I taste tranquility and savor it.

Training and bonding in nature soothes our souls. It is where we three come alive. It's right in our wheelhouse as a purposeful pursuit to problem solving. We have an insatiable desire to learn and grow limitless.

Emotional pain is the catalyst for turning a negative into a positive, by repurposing the learned fear and anger into desire and passion. Often the things I hook myself to are transient, leaving my soul to feel unsatisfied.

There is war within me of holding fast to shame's shaping, while God's voice beckons me to leave the habitual relationships and destructive behaviors. But how do you walk away from who you believe you are? How do you begin when you lack direction or tools and an understanding of your existence? Those tools don't exist.

This crossroad draws me closer to God. I start attending church. I real-ize my ways aren't working and listening to God's way aids me in finding a new course for my life, by being open to the Holy Spirit's leading.

Reflecting back over the people I married or had affairs with, it dawned how their behavior matched the passive-aggressive, manipulative maltreatment I experienced in my childhood. For us it was then a normal upbringing and wasn't viewed as abuse. But it was abusive. For me, this was a stark realization: We were attracted to other persons' trauma. We complimented each other's needs, agreeing to use or be used, to be both victims and victimized, feeding on one another.

Faith is inching its way up in me the more I nurture it, gaining a foot-hold. I desire a second chance. I seek a new normal out of the upheaval of ingrained darkness. I am amazed as I visualize and discover what it can be like to live in spiritual harmony and feel peace and contentment in my ill-tuned heart and home. Can life be balanced to feel one with nature? Or is that only a romantic fantasy?

Intellectually knowing does not change patterns. The learned demands of pleasing, peacemaking, acquiescing to others versus honoring myself yield anger and anxiety. Codependence drains me. Within me, warfare of the mind versus the soul is fueled by the pressure of society's road map for being successfully coupled and financially secure. My desires and goals collide with God's will for my life.

The Scriptures say if we believe in Christ's death on the cross and ask for forgiveness of sins, we receive the power of the Holy Spirit in our lives.

Sue knows a man from the obedience training center who has three golden retrievers and a rescue mix breed. He asks her if she knows a woman he could invite to an upcoming summer music festival. He gives Sue his phone number in case she thinks of anyone.

"Why don't you give him a try? He's got goldens. Here's his number if you decide to call him."

Realizing my past relationship decisions were poor, I recognized I needed advice from a therapist about dating this man.

I'm suspicious. It smells of a bad prank. My gut raises a red flag. My therapist advises me to take two years to heal from all previous relationships before engaging in another. Honestly, healing is an abstract concept for me. Healing what? Inner torment swirls between choosing to listen to friends and taking the therapist's advice and walking by faith. The pull to the old familiar patterns is strong. My mind convinces me to stay the course.

But maybe this man could be the support I need to help Saxon. Maybe, he could be a life partner for me. Maybe, my life could be fruitful. Saying no is difficult because codependence is my filter. Caring what others think and the need to belong and please others run strong in my veins. Fear keeps me there.

Emotionally fragile and spiritually weak, I find myself tethered and teetering. Head cupped in my hands, I ponder the decision of accepting a blind date against an undercurrent to walk away. Thoughts whirl of what is right and wrong. Angst saturates me. All my human insecurities bubble up as I weigh the pros and cons of living alone the rest of my life. I am sensibly leaning into saying yes to another potential rebound. The magnetism is stronger than my will to completely walk away.

I feel like a recovering alcoholic in the beginning stages, who is tempted to reach for the bottle and scared that the cycle will start again. What am I, a puppet of my mind? How does one stop the merry-go-round pattern of failing relationships?

After several sessions with my therapist in which she insists on prescribing antidepressants, I realize God is the missing piece in all my past relationships and the drugs would be a cover-up of the root cause. Drugs or God? I choose God. Going solo and shoving God to the curb failed every time. I promise myself that the next person in my life will be grounded in faith and hold God as their life's compass.

My Achilles' heel is Saxon taking me down a slippery slope. He needs a new dog pack for him to grow.

Pleasing my friends, balancing a professional life, and doing what is right for Saxon have created trepidation. Saxon is foremost in my mind. My devotion for him runs deep, much like my hell or high-water irrational self-determination. Surrendering myself as a sacrifice to save Saxon is invaluable.

Giving no consideration to the possible personal damage associating with this man, with tunnel vision I see him having golden retrievers that can broaden Saxon's exposure to strange dogs. This is my main motive to date him.

"It's only a date and it could be a fun weekend," Sue says. "Why not go? What harm could it be?"

"I guess you're right. Who is he and what is this guy about?"

"He's a businessman. He owns several businesses. He attends obedience classes with his dogs. So you have something in common. Besides, you're divorcing Burt. What difference does it make?"

I feel guilty, but she has a point. The man I might date seems to be self-sufficient. We are both professionals and have business and dog training in common. On the surface the relationship appears safe.

"Quit isolating yourself and call him. It's only a date. Go have some fun," Sue says. After a month of mental debate, her comment convinces me to make the call. Yah, I thought, what harm is there going to dinner and a music festival?

When he answers the phone, he touts the musical event. "I have VIP tickets to Rock Fest and we have front row seats and access to the food tents that are for the local businesspeople."

Well, special treatment, sounds like fun and a diversion from my messy divorce and being anal. For once, I am going to be respected and treated like a lady.

The July festival is a four-day weekend starting Thursday afternoon. "I am a car collector. I will pick you up in my red 1957 Chevrolet," he says.

Well, I love the classic muscle cars, the songs of the '50s and '60s, and all the rock-and-roll nostalgia of those years. "Great, I'll be ready."

When Thursday afternoon rolls around, I hear the car coming down my street. I have butterflies in my gut. Rock tunes blare out of the rolled-down windows of the red hardtop as he pumps the accelerator, creating the glass-pack rumble of the exhaust pipes. The car's rumble stirred a bit of naughtiness and adventure in me. The '57 Chevy is shined to the nines.

At first glance, this is exciting. Nice car, but not sure of the person. When the engine stops and he gets out of the car, there he is, all six-foot-five and three hundred forty pounds of man. His jolly belly flops over his belt. Oh, my, this is not at all what I expected.

He is a formidable man, wearing thick-rimmed glasses. The top of his head is bald enough to match a bowl ring with shaved white hair just above his ears. His shiny white teeth are perfect caps. His bulging blue eyes are widely set. He's freshly shaved and showered—spanking clean! Err go the reason for calling it a blind date, but anything is possible.

We meet at the front screen door. "Hello, I am Chester."

"Hi, nice to meet you. These are my dogs, Sadie and Saxon. Sadie is the oldest."

He tries warming up to Sadie and Saxon by rough petting and doing baby talk. I step back, giving him space with my dogs while I observe their reactions. It's natural for Saxon to be happy and grab a toy when he sees people coming. It's a ritual when dogs assess a strange dog in a pack and check them out. There's that tense moment of acceptance or not as the dogs circle one another, smelling butt, going nose to nose, sniffing the other's breath for aggression, deciding if friend or foe.

Once Saxon was near Chester and looking him directly in the eye, his joy changed to caution. He dropped his toy and backed away with half-raised hackles. Saxon gets a whiff of Chester's breath, then hones into his subconscious, feeling a dark undercurrent, triggered by reading Chester's negative energy field. Sadie is polite and retreats, staying in the background, as she did during the arguments with Burt.

My dogs love people, so this was out of character. Still, I dismissed their obvious reactions and avoided making a snap judgment. Maybe I didn't want to see what they felt and hoped that this time it was different, caving to motive versus reality.

Superficially, Chester is a very charming man who was worldly, well-honed, street-smart, smooth, keen, and savvy in style. A boyish, brash macho showiness grabbed my attention, stirring the rebellious part of me that stretched common-sense rules beyond healthy boundaries. His powerful

air made me feel feminine from his virile presence, as he was framing his
swift trust by befriending me into believing that he came with a high moral
compass and quality upbringing. That's where his flipside showed, slick
sly, and cunning. His performance was animal-like in trying to entice a
female prior to breeding.

Grabbing a jacket, I leave treats on the dogs' pillows before going out the
door. Cautiously optimistic yet vulnerable and nonjudgmental, I accept Chester
at face value. When we arrive at the music festival grounds, he struts like a full-
plumed rooster ready to crow with me as his arm candy. At the ticket counter
he flashes a wad of $100 bills, making a point that he always carries twelve.

We are seated in the front row where the speakers' reverberation vibrates
our bodies and deafens our ears.

"Are you hungry?" He wants to eat and get acquainted.

"Yes, I will follow you." We walked into the VIP food tent.

In the VIP tent he loads his plate and heads toward the beer taps, filling
two glasses. Onlookers put their heads down with eyebrows raised, peering
inquisitively at me as to why I am with this man. "What's wrong with her?"

Their reaction gives me chills as my gut twists. I wonder what they
know that I don't.

With the music blaring, carrying on a conversation at our table is impossible.
I move, so my ear is at his face. The entire evening is a one-sided conversation
of victimhood about the wife he is divorcing, and he makes a public scene,
bawling. Eyes glare from those seated nearby witnessing his disturbing the-
atrics. I am uncomfortable expressing sympathy and compassion. My flawed
fixer-pattern reignites. Gullible, I take the bait. Reliving his marriages and
divorce becomes our common ground. He doesn't ask about me or my interests.

"What was your reason for getting a divorce?"

"I expect a woman to engage in sex at my demands and the wife won't."
Well, that gives me pause.

"Are there children?"

"Yes, a thirteen-year-old daughter who has been in and out of alcohol
treatment since eleven. My wife won't let me see her." That rallies a fight-
flight-freeze response in me to what abuse had been inflicted on her.

We leave the festival before the last band played, but the amount of alcohol he's consumed across the evening makes me concerned for my safety going home. His driving is reckless.

Saxon and Sadie greet us as we come through the door. Once their excitement settles, Sadie slinks away, keeping her distance, yet watching guardedly from the floor as we sit on the sofa and talk. Sadie's paws are outstretched with her head resting on them. She intermittently raises her eyebrows with weary glances in our direction. Saxon places his body at my feet between me and Chester, serving as my protector. A second cautious indication is unheeded on my part.

One admirable quality that catches my attention is his defense of the penniless and the less privileged. Here he is generous, expecting nothing in return. From my past childhood experiences, then with Al, Africa, and Saxon, I understand and connect with how the impoverished feel. Simply listening and remaining silent, I figure I've found additional common ground.

He tells of a close fishing buddy who is financially strapped because of his medical condition and inability to work. He is helping him pay the bills. Chester is a man of means being generous to the downtrodden. Simultaneously, he shows me his soft side and reels me in.

It's deeply satisfying to have an intelligent and intimate adult conversation that goes to the heart of generosity, helping others, and the greater good. Fluctuations of emotions and varied topics of shared interests feed into the possibility of a valued friendship.

He gets very personal and quickly to the point. He's looking for a woman to bear more children. That is his motive. When he learns the full scope of a tubal ligation and my choice to remain barren, it's a strike against me. Not good enough!

Still, he makes his sexual advance, expecting sex in return for the festival. Saxon puts his body even more between us, pushing Chester away. Saxon and Sadie saw him as a predator and I didn't.

Things quickly cool off. We continue to talk on the topic of his faith. He has no regard for God and doesn't believe God exists. I am disappointed since it was my hope to find a Christ-centered person at a time when my fragile faith is gaining traction in my life.

The next three nights were a repeat performance of the first. He told his same sob story, weeping in his beer, being a glutton with food and alcohol. Somewhere across Saturday and Sunday, the dogs came up in our conversation. I mentioned Saxon's aggression and my interest in identifying resources to modify his behavior, luring Chester in. Unknowingly, we were greasing the other to satisfy selfish motives. He took the bait, offering to help tone down Saxon's aggression, though not explaining how. Chester's ego was fed and it was my step onto a slippery slope.

We discuss Sadie's accomplishments in obedience, tracking, and therapy work, along with the subject of training my dogs for field and hunting. He boasts his dogs don't need to be trained for hunting. They are naturals, above any rules that reflect on his actions. His competitive drive aims to one-up me. By Sunday evening, he has worn me down like prey and made his sexual advances again. Unfortunately, I succumb to his desires and give into his wishes. Feeling intimidated and pressured to be nice, I crumble. The hook was set giving each other a reason to be together. He got sex and Saxon got an open door to be helped.

Before leaving, he asks, "Can I call you again?"

I invite him to come along to a hunt test in Minnesota. My purpose for going is to learn the skills expected of dogs to qualify in a Junior Hunt test. Attending gives me a good idea of what test skills my dogs lack and where to focus my training efforts for Saxon.

Looking back over that weekend, like in previous relationships, dismissing his family situation, drinking, lack of faith in God, and several outlandish negative aspects was my self-sacrificing pattern being repeated. Inviting emotional pain into my life was normal. It struck me that this was Saxon's chance to get the help he needed. Saxon took priority. That's what mattered.

Chester's influence is stronger than my faith. Other people's opinions matter more than mine because I don't feel worthy. I'm consumed. Saxon's growth supersedes my spiritual growth. Faith is put on the backburner.

The Minnesota Hunt

Driving into the Junior Hunter test site, dog trucks are lined along the field fence line. Dogs are barking excitedly. The field is abuzz. Determined people wearing camouflage are airing their dogs, feeling the excitement of competition, waiting in anticipation for their number be called to the test line. All are there for the purpose of meeting the Junior Hunter test standards and grabbing an earned ribbon.

In the field are two gun stations ninety degrees apart and at a distance of one hundred yards where the gunners were behind the camouflage holding blinds. The judges are finalizing the test set-up and the mechanics for land so everything is safe and operates without a hitch.

Parking my van on a hill, we pull out the camp chairs to watch from a distance. Saxon and Sadie are in the van with the hatch open so Saxon can see the other dogs working. Saxon needs to feel safe his first time here. Zeroing into the test silences any conversation with Chester, which draws out an edginess from him. He's rattled not being the center of attention. The test is.

We watch the judges call the handlers to line. The test dog demonstrates how the test is run and its challenges. According to the rules, the judges tell the handlers their performance expectations and the dogs' line manners.

"Guns up," a judge calls, telling the gunners to get ready to throw and shoot.

We watch the handler of the test dog come to the line at heel on lead. He holds the dog's collar with two fingers having a slight restraint and watches the first bird go down. I picture Saxon at the line, doing the same, but skeptical how he will react knowing another dog is directly behind the holding blind. The handler releases the dog on the judge's command, "TEST DOG," to retrieve the duck and swiftly return to heel, holding the bird in his mouth until the handler takes it. The same is true for the second mark, which completes the land series portion of the test. Fear wells up in me, knowing Saxon is not ready for this situation. My immediate fear is him coming back with his bird and attacking the next dog in the holding blind. Saxon needs training to be steady on first-time command, desensitized to strange dogs, and focused out in the field.

The dogs that pass the land now perform two separate marks in water. Chester can't restrain himself. He's a blowhard. "My dogs can do that without any training. They are natural hunters."

Pompous ass is my first thought. His primal response is out to prove his dogs are better than any other. He locks onto the competitiveness, and the hunting aspect feeds an outsized ego. He's the man!

My training remains practical, focusing on Saxon's needs. Sue and I train together as often as we can with our dogs. Chester digs into dog training like a ferocious bull whirling and ricocheting in a pen. He seeks field-training techniques then disregards them, doing it his way and his dogs suffer embarrassment for this conduct.

He's the wolf in sheep's clothing. I'd assumed he was monogamous, but I was wrong. He tells me he's dating another woman, and explains her situation and how he is her rescuer. He likes that role and then complains about it. She was raped by her ex-husband and suffers from severe depression and an autoimmune disease that embarrasses her during sex. My traditional thinking clashes with his womanizing and wishy-washy morals, causing me to question my beliefs. Am I too prudish? How far is too far to be unscrupulous and still achieve for Saxon?

I rationalize he is free to date anyone and we're not committed. I guess it is my monogamous conscience that side-rails me. His mind games cause me to second guess my morals. An ingrained mental manipulating technique causing me to believe I'm wrong and he's right. This is his way of controlling people.

Our focus turn to the dogs and mine to helping Saxon.

Our stronghold is training the dogs for hunting. He has the guns and becomes the gunner for pheasant hunting. Saxon and Sadie can benefit greatly from being in the field retrieving birds. Saxon is working on his hunt test skills. When one dog is in the field at a time, Saxon is not threatened. We join a local hunt club, which offers timed-competition pheasant hunts. This venue feeds the competitiveness between us and our dogs. Our matching type A personalities stitch us together. Chester's true colors are blinding during the hunts. He's constantly berating and yelling where and how to move through the field and what quartering distance to hold between the gunner and my dogs. Nothing I do is right in his eyes.

Pheasant hunting is meant to be done quietly.

We are in the pheasant tournament with Saxon at the beginning of the corn strip and prairie grass waiting for the starting gun. Saxon is at heel, ready to go. The gunshot reports. Saxon is leading, picking up bird scent, running straight, and not quartering. Chester is running, gun in hand, which is ill advised. I'm falling behind and stumbling across the rough, uneven terrain.

"Get up here. Call him over to you. Why can't you move any faster? Call him! Call him! Get on it! We're supposed to be forty yards apart calling him back and forth." His tone is demeaning and degrading, insinuating a stupid woman that has no business being in the field and only virile demeaning guys can handle a gun in the field.

"He's on the bird. Shoot." My shot misses. He is pissed.

"Call him in. Because of you we lost. It's your fault."

He gets in my face, towering over me, arms threatening me during his verbal rant, just for the purposes of control, bullying, and intimidating me to feel I'm an imbecile, small, and worthless. He uses my lack of knowledge and inexperience to shame and instill fear.

Inside, I hear my sister yelling, "You dummy, you're nothing. Don't know why you're even here." I'll tolerate his verbal slap-downs, if they lead to forming healthier patterns for Saxon and minimizing his aggression.

Saxon Meets the Pack

Three months later, Chester invites me to stay at his apartment on weekends, offering to care for the dogs during the week while I travel. I accept his overture. This is Saxon's chance to break through his aggression by acclimating to a new pack. Chester wants to see Saxon in action. He thinks I am exaggerating.

It's a warm and sunny September day. I bring Saxon on lead into Chester's apartment. The kennel runs are in the backyard. His kitchen is filled with stacks of paper, leaving room only for trails that lead to the back hallway and the door to the outdoor kennels. Sadie follows behind.

Saxon feels fear and anxiety ramping up in us as we approach the hallway. My stiff arm and tight grip on Saxon's pinch collar send shock waves down the leash. His body is on alert the instant he smells the dogs, and his insecure demeanor shifts to raised hackles, forward-leaning, rigid body, and high-curled tail over his back, white elephant eyes, and the final jolt that transmits fearful chills up the lead. His low, guttural growl vibrates in me. My conditioned psyche experiences trauma hearing it. The negative energy, my fear, and Chester's deep-seated anger surrounding us are Saxon's fodder.

Pausing at the door to the outside, Chester starts petting Saxon, attempting to calm and reassure him. The petting is counterproductive. It only reinforces Saxon's anger and intensifies his aggression. Never coddle a fearful dog. When the door opens, Saxon sees the other dogs in the kennel. It takes all my strength to hold the leash as eighty pounds of raw power rises up like a mustang stallion. He's lunging, dragging me down the cement stairs. His eyes roll back. He is out of his mind in rage, charging the kennel's wire fencing, writhing and rebounding from the surface, and snapping his teeth with a ferocious bark. Survival propels him to kill. Never noticing their wagging tails and the playful bows, their mere presence triggers his flash anger. Chester's dogs are confused. They retreat, all cringing in terror from Saxon's blow. His male pup, Moonie, crouches, turning his body away, trying to tell Saxon that he isn't a threat. Saxon's patterned blind rage and improper socialization don't allow him to recognize Moonie's body language.

We confuse Saxon by first petting him when his fear was aroused, reinforcing his aggression, and then reprimand him for acting on his fear. The stimulus was overwhelming. We pushed him into a situation rather than allowing him the distance to acclimate on his own. I'm grateful that the fence held, because Saxon was fixated to kill them all.

Grabbing Saxon, I take him away from the kennels to give him distance to calm down. Sadie sits off to the side of the fracas. She approaches his dogs, showing Saxon the proper way to greet each one by slowly approaching the kennel and submissively touching noses, presenting a casual tail wag and a play bow. It deescalates the episode and reduces the tension.

"Well do you believe me now?" I say.

Chester stands mute and wide-eyed. He's paralyzed with disbelief by Saxon's ravenous rage and realizes my challenge. Being on lead at a distance on a long line, separated, is the only liberty Saxon can be allowed around his dogs.

Saxon's confusion worms into his depression. He longs to belong, but he is barred from any chance to show his good side. At my core is the same need for belonging, acceptance, and being loved as a normal person.

Each weekend at Chester's, before bedtime, my gut twists and heart aches when I take Saxon into the dark isolated hallway, excommunicating him from the pack. I smother Saxon with long loving strokes over his broad golden head and down his back, then kiss him good night. I am guilt-ridden. In my mind, I see Saxon's sad, dark eyes talking to me through the night.

Being invisible and isolated is shameful punishment. It's nearly the worst kind for a golden. Intuitively, I perceive that Saxon understood the reason for his separation. Chester's walls separate he and I, but our souls are bonded. He understands my struggle in isolating him, desperately wanting to help him and avert an order to kill him. The thought of euthanizing Saxon sickens me.

His unpredictable anger and aggression were dangerously real. Any indication of aggression brought a reprimand, and adds to his aggression. It proved to be counterproductive. He pushed his anger deeper, stripping him of any warning signs. Whose fault was this? Chester blamed Saxon for being an opportunist. Saxon was innocent. There had to be another way other than euthanizing him. Dedicated to my promise to love him to his last breath now meant after he could live a full life.

Every day with Saxon, the nagging voices of my friends, his trainer, and breeder looped in my head, saying, "You can't use him for anything? What good is he? You need to kill that dog. Just get rid of him and get another dog. He is not worth having for a show dog. He is genetically a bad seed. Why would you change the next fourteen years of your life for *that* dog?" Their remarks inflamed me, especially when I realized how easy it was for them to dispose of an animal. Here was where other people's opinion meant nothing to me. I knew this was not Saxon's fault despite what others thought was unsolvable. Somehow, I was going to figure this out for him. Whatever the cost, whatever the sacrifice, Saxon would succeed and be allowed to live a full life.

Overwrought and blank-minded for the Saxon's next step, I needed someone else to help me think. As I mentally wrestled, Chester welcomed the opportunity to provide his input on how to save Saxon's life because

Saxon, in his mind, was a victim. My love and protection for Saxon drew Chester in. Saxon became our joint cause.

Chester agreed to introduce his dogs one at a time to Saxon, but not until there could be a level of safety. This was Saxon's next step. I was grateful to Chester for giving Saxon this chance.

With winter encroaching, leaving Saxon in the hallway with subzero temperatures was cruel. Deciding how he could be inside with all of us and remain safe in a tight, cluttered space required setting boundaries. I was unaware and unfamiliar with any professional resources. Chester suggested consulting with a canine behavior veterinarian at the University of Minnesota. His willingness to partner and provide valid suggestions gave me hope both for Saxon and a stronger personal relationship. I was all in, despite Chester's raucous berating and womanizing. Saxon would benefit being with his dogs and hunting in the field.

Muzzled

At the end of January, Chester, Saxon, and I are sitting in the exam room with Dr. Petra Mertens, assistant professor of behavior medicine at the University Of Minnesota College Of Veterinary Medicine, discussing Saxon's aggressive behavior. Hearing Saxon's life history, she requests an observation case study. Videotaping Saxon among Chester's dogs for one week will be used for determining a behavioral plan for Saxon.

"Saxon should be wearing a muzzle when he is around Chester's dogs," Dr. Mertens tells us. Watching Saxon's reaction, I relate to his sadness. Shame wells up in me as I feel myself shrinking internally. Saxon knows.

The words don't matter. He visualizes the contraption from my mind, the tone of my voice and body reaction, which relay a negative message. His mouth must to be strapped shut, pressing his feelings even deeper than before. His ears flatten and his body shrinks low. He turns to look sorrowfully at me, nearly asking, *Why?*

The embarrassment and the outward visual persecution of wearing an apparatus around other dogs labels him abnormal. In human eyes, he is dangerous. It is an emotional torture we relate to. Being forced to zip it only increases our stored bitterness. Hopelessness blankets him. From Saxon's perspective, this is shameful punishment. Never intending to douse him with shame or add more pain, I hold hope he can safely be with Chester's dogs.

Optimistically, Chester and I look to one another even as we realize the risks, responsibility, patience, and uphill climb we are assuming. We are heading down an unfamiliar path. I am pleased that Chester is supportive and committed to helping Saxon. For now, this is Saxon's best chance to survive.

Dr. Mertens demonstrates acclimating Saxon to the muzzle and head halter using a positive training method. Slapping it on was counterproductive which would add to his fear. Using positive association allows him to accept wearing the muzzle before meeting strange dogs. Each microstep forward has to be perfectly executed, rewarded, and praised. Saxon's successful reprogramming depends on building upon each positive connection to change past learned responses.

Dr. Mertens lays out the steps. "First, without any dogs around, show him the muzzle and halter and give him a tasty treat over the course of a couple days. Then begin to slip it on for a few seconds and take it off praising and rewarding him for complying until he is wearing his gear. Advance that to attaching your leash and doing short walks in your yard away from any strange dogs, so he can gain comfort, confidence, and trust."

Starting the case study, communicating daily by email with Dr. Mertens, I follow her instructions. I write to her about the multiple, five-minute training sessions using meat treats and praise each time he begins to accept the head halter and muzzle. Although reluctant, he is obedient, redirecting his attention to do a sit-stay for three minutes, reverting to a command he confidently knows. It is heartbreaking, seeing Saxon muzzled. I trust this is in Saxon's best interest, yet I feel his shame and relate it to myself being told to shut up. Saxon hates the muzzle and the treats are meaningless. His nose is raw trying to rub it off with his paw. He shakes his head from the pressure of the head strap. Despite his resistance, he continues to work with me and learn. Each session is extended until a time he can wear it like a normal collar. The end of each training session is food, praise, and retrieving as a release to play freely with Sadie and shake off his stress. Dr.

Mertens is pleased with Saxon's progress. Relieved, I gain hope for him that he can overcome his aggression. It's only one small step of many to come.

The one-at-a-time introductions of Chester's dogs begin in my three-season porch. Sadie's stable temperament counterbalances Saxon's emotional instability. He trusts Sadie. She is his anchor.

Jule, Chester's oldest female, goes first. Chester holds Saxon by the collar while I bring Jule into the room. She makes casual eye contact and immediately lies down on the dog pillows, turning her body away from Saxon, offering him no threat. Chester takes off the muzzle against the doctor's orders and cautiously step by step, listening for any growl, walks Saxon over to Jule. I'm standing back, arms folded, clenched jaws, expecting his aggression to spike. Jule makes no effort to move as Saxon appears meek with a soft tail wag and submissive eyes, but stressed as he pants and yawns. Checking in with Chester for reassurance that he is behaving correctly, Saxon shows Jule gentle and cautious kindness and respect as they tenderly touch noses. He offers his paw pledging his commitment. *Please trust me. I am trying to be good and learn not to be angry. I just want to be normal and play.*

Saxon senses we are helping him reverse his anger. We pet and praise him. This time the petting is an appropriate reward. Once the initial introduction between Saxon and Jule occurs, it is as if they had known each other in the past and are now reconnecting. Tensions evaporate. Relief fills the room. This is an encouraging breakthrough. A positive shift comes over Saxon. His body softens. He's proud as he smiles through his stressful panting, wagging his tail, and communicating his success. Faith in Saxon's ability to modify his aggression is possible once again, showing us he has the elasticity to transform. We end the session on success and will come back in a few hours to be with the other dogs.

Rachael, Chester's three-year-old female, is next. Chester grips Saxon's collar, minus the muzzle again. Rachael begins barking. Her barking ratchets up as her anxiety increases. Chester silences her with the stimulus of the bark collar. Chester's fear surfaces as he tightly grips Saxon's collar, feeding into his aggression. Rachael simply sits at his side while Chester pets them both. Saxon is polite to Rachael and careful not to be angry. Rachael's glances say, *I know you are uncomfortable with me, but I am no threat.*

Chester releases Rachael to wander around the room, sniffing the floor as a canine calming signal. Chester's grip tightens, triggering Saxon's fear, hackles raised causing him to dominantly posture. Rachael stops to growl: *Don't go there.* We interrupt the process, correcting Saxon and not Rachael. I feel sorry for Saxon. He gets the brunt of the punishment, like I used to with my sister.

In human terms, I associate the dogs were mirroring the maltreatment of my sister's teasing, the passive-aggressive name-calling, vindictive tricks and my parents' blaming me while overlooking my sister's actions as "kid will be kids."

We introduce Chester's third female, Babe, a farm rescue dog of his daughter. Babe's introduction is like Rachael's but with more of an alpha response. Abnormal aggression is in her. Last is Moonie, the puppy, being pushed into a fearful situation. Moonie remembers Saxon's kennel attack. Deliberately accentuating Moonie's body language, he carries his body low, slinking as he runs to escape toward the closed sliding glass door, cowering. Cornered, he sits there, panting, nervous, trembling, and turning his entire body sideways. He deliberately raises his head, rotating it away from Saxon and Chester. His ears are pinned down on his head. He is trying hard to tell Saxon in as many ways as possible that he isn't a threat. Chester turns to pet Saxon and then he turns to pet Moonie, showing them they can be friends. For now, this goes without a hitch.

We increase the risk by replacing the muzzle and sending all the dogs into the backyard together. Saxon stands outside the other dogs, watching as they run and play. Saxon separates himself from the group, rubbing his nose against the old oak tree to get the muzzle off. Sadie occasionally comes over to Saxon to include him. He doesn't know how to play, so he lies down to watch. Sometimes, it is more how I feel, seeing Saxon sidelined, confined in the muzzle and how much it emotionally reminds me of how I felt being the playground dunce, bearing shame and embarrassment through my grade school years. Saxon is scratching at my subconscious and showing me snippets of myself as my amygdala fires flashbacks to a mindfulness.

The follow-up with Dr. Mertens brings disappointment. She tells us, "Dogs need to work out their issues without interruptions. The constant interruption only increase the aggression with each interaction and taking off the muzzle gives Saxon free rein, encouraging a fight with Rachael. Furthermore, Rachael gets reinforced for her growling. You need to learn to either counterbalance the situation by remaining calm or leave the room because you are adding to the tension, confusing and causing the situation to worsen. Use a high-pitched puppy voice for counterbalance."

Phooey, Chester thinks using a puppy voice is silly. He puts the kibosh on it.

Watching Saxon makes me see more of myself as child. He bears the burden he doesn't deserve. Changing patterns is a slow, arduous process.

A few weeks later, following Dr. Mertens's instructions by having no interruptions among the dog pack, we allow Saxon outside without a muzzle with the girls as we watch from the porch. Saxon responds with small but positive behavioral changes, lessening his aggression and exhibiting self-restraint, despite his dominant body posturing. His demeanor changes. He is surprisingly playful. He picks up a big tug rope and begins to play. For a split-second, Saxon experiences a flash of being normal and is learning how to be himself. He is learning social skills he lost as a puppy. Being part of a dog pack is new. We recognize the simple changes. What seems like a microstep is a giant leap, chipping away at patterned fear and anger.

Observing Saxon's progress, it is as if Saxon pinches himself before reacting. *Is this the same me?* A new and positive sense of reality strikes him.

He'd freeze in place, momentarily reorienting himself to follow the lead of the other dogs' playful behavior versus responding with fearful aggression. Every time he interacted positively, we praise and reward him, instilling support in his knowing he is safe and learning right from wrong. My heart smiles for him. I love him more each time he succeeds. My faith strengthens that he can overcome his learned anger and find his true self. For the first time all the dogs have their place on my living room floor. What a wonderful sight to behold them all asleep together as a civil pack.

Along with the peaks come the valleys. Chester's hair-brained idea is putting Moonie and Saxon together without the muzzle while holding Saxon by the collar. This time the quarters were tight, having no escape, and both felt trapped. Placing the two male dogs together carries its own anxieties from previous history. Chester is on guard holding the collar tightly. We are tense and on alert. Chester's nervous energy convey caution, signaling Saxon. Passively standing aside and allowing Chester to take the lead, we realize a fight could ignite, and it does. Moonie's body language says he isn't a threat. Dog to dog, Saxon charges Moonie, knocking Chester off his feet and loosening his hold. Kitchen chairs tumble as Saxon takes a death grip, snapping Moonie's neck back and forth. Death cries erupt from Moonie as blood streams from his neck. Saxon's gnarly growls muffle through his neck hold. We are screaming at Saxon. Saxon's front canine grazed Moonie just above the eye. Moonie fights back in self-defense as both dogs battle on their back feet. Chester grabs Saxon's rear inner flank. Saxon's reflex is to turn and snap, thinking it was Moonie during fierce flurry of growling and snapping. He rips open Chester's hand with his front canine teeth. The instant Saxon realizes he bit a human, the fight halts and his body sinks, never having intended to bite Chester. Moonie cowers. From then on, Moonie will keep his distance and hide whenever Saxon is around.

I'm distraught that Chester got bit. He could report Saxon, putting him in quarantine or having him euthanized. Surprisingly, while he attends to Moonie's wounds, Chester dismisses Saxon's actions and refuses emergency care, realizing he was wrong for removing the muzzle.

We report the incident to Dr. Mertens who reprimands us. "Your mistake was pushing the dogs together in confined quarters, threatening them both to strike out, increasing aggression. Putting Saxon in a group situation outside gives the dogs a chance to choose distance."

The division between Chester and me increased concerning Dr. Mertens's approach to behavior modification. He always knew better and rarely listened to her advice. Our infighting and inconsistencies caused Saxon confusion and setbacks. Chester's flash anger intertwined with his compassion to help Saxon left me confused about Chester's inflammatory nature. Balancing the dogs' fearful reaction of Chester and my devotion to Saxon, weaves my entanglement deeper in the relationship. I need his dogs for Saxon's progress.

The previous pack fight left the pack order unresolved and Saxon continues to attack Moonie, trying to settle it. When that happens, Chester yells, "NO!" and the interruption increases Saxon's unresolved aggression because the dogs can't finish the pack order.

Dr. Mertens again warns us to stop interrupting the dogs. While we think suppressing Saxon's anger was correct, she swiftly corrects us, stressing that it is counterproductive and, in fact, increases his aggression. Our minds tell us, it doesn't make sense. She cautions us to avoid any physical corrections that can compound the aggression. We have it all wrong. Saxon's emotions have been suppressed since puppyhood. He stored pent-up anger, which needed an outlet and resolution. The more he tried to expel his emotions, the more he was severely shamed and punished, which compounded his internal stress. Hearing Dr. Mertens say that physical force exacerbates aggression inflames me, recalling earlier experience with the obedience training and hitting and yelling at him as a puppy. The past circumstances are circling back piece by piece. I'm beginning to see and feel the greater parallel between Saxon and me being revealed. He emotionally is so much like me.

The environment at Chester's apartment replicates the one living with Burt. Chester is in a recliner, an alcoholic drink in hand, big-screen TV blaring, and we are bickering about something trivial. The dogs fearfully hide because Chester's rage inevitably targets one of them, throwing the most vulnerable dog against a wall. Babe yelps and limps away, and he has no remorse. He antagonizes the dogs, inciting chaos, so all are edgy and hypervigilant. Our guts twist, feeling trapped with nowhere to turn for safety. The dogs learn to mirror the behavior of others in their home, just as I did as a child. Their anger is our anger rebounding, and it fuels the infighting cycle. Chester's violence deepening Saxon's aggression is something I notice more and more. Yet I need his dogs for Saxon.

It breaks my heart as I watch him lying among Sadie and Chester's dogs. Dejection and sadness carry across his body and are seen in his eyes. Sadie is right there, sympathetically watching Saxon. Her eyes are loving but sad. She is trapped, maintaining her self-preservation by staying in the shadows, motionless, enduring the anger. The only parts of Sadie that move are her eyebrows, eyes, and her chest as she breathes. We were all emotionally detached, suffering in dissonance.

So why stay when the obvious choice is to stand up and confront the abuse and walk out? The same reason I had as a child when Dad slapped me down and told me to shut up: fear. My body remembers. I've carried forward a learned pattern into adulthood of accepting abuse as normal and thinking there is no option but to stay. So I block out my awareness to survive and act as if it never happened, and go on and on and on, time and again. It's a life pattern.

From the first day Saxon met Chester's dogs in the outside kennel up to now being able to be with the pack muzzled, he's progressed. He can be outside mingling with the pack. I believe Saxon is on the right course and it's one we can build upon. He sets the pace for change. That he can slog through a toxic environment and our hostile relationship feeds my hope.

We've neared an end point with Dr. Mertens. She reassures me, saying, "Saxon is a great dog and you are doing a wonderful job working with him. Progress will be slow. Have patience with yourself."

Her future recommendation for Saxon is to focus on just the existing pack of six dogs, working out the bugs in it. Work on being calm. Once that plateau has been achieved we can go beyond his dogs and consider unfamiliar dogs. In my mind, this meant a long-term relationship with Chester for Saxon's success.

She refers us to an obedience club in Minneapolis where they offer a snarly-dog class designed for reactive dogs like Saxon. Trusting her advice, I register Saxon for the class. Still naïve, I'm hoping this is the answer to his aggression.

Dr. Mertens offers me these final words: "You have done a great job with Saxon. I would like you to think positively. He's a great dog. I feel confident that we can get him to be much better. Be patient. He can be saved." That is why I was fighting for him. I hung tight to her words, *he can be saved.*

I weep, knowing there is hope for his life and that someone else has seen deeper into Saxon and finally believes in him as I do.

Snarly Dog Classes

Flooding is one method of desensitization used to change behavior patterns with reactive dogs, exposing them to the highest stimulus, letting them work through their interactions without interruption while learning good pack behavior. They mingle. The owners are supposed to observe the body language and the triggers that ignite the dogs.

I'm skeptical. It seems counterintuitive how this class will work positively for him if he is with other emotionally unbalanced dogs like himself. Where is the counterbalance to demonstrate correct behavior?

The class is designed as a form of socialization in a controlled play group. These dogs don't understand good play and are poorly socialized. Saxon becomes the aggressor. He postures dominantly. He attacks an intact Rhodesian ridgeback severely enough to send the dog to the vet for stitches. The ridgeback didn't back down and neither did Saxon. They both went at it with a killing vengeance, like a feeding frenzy igniting a united vicious pack, piling and fighting in the obedience ring. All the owners' sprung to their feet, bolting into the ring, to keep their dogs from being killed. The instructor threw a pail of water on the dogs and stopped the fight.

Saxon's fear and anxiety are reinforced as are mine. It is a tremendous setback for both dogs. Expressing my remorse to the owner, I offer to pay for the ridgeback's medical expenses. Later, I receive a letter from the dog's owner, saying, "I could tell by the expression on your face and your words that you felt as bad as I did about what occurred. I am asking that you share the medical expenses." She went on in her letter to say, "We will not be coming back to this class. I am not cut out for the hands-off approach. I am not sure if it is the Quaker side of me that reasons that if you would not let two kids duke it out in the backyard, why would you let two dogs do the same?" We agreed. The method of flooding was overwhelming and wrong for Saxon.

Caught in a mental maze, with outcasts who are unwelcome, I look in Saxon's eyes as he sits at heel, knowing he did wrong yet knowing no other way to live. Feeling guilty, I understand it's not his fault and he couldn't help himself. I'm troubled that I am at a loss for answers. I feel it's my responsibility to know. I stroke Saxon's broad head gently to calm him. He leans against my knee. We both feel at a loss for what to do next. Quitting is not in us despite just having been rebuked and covered in shame. I feel betrayed after I trusted. What is out there for him? It's a dilemma getting gut-punched and not knowing which way to turn.

I get booted out of class. I'm on my own again, on a mission to find help for my dog.

Slimed in shame, we stand stunned and unwelcome outside the training center. Saxon cowers, knowing he has disappointed me. He's confused about what to do with his emotions. The anger controls him. It's the opposite of what his heart tells him he is.

Unbeknown to me, another door shuts in hopes of me looking to Him for guidance. Like a ticker tape, the Bible verse from Proverbs crosses my mind: *Trust in the Lord with all thine heart; and lean not unto thine own understanding. In all thy ways acknowledge him, and he shall direct thy paths.* There stands the Holy Spirit extending the unseen hand to me when I am at the rope's end, hoping I'd turn to His guiding and let faith lead me. The choice is mine.

It's in the Field

It's right in front of us. We just don't see it. God's finger points us to working Saxon in the field. It's where love is found.

After dating Chester for some time, we decide to find a professional gun-dog trainer and enter the American Kennel Club Hunt Test circuit. A gun-dog trainer can accelerate a hunting dog's skills and determine if the dog has the talent to excel. Trainers depend upon the client paying them for their service. They feel the pressure to produce a skillfully trained hunting dog in a minimum amount of time. If the dog doesn't fit the professional's training program, they are called washouts. The trainer's reputation and the outcome command his livelihood. The client hopes the trainer understands the dog and trusts he does right by the dog. Most of the time, an inexperienced client doesn't get to see the trainer in action behind the scene.

Locating a trainer named Jack in Northern Wisconsin, we join his training group. Dogs need basic hunt test skills to pass the Junior Hunter test. We know very little about the process and lack the training birds, time, and people to help with marking and line manners. It is my vision and hope that putting Saxon in a new, positive situation where he can focus on retrieving birds, which he loves, will turn a negative history with dogs to a positive one. Shifting his mind toward birds and the ability might release stored anger. But I know that pushing Saxon too quickly produced setbacks. Moving at his own pace should allow him to integrate new skills easily.

Late one Monday afternoon we arrive at the training grounds. Immediately, putting on airs, Chester is schmoozing with the handlers, vying for attention, nosing to snatch pointers, showing interest in their dogs, but he could care less. Mostly it is about "beat or be beaten" in competition.

The student in me is minding my own business. I'm leaning against one of the dog trucks, with my arms folded, watching handlers run their dogs on marks and blinds when my eye is drawn to one particular man mingling with a few people in the training group. He is intriguing.

I watch him socialize. He seems kind and is listening attentively to people. He's not bullish like Chester. He's lean, muscular, medium height with salt-and-pepper wavy hair, and dressed in camouflage. His glasses slide down his nose.

He spots me standing alone, walks over, introduces himself, and strikes up a conversation.

"Hi there, my name is Bill. What do you have for a dog?"

"Male golden retriever."

"Hah! A swamp collie!"

"Ah, no, a golden retriever," I reply defensively. Putdowns rile me.

"Just kidding. That's what us Lab guys call a golden for the fun of it." He winks and softens the mood.

"Do you train regularly with Jack?" I ask.

"No, I'm just watching his setups. I'm with a bunch of other guys. Jack allows us to use his training grounds down the road."

"What's your dog's name?"

"BJ. She's six months old." BJ appears happy around him.

Bill's air is steadfast, reserved, and respectful. There's a quiet, gentle reverence seeing him move deliberately. His instincts appear keen and calculating. His ice-blue eyes reflect the wisdom of a man who has experienced much in life. His direct squint makes me feel naked and chilled as I sense his eyes laser through me. He pegged me, dialing in with an unspoken understanding of who I am. There is a mysterious likeness about him that draws me in. I don't understand why. I just know we have a connection.

"I am starting a pheasant farm near Sand Creek, so I can train my dog," he says. "You are welcome to come and hunt."

I smile politely and brush it off as a nice gesture and a bit of a come-on. But I like the idea of Saxon hunting pheasants. Bill takes a business card out of his wallet, and I reach for it.

Jack's training methods are cruel. Indian tricks are what he calls them. He tells the handlers, "This better stay within the group and on these grounds and never tell anyone outside about it." I see why.

It reminds me of Dad's chilling threat when he made me bury Toodle's puppies in a gunny sack, "I better not find out you told anyone."

The dogs are wearing e-collars. Jack ratchets the dial on the transmitter to its highest number, electrically juicing the dog that makes it scream in pain. That's hard to watch.

He hollers profanity, whips and kicks the dogs into submission. When the dog disobeys, Jack physically bounces them by their ears, dragging them a hundred yards, prying their mouths open, and slamming the dead bird in the dog's mouth. The shell-shocked dog trembles, then freezes from fear, often dropping the bird again. A dog that bites gets slammed to the ground and a cattle prod shoved up its anus.

A second e-collar strapped to the waist of the alpha Lab lets Jack juice the dog into a fit of mental terror to break its spirit and force it to comply out of fear. This revolts me, raising the hairs on my body. No ribbon is worth this abuse. Jack's methods applied to Saxon could ruin him permanently. Not just dogs, but people, too, would be targets of his aggression and doom him. Yet I stay, pushing aside the horrible treatment, to learn the concepts while disregarding Jack's methods.

When Chester and I train together he mirrors Jack's dispassionate ear-bouncing tactic, using it on his own dogs, dragging a suspended Moonie's seventy-five pounds of kyi-kying a hundred yards across the field. Chester is yelling, "BACK, BACK, BACK," and trying to teach a blind retrieve. Moonie's screams mirror the shrieking of a rabbit locked in a wild animal's jaws, triggering the primal instinct, titillating the attacker to sink his fangs in deeper. Terrorized, the louder Moonie's yelps, the more enraged and violent Chester becomes, kicking, beating, and slamming Moonie to the ground with his feet and clenched fists. Time and time again, Chester repeats the hundred-yard distance to the bumper pile until he breaks Moonie's spirit and he freezes from fear. Moonie is his bondservant, and it's all about Chester. Jack's training style gives Chester license to prey on the weak and innocent, releasing his repressed flash-anger for self-gratification.

I am yelling at Chester to stop. He won't hear of it. Chester won't stop, and Moonie's suffering continues. Soon Chester's crazed balloon head has swelled beyond instruction or criticism. He has assumed the identity of a professional dog trainer, acting like Jack, and nothing will stop him. He's on his own rampage.

In his backyard by the lake, Chester's profanity is inflicted on Rachael. Most days, she is flighty, out of body, insecure, and skittish, but especially when she comes into heat. Chester's physical brutality heightens, triggering his primal behavior, like a buck in rut itching for the chance to dominate a female. Watching him, Rachael is trembling, her mouth chattering, tail tucked and ears flattened, poised to duck at the slightest hand twitch.

"Rachael!" Chester sounds her name as a release command, sending her to retrieve. Rachael flares sideways instead of straight-lining into the water. His bullhorn voice had sent her lateral out of fear. He drills her repeatedly and she keeps flaring. Fear freezes her and she's scared to leave his side. Infuriated, Chester strikes with his gorilla hand so hard that she goes silent after a single yelp and her convulsing body is on the ground. Horrified, I run to help her. Chester warns me to stay away and demands I not tell anyone. He blames the dog. "She didn't listen and screwed up." He towers over her, posturing and acting justified in beating her. He lets her lie there, writhing through a grand mal seizure. The scene sets off flashbacks to my own childhood reminding me of how Toodle must have felt during the puppy screams.

Regaining my senses, my anger aroused, and my fear transformed into maternal protection, I stand in defense of Saxon and Sadie. "Listen to me right now, hands off my dogs. You will *never* do any training with Saxon. It is wrong and I will not tolerate you beating or mistreating Saxon or Sadie. If you do, I will call the police and have you locked up in jail." He knows I mean it.

The respectable decision was to leave with my dogs and report his animal abuse. No, I chose to stay and suffer through rather than be empty-handed for Saxon's access to another group of dogs and improving Saxon's ability to hunt birds, compete, and, most importantly, overcome his aggression. I somehow hoped Chester could change with my support.

Top Gun

In the pheasant field, Saxon is the only dog with Chester and me. The others are waiting their turn in the truck. The frequent flushing and retrieving birds can build Saxon's confidence, increasing our chances of achieving the Junior Hunter title while developing new thought-action patterns.

Saxon forgets his anger when he hunts. He becomes a fun, unencumbered pooch, and his confidence takes flight. Saxon is in his element, joyously using his natural talent, bounding through the field. He's purposefully put his nose to the ground, following a pheasant trail, halting to air scent of the pheasant's direction. Quickly, he turns a one-eighty, his tail whipping side to side, and he pounces with his paws to flush his prize, so Chester can shoot and he could retrieve.

Given praise and positive reinforcement, Saxon responds well to being built up when he releases his misguided aggression and redirects it into the natural prey drive. His marking ability is accurate and his love to retrieve shines bright. He prances with head and tail held high, the showman strutting his stuff, proudly promenading his bird, and delivers to my hand.

Saxon's field work is methodical. He's a thinker, moving to his own beat. Each time we hunt, our bond strengthens, and so does my belief that he will get through to the other side of his aggression.

The game farm sponsors a pheasant tournament. We entered the dogs in the Top Gun category. I have just enough handling skills to hunt alone with Saxon and Sadie. We are competing directly against Chester. The tournament, timed at twenty minutes, consists of four birds and eight gun shells. The score is based upon the least amount of shots fired in the least amount of time, and the most birds retrieved.

Saxon and I are at the starting line in the field. He sits at heel, excitedly barking, paws pitter-pattered with excitement, waiting for the starter pistol to fire and my command, "Hunt 'me up!" I am wearing my orange pheasant vest, and have a shotgun in hand and whistle in my mouth. The birds are dazed and hidden along a strip of mixed corn stalks and tall prairie grass against a background of colorful fall-leafed trees beneath a brilliant robin's-egg blue sky. The judge fires the starter pistol and clicks the timer. "Hunt 'me up, Saxon! Find the bird!" He kicks up the dirt behind him and shoots off the line. I am racing behind him as his nose picks up the scent and his birdie tail signals he is on the pheasant. He's found the first bird. He goes up on his back haunches and with his front paws pounces on the pheasant to flush it in the air. The beating of the bird's wings pumps adrenaline through his body. But as luck would have it, I miss the shot. OOPS!

The bird flies clear across the wide-open field and disappears. Saxon turns around in disbelief, as if to say, *where were you on that one?* He shames me for my inability and his loss of an opportunity to retrieve. Humbled that I better improve, we move on to find the next hidden bird.

Saxon flushes the pheasant from the grass. This time my shot is on target. Saxon retrieves the bird. He bounds back to me all wiggly-giggly and tail held high. Intuitively, I understand what he wants me to know: *Now that's better than the last one.*

The third bird was a miss again. If a dog could stand upright and put his paws on his hips that would have been Saxon, as he fixed his gaze on me in disgust. His look posed an uncomplicated question: *Do I have to do all the work here?*

Saxon is forgiving and gracious on the fourth bird, and he makes me look good. Without any instructions, he retrieves a dazed bird from the tall grass, sits politely behind me, holding the bird gently in his mouth. To my surprise our hunt finishes with three shots fired and he softly holds the bird and moseys into heel, looking up. Smiling at him, I could swear he winked at me to let me know *What happens in the field stays in the field.*

I chuckle that it will be our secret and a good one. Praise pours over him for being a wonderful partner and great dog. Our relationship is reinforced. We are knit together as a trusted team. It was pure love and it felt new to me. He awakened in me the realization that underneath his aggression was a very loving and kind dog. That deepened my dedication to him.

When the awards were handed out, we won Top Gun. Gratefully, I accepted our trophy, but most of all, took great pride in Saxon's ability, in front of all the men cheering our victory. Saxon proved he could anchor his physical talents in hunting, marking, and retrieving pheasants in the field.

Chester's jealous piercing eyes, his red-faced anger boils over. He's not cheering. We present a threat to his manly ego.

At home, Saxon's grounding was thriving in obedience training twice a day. One-time command, training sit-stays with and without a whistle, and heeling encouraged him to be steady on the Junior Hunter test line.

Chester chose to stay with Jack's training, where it was important for me to break away. Jack's punishing program was an ill match for my dogs. I was single-minded to design methods that matched their soft temperament and individualized their training. Hunting was meant to be a fun outlet for Saxon and me, not a horror chamber.

Mind-Bender

More than a year into the relationship, Chester introduced me to his mother, Vennen. Life had taken its toll on her. She was hunched and hobbled, self-conscious about her large body. She was also opinionated, tough, wise, resilient, and an independent, culturally self-made businesswoman who in her prime had raised two children as a single divorced mother.

In retirement, Vennen was socially active and volunteered in the Methodist church. Serving others gave her purpose. Faith in God was her stronghold, a reminder of my mother's Gibraltar faith. She had silver-coiffed hair, and the age lines on her face were those of a strong, determined woman who fought her way through a hard life. From her came that wise survivor instinct that I held onto in myself. As we developed a trusting friendship, Vennen would become an adult surrogate mother to me.

Chester, a restaurateur and businessman, invited his mother out to dine with us in a fine Italian restaurant. I was looking forward to enjoying a relaxing conversation while sipping fine wine and savoring a lavish meal. It was Chester's way of attending to the woman who raised him. The sense of family caring for one another seemed healthy. That night, she wore a stunningly coordinated amethyst ensemble and matching shoes.

We are seated at our table facing the entrance, chosen by Chester. He takes over, ordering the wine. When it arrives, he pours it for Vennen and keeps filling her glass against her will, dominating and intimidating her until she swallows it all. The tone at the table reminds me of the edginess sitting at the farm supper table.

We study the menu. Vennen chooses chicken Alfredo, but Chester rips the menu from her, telling her what he'll order for her since he's paying for the meal. This ignites a fiery exchange.

In my disbelief and embarrassment, my reaction is to hold my tongue, put my head down, and only glance cautiously at the two of them. Their loud and angry words draw the attention of the others in the restaurant.

When dinner finishes, we drive to her townhouse. Displaying his chivalry, he takes her arm and guides her inside. Then behind closed doors, he transforms into a raging, foul-mouthed monster. As he castigates her, my sister's image appears. I see sister hovering over me, telling me I am pathetic.

Chester towers over his mother with his large body. Face to face, he bellows and shakes his fist, threatening to bash her skull in. The root of the blowup is money she needs to pay her rent. Having taken control of her finances, he gives her an allowance, so she is at his mercy and has to beg for everything she needs.

Chester pretends to wind up and take a punch, watching Vennen recoil into a fetal position, her hands protecting her head. She is hyperventilating, sobbing, and trembling in fear. At the last second before striking her he says, "Gotcha!" And walks away shaking his head in disgust.

Holy Cow! What just happened? The yelling and screaming mirrored my upbringing. I am scared to go home with him, but I'm sticking this out, knowingly, entering my own hell, and risking everything to save Saxon.

There were occasions when Vennen and I talked privately and she could be open with me. She recalled gut-wrenching incidents with her ex-husband and Chester experiencing emotional incest, which robbed him of his childhood. He also witnessed the rape of his younger sister, hurled about like a torn rag doll. Chester's father made her watch as he wrings the neck of her pet rabbit to death, smashing it at her feet as she helplessly wept. He proceeded to threaten her to never tell, denying her existence as he walked away.

Vennen described the terror of being married to a man addicted to alcohol. "After his drunken stupors, he'd come home, find me, and brutally drag me by my hair, throwing me on the bed like meat, raping and sodomizing me. He was an adulterer and a horrible womanizer, lacking conscience who places himself above the law. After I mustered the courage to divorce him, he became crazed, stalking the house and doing drive-by shootings through the windows. If you notice, Chester always seats himself facing the entrance of a room. He always looks out his windows fearing someone is trying to get him."

Living with Chester on weekends, I was a witness to other egregious behaviors. The court agreed to grant him paternal visiting rights to see his daughter once a month because he said he loved her. His wife reluctantly dropped her off on a weekend. It was disheartening watching them interact.

One of the dogs in Chester's pack was his daughter's. She came to visit Babe and tried to talk to her father. He dismissed her and mindlessly puttered. A cold shoulder and silent treatment were her reward. She spent more time hugging her dog than her dad. It was as if I was watching myself as a child, as she sat in a near fetal position outside in the backyard, alone with her dog, crying. She wanted her father's love and acceptance. He rebuked her. So it was with me as a child.

When it was time for her to leave, she stood on the inside of his kitchen door, her hand on the door knob, waiting for her father to face her. He simply avoided her, by turning the food cans in his cupboard so all labels were perfectly front-facing. She wanted him to acknowledge her presence, and hear her father say, "I love you," and be hugged. It was not in him to do so. He took his anger out on her by silently rejecting her and an occasional grunt. Her tearful eyes met mine and our hearts connected. The pain in those eyes revealed her heart's longing. Her every effort to please and be loved was never good enough. She slipped out the door in silence. It made sense why she was in alcohol treatment at eleven years old. The reality of rejection was too great. Alcohol numbed the emotional and mental pain. She never felt good enough to belong or be accepted by her father for the beautiful person she was.

Chester was obsessed with procreation even though he couldn't love the child he had. He fired the question to me.

"Can you have kids or not?"

"No."

"So this won't work with you, will it?"

"It won't work, and at my age, it is dangerous."

Now that he knew this, I was deemed barren and disposable. Chester poured salt in my childhood wounds. I heard again what my father told me: "We should have had a son. It would have been better for the farm."

I bent over backward to please, hoping Chester would notice all my efforts to love him, hoping to break through his barriers and be accepted. Sacrificing myself to save Saxon seemed worth it.

I really didn't know love nor did I think I deserved it. Love can't go where it is not wanted.

In fact, perfect love sat at my feet with eight big paws, golden manes, and huge hearts looking up. I didn't see it.

Where Heart and Mind Collide

My career was the flip side of my personal life. On the job, I held high ethical standards. My livelihood depended upon it. But underlying that was my earnest belief about making a difference in people's lives. Caring for the patient was of utmost importance, and the doctors I worked with saw in my commitment to that genuine straightforwardness, which brought strong, trusting, valuable relationships.

Anesthesia was my area of product expertise. The anesthesiologist in Minneapolis organized an international medical mission trip to Guatemala. One of the lead physicians asked if our company could donate product. I made it happen. The mission interested me, so I spoke with the doctor to gather some more information.

"The poorest of the poor who live in the hills come when we provide free medical care to the women. Most surgical procedures are hysterectomies because the women have prolapsed uteruses and fibroids."

"Do you have tasks for nonmedical personnel?" I asked.

"We do need help assembling surgical packs in central supply and sterilizing the instruments."

My background qualified me for those tasks. Stretching the conversation, I asked if Chester could also participate. My hope was that seeing a different way of life would wake in him a change of heart and lead him to develop compassion. The physician paused with his hand to his chin, thought about it, and then said they could use a runner for odd tasks and for lifting heavy equipment.

This was another chance for me to contribute unconditionally to something larger than myself, to the greater good. I was hungry to learn and experience life's inner force that was directing and inspiring me to find wholeness and new horizons.

That wonderful feeling wilted with renewed dissension between Chester and me as his ego took over at the thought that he would be among doctors. Three months would pass before the surgical team left for Guatemala. During that time Vennen's health was failing, but because we needed someone to care for the dogs, we asked her to stay in my home for the two weeks while the neighbors provided back up.

In February, the surgical team arrives in Antigua. We board a bus into the hills of Chimaltenango at the Berhost clinic compound. The surgical suites were MASH units assembled in preparation for the morning surgeries. Each team member knew their role. Working in concert, we would be akin to a beehive or a dog pack, with each member knowing their role and contributing to the unit.

Our accommodations were meager. When the group sat down to the evening meal, guilt swept over me, knowing these people had nothing and we were indulging. Their education was practically nonexistent. Disease and birth defects were common for lack of good nutrition. Fruit rotted. Fly-maggot-littered meat hung in open-air markets where children sat hoping for a buyer. Shame hovered over children with a common birth defect, cleft lip and cleft palette. Sometimes, those babies were cast along the roadside to die. Families shunned mothers who bore them, compounding the lack of self-esteem. Latino women were property, so the men could justify their manhood by the number of children they procreated, regardless if the woman's uterus was prolapsed. In this, I recognized a perfect alignment with Chester's narcissism.

My eyes and heart opened and ached for the people and for the animals too. Feral stray dogs, starved, hoping to steal a morsel from the marketplace. Diggin' in the dirt and coming up empty, they would rely on village garbage for their existence.

This took me out of myself. I wanted to serve unconditionally. My experience changed my understanding of how important it is to help the less fortunate. At the same time, I gained an appreciation for how my life was blessed in comparison.

The surgeons asked Chester to assist in one case where the woman's uterus had a twenty-five-pound fibroid attached and they needed extra hands to hold the retractors. After the operation, he strutted about and bragged that he was now known as Dr. Chester. I was embarrassed by my association with him and ashamed I'd asked him along. I came close to asking forgiveness from the lead physician who gave his permission for Chester to participate.

Though the families we met were poor, they stuck together and helped one another, in contrast to the infighting and division in my life. Mothers were devoted and hard-working. They fearlessly clung to their faith, which shined its light through the darkness.

Fifty-five operations were successfully performed during our time there. On the last day, the women of my crew were met with a surprise when a young, poor teenage boy came into the central supply area. He didn't speak English, but we had picked up some Spanish. He walked in with an armful of bananas, handed one to each of us, and gave us a hug as tears rolled over his face. It was all he had, expressing his gratitude for saving his mother's life. He was alone because his siblings were dead and his father was gone. In a way, he reminded me of the Maasai girl. Both were angelic. His presence was about heart and giving. He had imprinted differently because his heart beat separately from the nature of the other macho men. He embodied innocence and humility.

There's a Bible parable of Jesus and the poor widow at the well. She gave two copper coins while the rich gave so much more. It was everything she had. Christ replied, "Truly I tell you, this poor widow has put more into the treasury than all the others." This was true for this boy.

He loved, respected, and took care of his mother. Maybe he was another divine intervention placed before me with an angelic message. It was: With full surrender, give everything you have unconditionally and do it out of love with an open heart. There wasn't a dry eye in our room. Divine moments stamped on my heart taught me about life's meaning and purpose.

He backed out of our room with praying hands to his heart, bowing in gratitude. Unknown to me then, the praying hands symbolized "I see the God or Christ in you." I was intellectually unaware but I felt it in my heart. This was God working in me to serve a greater purpose beyond my divided life. When I returned home, I would heed what I'd learned.

Ribbon Crazy

The snow on the farm fields was melting, which meant we were back into training mode preparing Saxon and Sadie for the Junior Hunter title. We were honing our skills to AKC standards, refining line manners, so the obedience requirements were met.

Reading through the test standards, role-playing in my mind how the test happens by visualizing Saxon in each requirement. Entering him in a test was a risk. It was more or less a progress check, finding the training holes and establishing a base line of his progress.

His first hunt test was memorable. Standing at the test line with the judges behind me and one dog hidden in the holding blind, Saxon sat at heel, signaling to the judges to call for the bird from the gunners in the field.

The field gunners behind the holding blind sounded a duck call, threw, and shot the live flyer. Saxon marked the bird, but instead of retrieving, he went into the holding blind of the gunners for a visit and found the crate of live quacking ducks. The live birds were more fun and he loved people. This was a no-no! His tail wagged with glee, but the judges wanted to see if he could retrieve the shot flyer. Eventually, he did pick up the bird. But he came within ten yards of the test line, dropped his prize, and instead of delivering to hand, he proudly peed on the bird. Well, that automatically disqualified him. Saxon was a very comical dog. No ribbon today, but he passed his line obedience and spared a dogfight. For me the test was a success.

Many never saw Saxon's comedic nature. He could be quite the clown when he felt safe.

The judges laughed and said, "I guess he told us what he thinks of this game." The laughter broke the tension and my concern about a dogfight. Saxon was quickly leashed and whisked off the test line. He was petted and praised for his effort and not fighting. He understood he was safe and loved by me. Regardless if he passed or failed, he was met at his kennel with hugs, praise, and a tasty morsel of meat supporting a positive association to the field and his effort.

Sadie was indifferent to hunt tests. She did what was required and was methodical about her work. She passed this test. Competition was not in her, but service to others meant everything. She wasn't built to acquire ribbons and undergo hardcore training.

Chester's dogs trailed several months after Saxon and Sadie earning their Junior Hunter titles. All knotted up, Chester couldn't stand being beat and was driven to win.

Achieving the Junior Hunter title was a landmark accomplishment for Saxon. It built in me the confidence to trust him, advancing his skills.

We entered a field event put on by the Greater Twin Cities Golden Retriever Club called the Working Certificate. Here, Saxon and Sadie passed the test and Chester's Moonie failed. While on the surface Chester shrugged off Moonie's disobedient line behavior, underneath he boiled with resentment, jealousy, and anger that Saxon passed, which proved his dogs were not naturals and my training was advancing Saxon.

Saxon made me proud of his accomplishment and how he held himself together in new situations with new dogs. Of the four stages of learning, a dog passes through when gaining obedience and social skills—acquisition, automatic, generalization, and maintenance—Saxon was floating between automatic and generalization.

Behind his registered name he held the designation of a JH and WC. With determination to raise the bar for him, the next goal was achieving his Senior Hunter title. This would be a remarkable accomplishment both in hunt test skill and changing patterned aggression.

The differences between Junior Hunter and Senior Hunter exist where the dog's marking memory is scored when two marks are down both on land and water. The senior test requires a team's ability to handle remotely in the field and water to a blinded retrieve at one hundred yards distance. The handler knows where the bird is, but the dog must sit to the whistle, facing and watching the handler's hand signals, steering him to the exact location of the bird. The fearful part of the senior test was another off-lead dog sitting on honor at the test line, five feet from Saxon without a leash or collar. Self-control and steadiness had to be solid, with focus on the mark despite distractions from the honoring dog who might break the sit stay, then race past Saxon and steal his bird without a dogfight. He wasn't ready, and with my inexperience I chose not to compete.

My training approach was working. Chester's ranting and inconsistent approach caused fear and confusion. His dogs mistrusted and cowered like his mother fearing a hand across the head. Our training together ended. I find opportunities to break free of him.

Saxon and Sadie were registered without Chester's knowledge, with the United Kennel Club located in Kalamazoo, Michigan. They offered four levels of hunt tests: Started, Hunting, Finished, and Grand Retrievers. Reading the rules and requirement I visualized the tests and the training that was necessary to pass. The Started test was a confidence builder for him since he'd already accomplished the skills in his Junior Hunter tests. It was encouraging that whether we passed or failed, we still got to run both the land and water. For Saxon that was great group training.

Each new location and new dog moved him closer to generalizing his need for restraint and obedience. I was hoping for a positive association that bolstered his confidence and dissipated his aggression. And each time he succeeded, his old pattern responses lessened, proving to me that he could hold his own around another group of excited and strange dogs that loved birds. We were moving him away from an abnormal aggression and welding another link to positively strengthen a progressive chain of healthy behaviors.

Believing that the other dogs were there for retrieving birds helped Saxon settle in. He was reading their right intentions and didn't feel threatened. It was another chance to lessen my anxiety at the line and establish confidence and trust in Saxon.

Through all this effort toward Saxon, Sadie eventually took to the shadows. She was always along but rarely involved. Saxon was making progress. My game plan was the more Saxon could hunt and retrieve pheasants, the more his skills would increase in the field, and his aggression could turn into a normal prey drive.

Bill, who handed me his business card at Jack's came to mind, inviting me to come to his game farm. By now, he was taking clients as a professional gun dog trainer. Stepping out on my own, and needing a gunner to hunt pheasants for Saxon, I contacted Bill and he willingly agreed. Every spare minute, my dogs went to the game farm to hunt. I never told Chester what I was doing or where I was going.

Hunting with Bill was a pleasure. He was a calm, self-contained gentleman, of a connected nature, respectful to me as a person, never viewing me as an object, and yelling was nonexistent. We connected based upon his keen insight into what we needed to be as a team.

The more we hunted with Bill, the more Bill enjoyed it and commented how Saxon was such a smart hunting dog. Finally, another person saw beyond Saxon's aggression and into his soul.

Then Chester started asking what I was doing during the week with the dogs. My telling him the dogs were out pheasant hunting pissed him off. See, I didn't ask him first. He felt insulted. How dare I go off on my own without his permission. His ego was bruised both by his possessiveness and competitiveness. He didn't like that I might learn something to beat him. So he bullied his way in, by coming along persistent to control the situation. Territorially, we were his property. Bill recognized Chester's true character.

Chester bristled when I told him of my intentions to handle my dogs in UKC tests. His clenched teeth, flushed red face, balled fists, and stiff body combined in a pressure cooker of repressed anger. The thought of me being one step ahead and losing control of me infuriated him. How dare a woman to have the audacity to step out on her own without his knowledge. In an attempt to manipulate and intimidate me, he blew into hysteria. But his ploy failed, as I stood strong against his bully tantrum.

He immediately registered his dogs with the UKC. The race for who could get the most titles the quickest was on. But it would wait until spring.

Snipping Ties

Chester's actions are hardly a surprise, yet they shatter me during our ski trip to Austria. He's been having a long-distance affair with a woman in New York, who is an executive of a major tech corporation. He's planning junkets to New York and Paris with her. For Chester to have intentionally betrayed me by destroying my every effort to love him is appalling. I confront him about it.

"You seem to have trouble knowing or accepting real love. Love stands right in front of you, and you reject it, maybe because you think you don't deserve it." I'm standing limp as a rag, weeping. "I'm good enough to be your sex mistress, but not good enough to be a respected equal partner."

Choking from this revelation, I am still able to buck up, reach deep into myself, to be holding out and giving him space, even though his actions made me question my values and morals. A memory of my mother surfaces. I remember how she silently suffered, swallowing moral indiscretions that misaligned to her conscience from my father. Here I am doing the same.

Resolute, a heart can't go where it is not wanted, and right now mine was not wanted. The rejection cut deep. I was learning I couldn't make someone love me no matter how hard I tried. Sensing another door in my life closing, I find myself being steered toward faith, which leads me to silently step back from this relationship. Living alone with my dogs is where life is heading. That was not the life I envisioned. The reality, I was already alone in relationships and embroiled in constant conflict. In contrast to that, being with my dogs was peaceful.

Learning about Chester's womanizing, Vennen flares. "Don't you ever marry him, he's no good. He's the reflection of my ex-husband. He will not change. That's who he is."

Her sharp-tongued words tingle my neck hairs, heeding me to listen, yet question. Could it really be that bad?

Chester and Burt were twin characters. Discreetly, I'm separating myself and silently retreating, until another option opens for Saxon. His dogs were Saxon's bridge.

In April, Chester flies off to Paris for a week, and his dogs are in my care. Since he is preoccupied, Saxon's field training and researching behavioral modification are where I redirect my focus. Saxon, Sadie, and Chester's old dog Jule are loaded in the vehicle, with Vennen coming along too. We head north out of town to meet Bill at the Hay Creek Game Farm.

For the past two years, Jule suffered from advancing leukemia. Giving her an opportunity chasing birds with the little life she has left is a good thing. After all, she was the first strange dog Saxon met; she was gracious to him and him to her. The hunt is my way to return the favor and honor her.

"Where is Chester?" Bill asked.

"He decided to run off to Paris with a rich woman and I get kennel duty."

Bill simply raised his eyebrows looking over his glasses and disgustingly shook his head. "Doesn't he understand what he has?" Bill's comment jolted me. He implied I had value and respected me. This was a revelation to me.

"He is never satisfied."

An attraction sparks. Bill could be a supportive friend who cares deeply and is interested in helping people and dogs without condition. So opposite of Chester.

The pheasants are caught, caged, and bungeed on the back of the four-wheeler. Bird scent, hunting vests, a wide-open grass field, and the sound of the four-wheeler rile the dogs to bark and spin in the crates, craving to be the first one to hunt.

Bill speeds out and hides one bird at a time for each dog. Back at the vehicle, he pulls out his slide-action shotgun and loads. The gun's cocking sound increases the dog's anticipation.

Jule is first. Vennen positions herself in the car to watch Jule hunt. We're spaced, quietly walking the field, so Jule quarters between us, catching crosswind scent. We watch Jule to see when she gets birdie. She finds the bird and flushes while Bill is polite to let me take the first shot—Bang! Got it.

"Wow! Good shot!"

Walking the field toward Jule, we are relaxed, enjoying the teamwork and nature. When Jule got to the bird, she was stumbling and her breathing was labored. She was barely holding the bird.

Getting her back to the truck was a slow go, and we let her lie in the shady grass to rest. Winded from her adventure, her essence glows with delight. The old girl still has it in her to hunt. It was the one pleasure she had. I'm pleased to give her this memory. Chester has missed it. Vennen is delighted and claps for Jule. This is the first time Vennen has seen the dogs hunt.

Another bird is hidden in the field. Saxon is clawing and barking in his crate to be next. When I open the kennel door, he waits for my okay, then bolts. He leaps out as he's called to heel. Bill is ready, and off we go. Nose to the ground, Saxon is naturally quartering. We are nearly running to keep up. Several times I blow my whistle to slow Saxon down and bring him in closer. He skids to a stop and turns with his tail whipping from side to side. He's found the pheasant.

Bill points and sounds out, "Birdie. Saxon is Birdie. Get ready."

Saxon rears up on his hind legs, pounces down hard with his front paws, and pushes under the bird to flush. As soon as the bird flushes, Saxon is chasing and chomping on the tail feathers until Bill can get a clean shot. Bang! Down goes the bird. Saxon fetches it and runs to me full tilt, head and tail high, with the pheasant wing covering his eyeballs like a mask in a Mardi Gras parade. This is where he shines. He is proud, happy, and free, prancing and parading around with his bird. What a thrill to see his joy.

"Wow, can he mark. Not bad for a golden." Bill is clearly impressed.

"Yes, he's a good marker and smart, even though he is not black like your dogs. He can hunt." It's my turn to wink at Bill. He smiles back.

Sadie's style is quiet, reserved, and methodically accurate as her nose searches out the bird. Daintily as she retrieves it, she trots in into heel, sitting politely until I lift the pheasant from her mouth.

Such a balanced day of camaraderie, exchanging pleasantries, and seeing the dogs in their element doing what they were bred to do. The friendship we share is genuine and relaxed. Bill invites us back.

Before leaving the game farm, he demonstrates how his puppy has advanced since I first met Bill at Jack's. He is training his female black Lab, BJ, for an AKC Master Hunter title. He puts her at heel, lines her up for a blind retrieve, sends her, sits her to the whistle, and casts her to the bumper he placed in the field. Next, he turns her to watch three bumpers hand-thrown in different directions as she waits to be sent on her name. Precision work.

How does he know those are the skills Saxon needs? Seeing the skills in action inspires me, and I hope one day Saxon can do the same.

Remembering Saxon's behavior as a puppy and seeing his progress in the field, inspires me to surge forward to discover how far we can rise together. Saxon's heart is wired for greatness.

I grasp that earning Chester's love would be futile. Too much rejection and exploitation are wearing on me. We are outgrowing the relationship with him, heading in a new direction.

Pretending nothing changed when he returned from his Paris junket, we pursue the UKC hunt test, improving Saxon's foundational obedience and impulse control around strange dogs. We are rewiring his brain with new behavior patterns and subliminally mine.

Each time, Saxon behaves at the test line and passes his hunt tests, we snip ties connecting me to Chester and his dogs.

Saxon earns three passes for his first UKC Starter Hunter title. Having no dog fights was the greatest victory. My competitiveness and ambition surge with each ribbon achieved. I am driven in a myopic pursuit of raising the bar each time to achieve even steeper goals for Saxon.

My increased confidence, competitive nature, and independence haunt Chester. He doesn't feel needed and his control is threatened by my emotional distance. He's annoyed that he underestimated us, now realizing the traction we are gaining right under his nose.

Sights are set for Saxon and me to move up to the intermediate hunt test level with UKC, the Hunter Retriever. That requires off-lead and handling to blind retrieves, for which Saxon is not yet prepared.

At the Crossroad

I sense an angel over my shoulder whispering in my ear, *Grow, grow, you need to grow.* The call to grow is a call to walk the way of the Holy Spirit. It's His voice inside offering direction, nudging for attention, encouraging me to leave the darkness and walk in the light.

Now fifty-five years old, I discern that my life is stale. Its architecture is parched intellectually and spiritually. I can see Saxon's progress. He's moving forward and I'm not. Lagging behind I ask myself, who am I? What is my life's purpose? Why am I here? I asked these same questions when I was five years old. Not much has changed half a century later.

I enrolled in an accelerated MBA program in Minneapolis to satisfy my intellectual craving and lay the ground to advance my career toward a secure financial future.

The next thirty months are dedicated to weekly night classes, written case reports, and research and group collaboration with my peers. The workaholic in me is immersed to graduate with straight "A"s, bolstering a successful sales career and advancing Saxon's training.

Research came easy for me, writing did not. English and grammar in my early schooling was poor, because of the home environment. Reading for pleasure was sissy and frowned upon when farm chores took priority.

An initial consult with Patricia McConnell, PhD, and her associate, Karen Lund, directs me to Dr. Susan Krebsbach, DVM, in Oregon, Wisconsin, whose veterinary animal behavior consulting service is called Creature Counseling. I arrange a meeting with her for Saxon. She would become instrumental in teaching me how to rid Saxon's rage around strange dogs and restore him.

Saxon's inward emotional dissonance blossomed physically at four years old as increased hip dysplasia, ear infections, periodic allergic flares, hot spots, and other skin sores. His inability to down-regulate adrenaline and constant stress boiled inside, weakening his immune system.

Dr. Susan evaluated Saxon's emotional condition and behavior toward strange dogs from his history of interactions. She prescribed protocols detailing the steps of desensitization, counter-conditioning, and operant training. She explained those concepts for me.

"Desensitization is a process used to diminish his negative emotional responses, after repeated low-intensity exposures with positive outcomes. Counter-conditioning is the process of forming a different response to the stimulus. Operant training has four aspects. Positive reinforcement, which means when Saxon sits, he is reinforced with a treat. Negative punishment is applied when he makes a mistake or lack of effort, and there's no treat when the command must be repeated. Negative reinforcement is for when he stays locked on the stimulus and is not watching you. He gets a leash correction for not obeying. Overtime, pulling on the leash and releasing the pressure to a loose lead, Saxon will learn to avoid the leash pop before it happens. Positive punishment in Saxon's case is not appropriate; the aversive physical methods hitting, yelling, manhandling increase the possibility to Saxon's heightened aggression, directing it both to other dogs and people. Positive punishment is overkill for the behavioral infraction.

She added that impulse control was another aspect he needed to learn. "He will wear the Gentle Leader during his training. He's going to resist the head halter."

This brought dark memories of the muzzle and the embarrassment we shared. But I put those thoughts aside, since these positive methods could work for Saxon. They were the right thing to do for him.

Saxon was accustomed to being put in situations that were intended to help but ended badly and left him feeling tricked or betrayed. The same had been true for me. I watched Saxon's reaction. Emotionally, his gut was knotted. His low-crouched body and ears pressed against his head with upraised eyes said he hated the muzzle. It was a throwback to the isolation and fear he endured as a puppy with Chester's dogs. This was different. The anger was gone. The process was positive, his ability to adapt caused him to feel safe to comply and he trusted me.

"The dog that resists this the most is the dog that needs it the most," Dr. Susan told me. "Never jerk or yank on the leash. Pull horizontally so Saxon goes with you. He will eventually learn his reward is to walk without pressure as you lead him. Make it fun and give him high-value treats." Conforming to new behaviors was going to be Saxon's freedom to the other side of anger. He was laying down an example of my heart's work to follow. That had not occurred to me.

Next, she recommended using a citronella collar for correcting natural dog behaviors that were destructive, such as digging, chewing, excessive barking, biting, jumping, puppy nipping, which can be corrected with a remote spray release of citronella, catching the dog in the act. It is a negative consequence followed with praise for stopping the behavior. Hearing the list, I realized Saxon was a well-behaved dog at home with one exception. He was a digger and a good one. I couldn't wait to try the collar, so he'd stop diggin' in the backyard. But this went beyond natural behaviors and into communicating to me about my family behaviors. The backyard represented relational issues of the past. His diggin' planted seeds for me to dig inside myself. Then, I missed his cues.

After several of his frenzies and a full face of citronella, the backyard diggin' ceased. He dug long enough to plant the necessary message for me. Diggin' was in him, so the situations where he could dig, were along the bike trail walks. Because dogs understand that diggin' in one location is naughty, they may not transfer that training elsewhere and wind up erupting a sandstorm, as Saxon often did along the trail. I didn't correct him. I allowed it, giving him another physical outlet of his frustrations.

Training inconsistency is often a reason a dog is confused and where most dog training falls apart for a normal dog. Saxon was not a normal dog. Generalization had not occurred. Just because a dog can obey at home doesn't mean he understands to obey in public. Saxon's discernment allowed him to differentiate where digging was allowed.

Saxon's Paradigm Shift

The focus game is the initial two-part goal for Saxon's desensitization teaching him to first look at my face and be rewarded. Then he is allowed to look at the stranger but needs to look back in my face, remaining calm while accepting the person sitting close by. This training begins in a distraction-free area and moves to different locations adding distractions. This shapes behavior leading up to having a neutral dog while using distance as a friend. Finding the fine distance line where Saxon's reactivity erupts becomes the point where the lesson begins. The distance decreases until Saxon feels safe and can calmly focus. This goal has two building blocks, which cement each lesson and layer firmly upon the other, before another is added. The key is Saxon remaining calm and volunteering impulse control.

Shaping or acquiring a new behavior is how we start. Shaping is the beginning of any new command for a dog with no corrections, much repetition, and positive reinforcement. A clicker is used to instantly mark the correct response or effort followed by a treat. Firing the clicker produces a stimulus-reward response. Clicking and treating ten times teaches him that when he hears a click, a reward follows and his actions are correct. It takes voice and emotion out of the training and makes the dog focus on actions.

No steps are skipped. Chaining, perfect execution, and consistent follow-up training make the protocols a success. Reversing learned aggression can't be hurried. Progression is based on Saxon internalizing it. His internal hard drive is being wiped and a new program downloaded.

Saxon's training begins shortly after New Year's Day outside in my neighborhood. Nancy, who rescues golden retrievers, volunteers to help me by acting as an approaching stranger. Setting up the exercise, Dr. Krebsbach observed Saxon for the point of reactivity. Now Nancy and I are on opposite sides of the street walking toward each other in a step-stop-start fashion. Nancy makes no eye contact. I am supposed to lure Saxon's focus walking at heel with a high-value treat, like chicken. We repeat the process by adding types of distractions, as Nancy gradually includes scuffing shoes, irregular awkward steps, jangling keys, banging pots and pans, coughing, dancing, and odd behaviors and dress until he is laser-focused on me.

Then Nancy walks toward me on the same sidewalk, without distractions, and stands beside us. If Saxon's response is an automatic face focus on me, without lures, we'll know he understands and is ready for the next stage of desensitization. Treats and praise come when Saxon chooses the correct response. He learns from his mistakes, which don't result in treats and praise but do make him behave in ways that are rewarded. I never yell, wave threatening gestures in his face, or use physical force, allowing him to make mistakes and still feel safe. He is shown what is right and expected. If that doesn't register, the task gets simplified.

Phase two is adding a strange dog to the lessons. Until Saxon is more stable, an inter-dog aggression protocol designed specifically for Saxon is maintained. The fifteen-day protocol requires that Saxon and I train alone in fifteen- to twenty-minute segments in a quiet area free of distractions, starting in my basement. It combines short and long activities of sit-stays, adding brick upon brick. He has to unlearn to learn.

This is new software for teaching Saxon's mind and muscle memory to be calm, focused, and grounded by shedding his former emotional patterns of fear, anger, and anxiety.

It is also teaching me that the mind is a malleable organ. I am learning to be a better leader and consistent trainer. Still I don't internalize how any of this retraining applies to me.

For the fifteen days, every morning and evening before Saxon and Sadie eat, we walk down the basement stairs on lead in heel position, meticulously training according to each step for each day of the protocol as progress. A stronger bond, respect, and trust forms between us. Sadie peers down from behind the closed glass-pane door, patiently watching from above, laying head on her paws, waiting to eat. Sadie remains abidingly patient and supportive in our shared efforts to retrain Saxon.

Saxon's progress is linked to repetition, like rote learning. New action is attached to the previous day's lesson, whether he has progressed or regressed. Training starts from the new skills and behavior he was successful doing to rule out a fractured foundation liable to failure under pressure.

His entire demeanor lights up when he hears the clicker. He relaxes, his ears perk, his tail softly wags side to side, his eyes become bright, and his face softens with a smile in anticipation of his treat. "*I did good*," his expression conveys. He understood right from wrong. After our daily lesson, Saxon anticipates a fun game, never knowing if he'll tug or retrieve.

His defenses evaporate when the tug toy appears from behind my back. I make it a fun tease by waving it in front of his nose. He's a hoot to watch. He barks and does a play bow, telling me, *Yes, yes, I love you too. Let's play!*

He spins his back legs in reverse, like a car revving and spinning its tires in the mud, trying to gain traction. He's pulling with brute force, while bucking and jerking the toy to win. His powerful chest is strong enough to pull my entire weight. He'll win, I'll take the toy, and return it back, reducing chances of resource guarding. Resource guarding is when a dog presents aggressive, protective behaviors like growling or snapping, warning the approaching dog or person to stay away from his prize, such as his food, toy, a person, a yard, or the individual space. I'll end the game saying, "Saxon, sit! Good boy! Out!" Ultimately, Saxon learns the toy is mine, and not his to keep.

Dogs are natural problem solvers. Saxon is also a critical thinker and acquired the skill to put his impulse control in check. By his never moving a paw or break a sit-stay until he's patted on his chest, with the praise, "Good dog, Saxon, good stay! Treat! Treat!" He'll erupt with a *Woof* and spin like a top with joy expecting a game of tug or a fun retrieve. Throw his tennis ball at the wall across the room, and he'll charge after it. Retrieving it on the rebound in midair, he is happy bringing it back, confidently holding his head and tail high, anticipating another toss and treat, affirming a lesson well done. Saxon loves training. It's fun and has strengthened our relationship, confidence, and trust. We have teamwork, equality, and a great bond.

I pat him on his regal chest, eyeball him, and call out, "Chow! Chow!" In a split-second, he spins around and gallops up the stairs for his breakfast. Sadie sees him bolt and springs out of the way. Saxon knows how to press down the lever handle on the door and fling it open with his big paws. Once upstairs, he plants his butt and politely waits while his food is prepared. Sadie meanders around him with her sensual saunter. They kiss one another by licking their mouths, a gentle caress, and look in the other's eyes with affection. Their love is pure. A warm smile covers my face. My heart opens. We are a family united. Love flows through this house and peace is possible.

Across the fifteen days, the exercises are purposely varied, avoiding being patterned trained. Saxon, an active participant, learns to think and respond differently that he did with prior patterns. Repetition tests his ability to focus. He knows now to correct his mistakes if he breaks his sit, and he has repositioned himself to sit squarely tucked. Just a few fair corrections, followed by a higher number of successes and the rewards instruct him that compliance brings reward, the quicker the compliance, the quicker the reward. Saxon is accountable to obey to a first-time command. His compliance training was applied through respect, using positive balanced methods applied in a structured obedience regimen. A very quick study, he is held to a higher training standard than other dogs. The more complicated and unpredictable the exercises, the more attentive he becomes. Even though he anticipates the next action, he waits to be sure.

The times our eyes lock on each other it is never a threatening stare, but an observation and a conveyance of love, seeing the other's heart. It's what matters most.

Moving at his pace, he doesn't balk. He's making great forward strides, framing in his mind another game. Through his growth, his sagacity shines. Boundaries applied through his obedience are indirectly a signal for me to notice in my life.

"Catch him being good" is a game he quickly masters. He volunteers a "sit pretty" by sitting up, balancing on his haunches, or calmly lying down, waiting quietly next to Sadie when their food is prepared. Any voluntary obedience he offers merits a surprise treat between his front paws. Then, with raised head and perked ears, he returns a look of *Oh, where did that come from?* I praise him for being calm, sitting, being on a down, and waiting. Soon he offers those behaviors. More often than not, we grow to understand the deeper part of ourselves. He sluffs off his ill behavior and starts growing a new, shining self.

Helping Saxon transform gives me an outward purpose and a reason to avoid introspection, as I am unaware of what he is pointing out to me. But his retraining/rewiring process designed to untangle his aggression serves a dual purpose: to open my eyes and heart to my toxic internal patterns that need to be changed. Through his advancement of rehabilitation, he shows me that I can change as well.

The inter-dog aggression training that Saxon completes garners stellar results. But that was in my basement. The next challenge is applying it to new locations and situations, first free of people and other animals because the outside sounds and smells are enough of a distraction. Gradually we'll increase the difficulty by adding distractions and maintaining his ability to stay focused on me. Graduating from this protocol means performing the steps off-lead with a high level of distraction where no dogs are present. He still isn't ready to accept other dogs and stay focused and calm. By now he's been weaned off treats and functions with praise.

The next seven months involve more behavioral training protocols that advance Saxon's ability to focus and minimize aggression. Each builds upon the previous one while adding more difficulty and testing self-control. The different protocols encompass protective and territorial aggression, attention-seeking behavior, and counter-conditioning from strangers approaching with their dogs.

With the help of a few brave friends who volunteer to help, part two of the desensitization process gets underway. We are back in the neighborhood on opposite sides of the street. This time my helper has her dog. We were shaping Saxon's behavior to accept a strange dog and be redirected, calm, and focused on me. Again step by step, it's a start-and-stop progression.

Over time and learning from mistakes, successes, challenges, and regressions, Saxon perseveres and is able to sit side by side with another dog team and remain calm. It takes great restraint to not revert to old rooted fears, both his and mine. Some training sessions are not successful as his aggression fires to the surface. At those times, we regroup and sort out how to turn it around and help him.

The day he sits calmly within five feet of the other dog team is glorious. The impossible is possible. His new foundation is laid, and we are cementing one new brick at a time.

It's amazing what focus can do. Watching Saxon grow one step at a time, I am able to say Saxon made it. It's the thought of defeat and quitting that propelled us. Adversity served both as friend and foe.

Saxon's rewiring creates a new lifestyle. He has demonstrated he can be trusted around other dogs. He has shown me a life can be changed and grow from a new root system, while the harmful portions are pruned away. Shame and abuse had stolen my self-worth and caused me not to believe in myself. Helping reform Saxon's aggression gave me a cause to avoid taking a serious internal look at myself.

Saxon has overcome a hurdle, something long thought by others he could never do. He has exchanged his anger for an inner peace. His impulse control can remain intact beside another dog. Seeing this happen in a structured situation gives us confidence to test it in the field.

Now is the time to revisit the UKC Hunter Retriever title to help him apply his new foundational patterns while using the test as a proofing tool.

The ribbon itself holds little significance. Not engaging in a dogfight is the real goal.

Having both dogs off-lead at the test line, whether honoring or working, is risky and unpredictable. If either dog breaks the stay or both run down the bird, the prey drive could flip into aggression.

During his protocol training, he proved to me his sit-stays were reliable. I trusted he could succeed.

Chester is intrigued by the changes Saxon has made, and the possibility of chasing down Saxon's Hunter Retriever title sparks Chester's curiosity about my training methods.

"How are you training Saxon?" Silence, which spun him sideways since he wanted to train with me. He wanted competitive information, to edge in and see my training methods for his advantage.

Saxon and Sadie must pass four tests to qualify for the title. In late spring they both do just that. Later in the year Chester's dogs also pass the tests.

Saxon was now three for three and no fights. Although there are occasions he sounds a low guttural growl, his focus is quickly trained on me by indirect pressure of a sit command. Each test, my gut twists, and I hope it won't trigger him. Each positive exposure lessens his aggression. He has changed his response, but my body and mind have not made the switch. Hypervigilant, anticipating, listening for some indication of reactivity is how we walked on and off the test line. His guttural growl is locked in my fibers. I have not overcome the experience of his aggressive reactions in previous dogfights and still expect them even though he has proven his restraint. I still feel the muscle memory comingled with my own shame, knowing the risk I am taking with Saxon and the consequences, which puts us both potentially in jeopardy.

Jule

It's a Thursday afternoon in April, Chester calls. He rarely calls. His voice is solemn and broken, emotionally distraught. That, too, is rare.

"Jule is dying. She may not live through the day."

My thoughts go to Saxon, not Chester. Jule was the one that opened a new door in Saxon's life. He lay alongside her on the apartment cushions, when the other dogs distanced themselves. He felt safe with her as he did with Sadie.

"I'm so sorry you are losing her. I saw this coming on her last hunt. I'll load the dogs and come right away."

I find Jule lying in her igloo in his outside kennels. Her gums are shale-colored. I kneel by her side, bringing Saxon to her. Nose to nose, Saxon smells her breath and he is instantly horrified. He recognizes death's odor, which surprises me. How can he know that? He runs to the rear of the kennel, trembling in fear. His body is tight to the corner, curled in denial and sadness. He is broken and has a weeping heart.

From the first day Saxon gently touched noses with Jule, making a safe connection. Now he is losing the only other dog besides Sadie he trusted. Jule was Saxon's teacher and the bridge that opened his door to begin healing and escape being euthanized.

I coax Saxon toward Jule. He gently crawls inside the igloo, careful not to step on her, wrapping his body around hers, comforting her and keeping her warm during her last moments of life. He is ever-present, paying it forward with ethereal love, indebted to one who saved his life.

Through Saxon's grief, his heart naturally spills with overwhelming gratitude and deep affection. He licks and caresses Jule's face, lying with her in silence, putting his head over her back just like he does with Sadie. It's love so amazing, love so divine, and makes her feel safe as her soul transitions and rises to the heavens. She's gone.

Tears run down my face. Such an expression of compassion and unconditional love have opened my heart to feel what real love is. It's not earned, but freely given, gentle, kind, authentic, expecting nothing in return. Saxon loved instinctively. He gave of himself for her. This was not mechanical, but a dog's genuine expression of deep grief and ultimate tenderness. It is a life lesson this human needed to see. I see now why the anger confused him, because he is about love.

I am convinced that fighting, believing and protecting him, resisting others' influences was the right decision. His huge heart was overshadowed with anger imposed upon him through no fault of his own. He didn't know what to do with anger. Now I am increasingly aware by not seeing Saxon as a dog having aggression issues, but as a dog with a soul, whose true identity has a divine depth of untapped potential. This is a moment where I shift my perspective of feeling sorry for him, and he instills in me an iron faith committed to his unlimited capacity to grow.

Chester stands gut-punched outside the kennel. Jule's death cracked him, piercing a locked heart, making way for love to spill through the pain. It is something I once thought impossible. Grief wells up in him. He will fight back tears over the next two years. Finally, something has become real for him. Still my decision to distance myself remains firm. But the timing wasn't quite right to end the relationship.

A Body Crumbling

Ehrlichiosis is a tick-borne bacterial disease that affects the entire immune system by attacking and manifesting diseases throughout the dog's body. The disease is a clever hopscotching in the organs, compromising the gastrointestinal tract, kidneys, and liver. It causes lameness, difficulty in breathing, internal bleeding, and unexplainable infections. Skin staph infections are common and water consumption abnormal. Clinicians' tendency is to misdiagnose the disease in its early stages, elusively allowing Ehrlichiosis to worsen. The PCR testing now done was not available then or it was not offered or known about by the lay person.

Saxon was diagnosed with Ehrlichiosis, which exacerbated his hip dysplasia and caused lameness in his right elbow and difficulty breathing. Saxon self-soothed the pain in his legs, causing lick granulomas erupting in staph dermatitis. He was miserable. We shared many sleepless nights because of his allergies. His unrelenting itching and panting escalated his anxiety. He was continually conflicted, miserably torn to obey, fighting his fears, suppressing his aggression, struggling to be normal, a body trapped fighting a villain inside him. Antibiotics were ineffective, so he endured the maladies for the rest of his life.

Watching Saxon's declining health caused me to finally turn my eyes inside. I, like Saxon, marched and persevered through emotional pain. A tenacious faith allowed us to believe all things are possible. An inner driving force tugged at our minds, moving us onward to become whole and take back what was stolen.

Behind Closed Doors

Living alone was no longer possible for Vennen. She was falling, incontinent, and in the advanced stages of dementia. She needed assistance and supervision. Once a ferociously independent woman, she was now a body coming undone, assaulted by disease rooted in psychological abuse. She felt betrayed, vulnerable, and at the mercy of others.

In my kitchen, Chester and I discuss the gravity of his mother's condition.

"What options do we have so she is safe and cared for?"

"She's not going in a nursing home because I'm not paying for her. And I can't have her in my place."

"So you're suggesting she live here with me? Do you realize what you are asking?"

"Seems like a reasonable option."

"You better share the workload and not think you can run off skiing or with another woman and dump me with your responsibility. She's *your* mother."

Jeepers! What the hell did I just do? Juggling graduate school, traveling for work, leading Saxon's behavior training, caring for all five dogs, cooking most of the meals, and having no medical knowledge to manage the care of Vennen's progressive dementia—pile it on was my normal behavior. After all, Ma operated constantly on overload; it was expected. Martyrdom, at all cost, is the price of codependency.

Saxon's behavior modification stalled while the dogs received basic care. Luckily, his aggression eased. The early morning and evening walks with my dogs, were where I maintained my sanity by escaping the self-induced entrapment at home.

My home underwent a conversion for a handicapped person. My living room became Vennen's bedroom with a therapeutic lift chair and a walker beside it. During the sundowner stage, every day, 24/7, was an unending series of cries, hallucinations, screams, and wailing. She was delusional.

"Chester, help! Chester, help! Help me! You have to help me! Chester, where are you? Why aren't you helping me? He's hurting me again! Chester! Chester! Chester!" Vennen rarely slept. Her nightmares and hallucinations intensified. Multiple personalities emerged. Disorientation, fear, and confusion set off her mental fright in unfamiliar surroundings. Pleasing her was impossible. She profanely lashed out. Unpredictable, erratic, crazed, cantankerous, and violent behavior surfaced. She flung her arms and fists when Chester came near her. She threw her food tray when it didn't meet her standards and was choking when she ate because the disease strangled her ability to swallow. She was resentful and demoralized by being fed pureed food like a baby.

It was scary to witness. Growing up on the farm was pale in comparison. Random flashbacks of my mother bombarded me. Ma's toxic prison was verbal maltreatment rooted in shame. This situation was demonstrative belligerence. I was drowning, but the superwoman in me was driven to rise above.

Vennen, a betrayed mother, nearing the end of her life, just wanted to feel love and not live out her days in mental terror. This time, it was me protecting her, empathizing, and sharing her pain. Caring for Vennen lessened my guilt of not being able to do more for my own mother as she died of cancer.

I watched Sadie and Saxon often huddling at her feet, putting their heads on her lap, lovingly looking in her eyes, being a comfort in her despair. I saw love's tangibility, freely given, but stolen across her life. My dogs' unconditional love pierced through her fear, shattering its razor-sharp edge, absorbing life's victimizing blows. Their open-heartedness soothed her emotional scars. It was Christ-like, amazing love.

The ingrained fear in Chester's dogs made them dare not approach Vennen, dreading his forceful hand.

Vennen's wails hiked Chester's anger. She was his prey. Alcohol's numbing was useless. His altered mind snapped. He came stomping at her fist-swinging, a cursed madman yelling, exploding like a raging bull on a killing spree. Vennen screamed, recoiling as he towered over her, helpless to defend herself. He likes it that way. He feels a justified power refueling for the next go-round.

What had I done to lose the oneness and harmony of Africa or the Navajo for this violence and chaos? Where was God in all this? This was stealing my soul, and I allowed it.

Evil slithered in, engulfing me in a house of horror. To the outside world, all was normal and quiet. I was living a divided life, plastering on the good girl to mask the anguish percolating underground.

Fear's rapid firing kept the dogs on high alert, never allowing their adrenaline levels to down-regulate. Most of the time Sadie, Saxon, and I hit the deck, invisible, operating business as usual, hoping not to be a target. Toxic fear and pandemonium had run amok, as evil took up residence, pushing out any inkling of God in my house.

Like a locust infestation, Chester, his dogs, and Vennen overwhelmed my house. Chaos governed so much that it was unbearable to sleep inside. I moved a spare mattress onto my three-season, uninsulated porch, sleeping with my dogs beside me for warmth in below-zero temperatures. Love anchored us three together.

I coped using compartmentalization and denial to block the trauma; failure was never a consideration. I had too much at stake to let this suffocate me.

I felt guilty of dragging Saxon into a poisonous and vitriol environment, piling on prolonged stress. I put myself in this situation because of Saxon's need to be with other dogs and build on the social aspect while completely sacrificing myself. Was this the way to do it? In hindsight, probably not. But what I did was well-intentioned and the best choice based upon my knowledge about dogs and my mindset, then.

A nursing home was where Vennen belonged. She deserved to be treated with dignity, proper medical, and spiritual care. Head-strong Chester refused. The man was greedy and selfish; he was always about the money.

The contrast in the midst of the mayhem was the love Vennen received from Sadie and Saxon, bravely sitting at her feet as tears rolled down her face, comforting her as she petted them. Courageously, my dogs pushed through the violence to show that love is stronger than hate.

The physical and psychological violence went on for months. When Vennen cried for help, Chester retaliated by yelling, "You bitch, I'll give you something to scream about," and smacking her across the head.

Threatening to call the police, I declared, "She's not your dog to beat, she's your *mother*!"

He turned his rage on me. For once, I stood up to him. That's when Saxon placed himself between us. His attack growl was a warning to Chester.

"If you strike me, you better make it count because I'll make sure you're in jail the rest of your life for elder abuse. You're not taking me down like you're doing to your mother."

Saxon held his ground between us, and Chester backed away. Too many times, I'd turned a blind eye and let this happen. Now frightened by the thought of being his accomplice, I woke up to the importance to carefully distance myself from him. Living like this was unsustainable for me and the dogs.

My gut wrenched. All living here had been victimized and silenced. I'd been too fearful to stop it, yet not ready to take the leap. It scared the bejeebers out of me seeing what life would be like living with him as one grew older. It's what evil does. Shame and fear silenced the inner child once again, as was normal.

Now bedridden, the therapeutic lift chair is replaced with a hospital bed in my living room. Chester recognizes the weight bearing down on me, offering to move his mother to live in his apartment. That didn't coincide with his previous statement of not being able to have her in his place. It smelled fishy to me.

From the beginning when I agreed to have Vennen come and live with me, he stated, "I hope this gets over pretty quick . . ." He paused with a side glance. ". . . because I sure want to get back to skiing." Why would I not question his motives when a hospital bed would never fit in the paper maze in his apartment? She'd have been thrown in a back, cluttered junk room, with the rest of his trash. Vennen's existence depended upon staying in my house. Chester was very cunning at covering up and lying about his immoral actions, calling them accidents and walking away with the help of an expensive defense attorney, unscathed. If a fatal accident happened to Vennen at his residence, nobody would know and that's the way he wanted it, no witnesses.

Being with Chester for the sake of his dogs was still necessary. Protecting Vennen's life took the priority.

For her sake, I had chosen to endure the chaos. The pressure built as tempers flared. The dogs felt it, and they found distant corners to seek safety. Something needed to break and soon. My decision to leave was made. Again I find myself buying time.

Convincing Chester to have hospice come was a start to my getting some relief and for Vennen to have an outside advocate.

The man contained no common sense or empathy, nor could he apply it to a realistic situation. All things were literal. Vennen was an object to him. His fatal error happened interpreting hospice's care instructions.

Hospice's follow-up care sheet included instructions to have Vennen drink sixty-four ounces of water each day. Chester was obsessed to get the water in her, whether she wanted it or not and whether she could swallow or not. He physically forced her to drink, as he stood over her and poured. He yelled at her when she refused. Flat on her back, she drank and choked down the water out of fear. He was merciless to her defenselessness. It heightened his sense of power over her.

Our arguments were brawls over his lack of compassion. Yet there were times I felt bamboozled never knowing if he was saving her life or hastening her demise by pushing water and food down her throat.

Hospice caught him one day in July. I had left the house for a brief time when an angel screamed in my ear, "Leave and take care of the mail before hospice comes." God's voice rescued me from being the accomplice. Another warning about changing the patterns of my life before ruining it.

The hospice nurse checked Vennen, saw that her face was black and blue, and asked what happened. Chester lied, saying she fell out of bed. But the handprint by her temple was obvious to the nurse. His knee-jerk reaction had been to cuff her when she spewed projectile vomit in his face after he poured water down her throat.

I returned from my errand to find the police and an ambulance at the house. Chester was handcuffed and being hauled off to jail. The ambulance took Vennen to the emergency room where her face was photographed for evidence. I stayed with her at the hospital until she was admitted. She stayed a week and went from there to the nursing home. In Vennen's diminishing mind, this was her death sentence. Her son betrayed her, but at last she was safe.

The state of Wisconsin became her guardian. Chester lost any rights to make decisions for her. When I visited her, she reached for my hand saying, "Finally, I don't have to make any more life decisions." She was leaning into death.

Chester was allowed to visit his mother, but only under strict supervision. He managed to charm the staff at the nursing home into believing he was a caring, loving son who pampered his mother. Snowballing them, he got them to trust him and their watchfulness waned. When no one was watching, he forced food down her throat. She was paralyzed and powerless to resist. Having lost the ability to speak, her voice was silenced and trapped in her body. She was defenseless to utter words. Her hopelessness set the hay hook down in her. Her fading eyes told a sorrow-filled story.

Every night, I sat silently beside her bed, holding her hand watching her as she watched me. Eye to loving eye, both our hearts were connecting to God. Faith replaced her fear. Tears flowed. She knew she was dying. Her physical body was having the last word, failing piece by piece. But she was not afraid to die because she believed God's grace would hold her. Vennen's life demonstrated how maltreatment steals the soul's nurturing. She was God's opportunity to tell me not to repeat her life.

I passed forward what my mother gave me—scripture, music, prayer, and a sense of restoring hope through God's mercy, grace, and love. I provided her an assurance, so she knew that when her time came, she would be lifted on angels' wings and forever be safe and loved. Ma's essence was over my shoulder, smiling and watching, pleased she installed God in me during my formative years.

The moment Chester entered the room, the light in her eyes turned to horror. Her body stiffened, trembling, her jaws clenched. Her being remembered the trauma, and she felt all the pain, anger, and fear rumble inside.

Sadie and Saxon were so happy to visit Vennen in the evenings. They came into her room, tails wagging. With a toy in his mouth, Saxon put his paws on her bed and smiled at her. Her eyes smiled back. Fear had lost its stranglehold as faith and the dogs' unconditional love girded her. She and I had faith on our side despite the maltreatment ground into us. In dying she taught me to step out of a life of exploitation and not to take it to the grave.

Don't live the life I've lived is what I felt from her. Find a new path.

As our visit unfolded, Sadie lay alongside Vennen, resting her head on Vennen's stomach.

Vennen's body and mind relaxed, her eyes and breathing softened. Saxon peacefully rested his broad head on his paw, lying on the floor beside her bed, and listened to me sing *Amazing Grace* and read the Twenty-third Psalm. In the reflection of her soul, love and peace were shining through her eyes. Here was faith, the precious bridge to eternal life.

In time, she no longer recognized me, but she connected my compassionate touch and loving smile. Names didn't matter, accepting her as is, raising up her being, and transcending life's temporary existence did. Reaching out in faith, feeling love, hearing God's word, and sharing prayer brought peace to her soul.

Because of Vennen, God helped me to ask myself the hard questions. Was this all worth the emotional pain I put myself and my dogs through? What's been proven? My personal life was a mess. My spiritual life was fractured. What was I going to do to change my thinking? Did I want to find myself in Vennen's position at the end of my life? The Holy Spirit patiently waits for me to reach out and open my heart.

An opportunity opened when Chester, consumed in fighting for Vennen's guardianship, was away from the house most days. This was my chance to escape. Professionally, I was exceeding sales expectations. I had graduated with honors in my MBA program. Saxon and I deserve to be unrepressed.

By my presence and association, I had nearly been an accomplice to elder and animal cruelty. This was a bell ringer for me. I realized God's armor was protecting me from a life being ruined.

The hair-on-fire moment came when I realized the severe risk and danger my dogs and I faced. In my mind, I relived how Chester beat his dogs, threw them against walls, cold-cocking, whipping them into submission, and tormented his mother, how he victimized others by emotional incest, sexual improprieties, adultery, womanizing, and bullying, and how he was controlling and so much more that embodied a sociopath. My well-intentioned need to have Saxon be with a group of dogs where he could learn to be social and my need to have a life partner motivated and distorted reasoning put me in this conundrum.

God's timing is impeccable. What comes to mind is each time I am near disaster, I'm rescued. Noticing, walking toe to toe with me is His Spirit. He whispers to cling to my faith. God's net is always there when things get really ugly. I've come to notice as one door closes, another opens. The Holy Spirit clears away the obstacles for me to move forward. While the Holy Spirit continues His work in my heart, I march ahead on my own.

This relationship with Chester hits a headwall, but a special person enters my life to teach and guide me along my heart's awakening. The contrast between harmony and evil is brought to light. Patiently, Spirit hopes, time after time, that I may eventually see a trend, good or bad, and, ultimately, have enough nerve to examine myself and dig at the root cause. How else is this explained other than His perfect plan? It comes down to the choices I make and the decision to take responsibility for them. This is part of my mental processing.

Restoring me and making Saxon whole are the priority. Escaping this time, I choose faith to guide me. My way wasn't working. God's way never fails.

The place where my heart and faith unite in harmony was at Bill's pheasant farm. Hunting in the open air with my dogs and being with Bill felt safe. The pleasure of it was peaceful. The noise was gone. The freedom to be myself and laugh again was long overdue. In all this was an interconnectedness, an oneness!

Bill's entire demeanor beams on seeing us return. He is so excited to show me BJ's hunt test skills. He and BJ not only achieved her Master Hunter title, they qualified and passed their first Master National Retriever competition. Bill proudly pulls out his phone and shows me the picture of the silver award plate and ribbon and the article about them in the local New Auburn newspaper. That's big stuff for a self-contained, small-town guy. For me, so inexperienced to the hunt test game, the Master Nationals are beyond my comprehension.

Giddy and proud of their team accomplishment, Bill demonstrates one of BJ's attributes, running the test. He hides an orange bumper way out into the pheasant field, marking it with an orange ribbon on a stem of goldenrod. BJ lines parallel, sitting at heel and sent. Going off the line to the blind, he whistles and she instantly turns and sits facing him. Wow! Extraordinary!

He gives her a right-hand signal, straight up above his head, directing her back online and toward the ribbon. One cast and she lines it a hundred yards out, swiftly retrieving the bumper and coming back to heel. She holds the bumper until Bill takes it.

Impressive! Those are the next skills Saxon needs. Bill plants a seed, visualizing Saxon and me having that same partnership.

Invariably, when we finished hunting, Bill and I ended up on the tailgate of his dog truck, legs dangling and swinging forth and back, drinking a cold pop, baseball caps turned backward, like two buddies, with me talking and him listening. That tailgate is his mobile office.

"Please, have a seat in my office. So what's your story?"

That opener gives voice to my history with Chester and my struggle with Saxon's aggression. I tell him how I want Saxon to be normal. Listening intently and taken in, he appears preoccupied. The dog trainer in him is tooling ideas around of how he might be able to help.

"Chester doesn't know I'm here." I give him a side glance.

"Oh! I see." Hunched, gripping the edge of the tailgate, he nods with a sly smile.

"And you, what's your story, Bill?"

"I grew up with a father who beat me and my mother. Life was so bad I left when I was eleven. Never looked back. Mother stayed. I was a runaway trying to survive."

This paralleled my father. I listen.

"I ended up serving in the Marines in Vietnam and killed a lot of people, children included." That type of trauma is something I couldn't relate to. I can see by how he tells his story that it cuts deep as he relives the horrible atrocities in his mind. It changes people's hearts and affects one's soul.

"In the war, I was a sole survivor, and I will never understand why God gave me a second chance. It haunts me why my life was saved."

Faith saved Bill, as he grabbed God's hand on the battlefield, standing alone amid the bloodshed, crying up to survive. Bill's survival was another example of how one can elbow through life's hurdles and make it. So I knew scissoring the final strands with Chester and standing on my own was possible.

Bill's humanness was his surface face, but the real person beneath the surface was extremely real and insightfully wise. So much so, he read my thoughts and finished my sentences. His Godly energy drew me to him, as he spoke freely of God, prayer, forgiveness, and gratitude.

Reminding me, faith is where I needed to turn in order to survive.

Training hunting dogs for competition was Bill's passion. I began to feel I could trust Bill as someone with whom Saxon could learn and be safe. God saved Bill's life for a reason. He was a blessing in disguise, all because of Saxon.

Chester was oblivious of my changed feelings toward him. In the meantime, my survival meant acting in business-as-usual manner.

Corporate offered me an opportunity for a lucrative sales advancement after twenty-five successful years. My competition for the coveted position was steep. Every day, I hit the floor running, giving it my all, building on the day before. I loved my work and looked forward to being and belonging with intelligent, positive people. They inspired me, and they made a difference for their patients. I felt valued and involved having a purpose greater than myself. Yet the performance expectation, accountability, and ethics for the company were paramount and consequential.

I was motivated from a place of love and compassion, not climbing the corporate ladder. My approach taught me boundaries and the importance of personal growth and seeking ways to be better at being better.

The company was nearing final FDA approval for a blockbuster drug for treating Crohn's disease. Strategically, my resume was strong against my younger, less experienced and accomplished, hungry applicants. I brought to the table my MBA, years of award-winning sales performance, established professional relationships, and letters of recommendations from management and doctors. My driven-to-succeed attitude was grounded in perseverance, tenacity, dedication to solid customer service, and built-in resilience to rejection. The person the company selected would be deemed the best of the best whose focus was on making a difference in peoples' lives and ultimately caring about the patient. And that's where I hit the ball out of the park with recommendations supporting the company's priority. They hired me. I never told Chester.

Sales travel was 75 percent across North and South Dakota, Southern Minnesota, Iowa, and Western Wisconsin. One thing I never thought about when I accepted the position? The dogs! What do I do with the dogs? Saxon? Sadie? It hadn't occurred to me that I might have to surrender them over the job. I was gut-wrenched again about Saxon's survival. That's when serious prayer started and I began a soul surrender to God's will. I had to take the risk and allow faith to be my guide. This was my window of opportunity to leave Chester and take my dogs and myself in a new direction.

There were online testing requirements about the drug's science and research to hold our position or it would be given to the next candidate. It meant passing every test with a score of 95 percent or higher. Every morning, from August through October, I concentrated on my studies, in my office. In the afternoon, the dogs and I went to Bill's for pheasant hunting. The more I hunted with Bill, the more I came to trust him with my dogs. Remembering his blind-retrieve demonstration with BJ, I was confident Bill could train Saxon while I traveled.

Saxon was owed a second chance to minimize his aggression. Bill's training could expand Saxon's behavior modification, teaching him to focus with other strange dogs working in the field around him. The idea seemed logical. This was Saxon's shot at being normal, and safe, around strange dogs, developing into a well-mannered bird dog, and becoming whole.

In September, I asked Bill, "Would you consider evaluating Saxon? Do you think he has a chance of getting one Senior Hunter ribbon, just one?" To me, it would prove how far Saxon had come in battling through his aggression.

Bill peered over his glasses at me and withheld his answer, saying only, "You are asking a lot." He knew Saxon was a huge undertaking. Saxon would be his first aggressive field dog to train.

At the time, I didn't grasp the vast responsibility being asked of Bill. Naively, not understanding the extensive training, the drill work, and the remedial socialization involved to getting one ribbon. Senior Hunter skills alone were arduous and time-consuming. If Bill decided to say yes, Saxon would be a challenge for him. He understood the risk he was exposing his dogs and his clients' dogs to. Yet he understood my predicament.

"I need to think about this and discuss this with my wife." That answer was fair enough. That night, I prayed, believing God could find a way for this to work, that Saxon would get a chance to be trained and modify his aggression while I worked. The next day, Bill called me.

"Bring Saxon to the field. I will evaluate him and let you know."

Thank you, God. I was thrilled. Saxon passing one Senior Hunt test to earn just one ribbon would be a monumental accomplishment, beyond my wildest dreams come true. It would mean he could sit calmly near another working dog and focus on his work while not attacking the dog next to him. Phenomenal!

The next day, as I headed off to meet Bill for Saxon's evaluation, Chester stopped me.

"Where have you been going every afternoon?" His tone condescending and accusatory.

"I don't think that is any of your business." I was tight-lipped. He pressed me again for an answer. So I told him.

"I have been taking Sadie and Saxon pheasant hunting at Bill's game farm."

"Well, I am going along today."

"I really don't want you there. Besides, what about your mother?"

"Why, what's going on?"

"What about Vennen? Isn't she your priority?"

"Ah, she can wait. She is going to die anyway." Suddenly, his mother lost importance, even though he was anchored to her until her death. It irritated him even more that I was gaining ground.

"I don't want you near Saxon or Sadie."

Well, he injected himself. He sensed that competition was brewing and he was losing power over me. He resented my challenging him. How dare I liberate myself from him? After all, he viewed me as his property.

I was gaining strength as his control weakened. A cold silence prevailed as he rode with me to the game farm.

It was a beautiful fall day; clear, colorful and warm. Bill greeted us, looking suspiciously at Chester. It was like two snorting bulls before a face-off.

"He had to come along and see what we were doing today. He's jealous!'"

"Hmmm, get Saxon out of the kennel," Bill told me with pursed lips. This wasn't how he wanted Saxon's evaluation to get underway. "Chester, stay in the truck and out of sight of Saxon."

Chester didn't listen as usual. He had to interject himself, with his standard posture of dominance.

Bill had a handful of bumpers. He threw them one at a time for Saxon to retrieve. He tested Saxon's memory to see if he remembered where a second bumper was when he threw two. He evaluated his force-fetch and level of obedience. Saxon fetched the bumpers, but his delivery and hold were weak. He followed commands extremely well and his obedience was quite good. What about eye contact? What would Saxon do with direct eye contact? Would the stare trigger his aggression? His eye contact was neutral and focused. He seemed to understand more than I realized, this was a second chance for both of us. It was as if Saxon had insight to the future knowing why it was important for both of us to make this work.

An unexplainable vision and stirring deep within my core signaled that the three of us were embarking on a predestined journey. I was having an out-of-body experience, a reunion from a previous lifetime. We were foreordained to fulfill our soul purpose as we supported each other on our soul paths of transformation.

The presence of the Holy Spirit enveloped Bill, Saxon, and me, shining love's light around us. In those moments, the world stopped and all was surreal. Saxon and I were about to be blessed with something magnificent as we stood in Heaven's radiant beam.

Waiting to hear Bill's answer, I sensed God had orchestrated bringing Bill and Saxon together.

"Saxon is a very intelligent dog. His hunting prey drive is good. He has an acute sense of his surroundings. He's yellow and not very fast," Bill said, indicating that his peers were going to ridicule him for training a dog other than a superfast, field-trial black Lab. Why would Bill invest the time training a slow swamp collie who came with challenging issues? These are certain washouts for a pro trainer.

Bill understood the criticism he'd face taking Saxon, but he was out to prove them wrong and buck the system. The "I'll show you" was ingrained in both of us. He was willing to endure their criticism. This was nothing compared to Vietnam. He recognized Saxon's sagacity and my dilemma, and he cared.

Pro field trainers have an algorithm they follow in bringing dogs through the hunt-field trial competition. This is where they decide on continuing the dogs' training or washing them out. Saxon was the exception to the algorithm, so Bill had to redesign and customize it to meet Saxon's training requirement. Instead of the dog adjusting to the standard protocol, Bill was adjusting to meet Saxon's needs. The challenge would be to develop an individualized, balanced training plan to fit Saxon's soft-sensitive temperament riddled with health issues.

"The only way I am going train him is if I have your total commitment to train with me and bring him along."

Breathless, for the love of God, I realized he said yes, and so did I. I was blown away that another person who cared about Saxon as much as I did. How could I be so fortunate to find him? Or was I led?

I stood there limp and cried. Bill was giving Saxon a second chance in his life. He was going to train Saxon and mentor me as his handler in the hunt test. We were just given a gift from Heaven taking Saxon to the other side of his aggression and from being abnormal to normal.

"You have my undivided commitment to give every spare minute to working with you."

Bill and I shook hands.

"Let's take him as far as he wants to go. Let's get just one senior ribbon."

He agreed. "It's about making a difference, not the ribbon."

I smiled through my joyful tears and agreed. It was more than a ribbon we were chasing; it was about changing hearts and lives.

United as one, we were sealing a commitment to succeed, suffer, exist, whatever it took to recreate Saxon while unbeknown to ourselves, we were being recreated, guided by soul and Spirit to move forward courageously, in concert trusting faith, to break through our old nature.

Emotionally, I shunned Chester, jealousy and contempt was written all over him for being excluded. He lacked the aspect of faith to comprehend a greater power than the ribbon.

Between September and the middle of October, Bill invited me but not Chester, to attend his group client-training sessions with Saxon. Training was twice a week. Bill set up simulated hunt-test concepts for the junior, senior, and master levels, based upon the drills he worked each morning in his yard for proofing his training, to demonstrate to his clients their dogs' progress.

Chester bullied his way in, flashing his big-shot money, acting like an idiot, wanting everyone to believe he was a successful businessman who knew everything about anything, including dog training. Bill and with his clients recognized Chester's fraudulence. They all saw him for the brazen, disrespectful bully he was and gave him the cold shoulder.

Saxon is honoring on lead to the various working dogs, keeping a safe distance, but staying part of the action so he can acclimate. Bill informs his clients about Saxon's aggression issues, so Saxon is the last dog to retrieve. Fear washes over me, having Saxon off leash around other dogs. Roles reverse as one client is honoring on lead to Saxon, both were distanced.

Here on the test line the action starts. As Saxon and I are at the line, watching the field, one of Bill's clients role-plays being a hunt test judge, calling out, "Guns up, dog to the line." Pushing through my fear, hyperventilating and trembling, I release Saxon's leash. "Sit, and mark," I say, meaning Saxon is to sit-stay and watch where the bird is going to fall and not move until told. Saxon looks around, noticing the other dog. Keeping my composure, I tell him, "No, mark." He refocuses on the field. The person impersonating as a judge signals the gunners. We hear a loud duck call seventy-five yards out, Quack! Quack! Quack! We see the bird thrown into the air and a gunshot at the arc of the throw. Nervously, I keep my finger through Saxon's collar until the judge calls, "Dog!" Pausing before releasing Saxon on his name, I want to make sure he is focusing on the bird and not the other dog and he is. Then we hear it: "Saxon!" He runs out with his rear pigeon-toed gait and tail swooshing high above his back.

Sometimes, when he accelerates, his tail looks like a windmill, going in circles around his rump, which makes me smile.

The acting judge signals the honoring dog team to leave the line. Saxon now commands the field without feeling threatened. I relax, knowing the pressure is off. He skids in his tracks like a baseball player, as he reaches the scent cone of the bird. Head cocked, ears alert, he turns his body and bolts to the bird. This time his golden tail is wagging like a metronome ticking beyond its capacity. The pheasant is crippled and starts running, eliciting Saxon's prey drive as he pounces on it and places it between his powerful front paws. But the bird manages to escape, going airborne. Saxon leaps into the air, snapping at tail feathers, pulling the bird to the ground. The bird escapes and Saxon leaps again, demonstrating an erratic dance, pinning the bird between his paws, panting and spitting feathers. Seeing him so involved and having fun doing his work is a pleasure. Saxon even disregards the gunners sitting in the holding blind. In this moment, in the field, the bird is everything to him and strange dogs didn't matter. His natural ability shines, his true nature is alive, and Saxon is emerging into his new self.

"Saxon, fetch, fetch it up." He retrieves, intermittently dropping the bird, trying to get a better hold, hearing the whistle's toot-toot to come into heel. This is where Bill will retrain his force-fetch so he learns to immediately fetch and hold, and then deliver to hand. The process of force-fetch is about a dog understanding how to get out of pressure through compliance.

Saxon returns carrying his head and tail high, showing off his prize, practically parading, in front of the judge. Praising Saxon, I beam with joy. So does Bill. Inside Bill's heart is pride, hope and accomplishment, most of all, making a difference in a dog's life that is most gratifying.

"Good boy, Saxon. You are a good boy! I love you, sit, and give!" I say, attaching his leash and walking off the line. Bill's clients are cheering, offering their full support for Saxon's accomplishment and good behavior. Saxon needed a positive experience to counterbalance a massive amount of the historically negative assaults. This is all such a contrast to Jack's training group.

Sadie is content watching and cheering Saxon on. But when the group training has finished, Bill throws a few marks for her so she feels included in the training. Being around Bill and seeing how he works with the dogs and people convinces me he is a trustworthy person and his training methods are well designed for advancing a dog's natural talent. Three weeks of product training in Chicago are approaching. Until then, I ask Bill to board and train Saxon. Sadie comes home with me. Boarding Saxon with Bill will give Saxon the daily concept drills and field work he needs for the Senior Hunter ribbon.

Holding firm my commitment, I agree to train with Bill as often as work allows, so he can mentor me. With a tear in his eye, Bill agrees, knowing the difference he is making.

Chester busts in again. "My dogs can do this. I'll bring them and train with you."

Bill makes the situation quite clear. "You have to pay for your own training. She is paying her own way." Oooh! It drives Chester crazy that another man is stepping on his property, dogs included. Here Chester is ungrounded and suspicious, knowing his ties to me are being cut. His mind is blown by knowing that Saxon is going on Bill's dog truck, training every day. He feels disadvantaged.

At the end of September, I bring Saxon to Bill. I've packed his food, medications for chronic hip pain, supplements for immune support, and wire kennel. It's heart-wrenching, but my back is up against the wall. I am at the end of myself to help Saxon grow in his training. I need the job and this is my only option.

When I drive into the field, Bill is waiting. I go to Saxon's car kennel, open the latch, clip the leash to his collar, and sit privately with him, caress his flowing golden mane, and look him in his eyes. Intuitively, he understands what I am going to tell him. His eyes see into my heart. He grasps my intentions. Loving him enough to set him free to grow, I know and he knows this is not abandonment.

"Saxon, letting you go is the hardest thing I am doing. This is for you, to become your best. Bill can take you beyond the hunting skills you've learned with me. He will be good to you, helping you feel comfortable around new dogs. I promise you I will do everything I can that's possible for you. I love you with everything I have. I am not saying goodbye or quitting on you. I'll be gone for a while, so for now I can't take care of you and train you the way you need to be trained. I'll come back and work with you as often as I can. There's a champion in you. I believe in you. I trust you. Do your very best. Try not to hurt any dogs and learn how to be calm. I will be here for you, I promise, I love you, Saxon. I love you."

Grabbing a small bag with meat and my scented T-shirt, Bill transfers Saxon's things to his dog truck. Saxon slowly, obediently walks at heel looking in my face with a look that says, *I will be all right, Mom. I love you too.*

Saxon knew I would not quit on him and in return, he never quit on me, whatever the cost he had to endure. This was our partnership.

"Please, put the T-shirt in his kennel at night so he knows that I will be back for him and he can smell me and still feel close. Lock his kennel, and keep Chester away from him."

"I promise he will have the shirt in his kennel, protecting and caring for him like he is my own."

I am at peace, knowing Saxon is safe and getting the training he needs. Bill points out Saxon's name above the dog truck kennel, which tells me it's pretty special. Being on a professional trainer's truck qualifies him to be among the smart field dogs, or, as Bill calls them, the "big dogs," the ones with the talent to succeed. I think how far Saxon has progressed in the last seven years. Understanding his false start in life and where he is now, I feel certain that faith's guidance led us to Bill.

The truck kennels are constructed of steel bars and a metal bottom. Another dog is on each side of Saxon's kennel and the quarters are tight. Bill lifts Saxon into the kennel placing my T-shirt beside him. Saxon's anxiety surfaces, and he growls.

"Saxon, Saxon, look at me!" I say, redirecting and refocusing him. That calms Saxon down and I reward him with a chunk of meat.

I cup Saxon's head in my hands. We are eye to eye and head to head, two hearts connected one more time in silence. No words are uttered between us. I silently convey to Saxon that he has the talent and foundation to succeed, and he is valued as a great dog.

With a tearful smile, I must let go. I kiss his big black nose. Then, as Bill is closing the kennel door, I realize one more thing. "Wait, Sadie needs to see where Saxon is."

Bill lifts Sadie to Saxon's face as she licks his nose and reminds him, "I am your best cheerleader. I know whatever you are faced with, you can do it."

Time after time, Saxon seemed more human than canine, mirroring my emotions and actions, hoping I'd shift from an altered consciousness. Leaving Saxon was tough, but it was the right decision. Moving forward was life-changing. By faith, I can keep my dogs.

In doggie boot camp, Saxon persevered under pressure to perform. The adjustment and adaptability were substantial. New rules, new surroundings, smells, sights, strange dogs, drills, people, an e-collar, more self-control, and being housed in a kennel all pressed on his mind, mood, and health. I'd imposed on him my need for accomplishment and overachieving, going on and above normal expectations. Engrained human patterns were being passed forward to a generation of dogs.

Individualizing Saxon's training plan required Bill to have a baseline evaluation of his foundational obedience, temperament, and gun shyness. The temperament test would reveal any signs of resource guarding and Saxon's sensitivity to correction. All were essential to understanding Bill's approach to training Saxon.

Saxon easily passed every aspect including direct eye contact. He was soft-mouthed holding birds and bumpers and never froze in possessing them. He waited patiently for his food and never guarded his bowl. The gunshot meant fun and birds. The new challenge was understanding the e-collar and what the corrections meant. Here he needed to understand the concept of pressure on or off, which teaches the dog how to get out of stimulation through compliance. The instant the dog makes the right decision after being taught the basic foundation commands, stimulation stops and the dog is rewarded. When the stimulation of the collar is applied to a dog, it is usually done for lack of effort or noncompliance. It is commonly used for field training when the dog is far-ranging to correct the dog's error. An example is when a dog doesn't come to heel and continuous stimulation on low level is applied until they are at heel. That is when the stimulation stops. It compels the dog to comply, avoiding the aversive consequence.

There are three basic commands used in the field: heel, here, and sit. Saxon already knew them. Usually he'd heel on the left, Bill introduced heeling on the right as a strategy, sending Saxon into the water so he was straight-lining to the mark.

In the afternoons, Sadie and I meet Bill and Saxon for a private lesson and later join the training group.

Barking inside the truck, Saxon knows I'm in the field. When Bill lifts him down, he runs to me, exuberantly, spinning in circles. I reassure him I haven't abandoned him. He licks my face, smothering me with doggie kisses. Sadie and Saxon get a moment to reunite and briefly play. Then it's all business.

Bill demonstrates Saxon's morning lessons, giving me a detailed understanding how to better handle Saxon in a test. Saxon is reintroduced to force-fetch, blind retrieves, honoring another dog with sit-stays as another dog gets to retrieve. Stopping on the sounded whistle with a front-facing sit, taking hand signals to steer him in the field, all this is done on land first and then applied to water.

Saxon left behind a toxic environment and was on his way to wholeness. His reformed life lies in front of him as I contemplated my future. Saxon has purpose, routine, and structure, which grounded him. He's making forward strides, working, learning, and socializing around a new community of dogs.

My insecurities spill out, showing a lack of confidence when Bill is mentoring me about leadership skills Saxon has learned. Since dogs read body language more than words, my inward weakness transfers to Saxon.

"Carry your body tall and upright with confidence so you can counter your fear. Saxon knows when you are fearful by your breath," Bill tells me.

The counter-conditioning, desensitization, and operant learning Saxon acquired are designed for me to take notice of my own need to change behaviors. Saxon's future success depends upon me reorganizing my emotional conditioning.

"It's important to be bonded to your dog before any progress is made," Bill says. He bonded with Saxon by bringing him inside the house every night, sleeping with him on the sofa, nurturing him with love and compassion.

He has upended and erased Saxon's uncertainty while instilling new messages of safety, confidence, security, trust, and respect. Bill was the leader, so Saxon lost the need to protect and he relinquished his fear. Leadership and pack order had been lacking across Saxon's life.

To teach him pack order, Bill introduced Saxon to his dogs, using a long line, walking the dogs together in the pheasant fields, giving them space. Saxon's socialization continued by bringing him in the house with his dog pack as part of the family.

Saxon learned to remain calm, lying with Bill's Labradors. He added other clients' dogs along with his own. Saxon's aggression stabilized. It no longer overpowered him.

Vennen died two weeks before I left for Chicago.

The night she died, Chester, his sister, her husband, Chester's niece, Sadie, and I encircled Vennen's bed. For the last time, I held her hand, sang "Amazing Grace" and recited the Twenty-third Psalm to her. Sadie gazed toward the ceiling and saw Vennen's essence. Her soul was hovering in the room. Briefly, it stood behind me, as she lay her hand over mine, thanking me for loving her for the real person she was. I felt my mother's eyes from Heaven. Ma was smiling because her last words to me, "Always be kind and have a pure heart," were being lived out in that room. Vennen was free the instant her silver cord snapped. Death unlocked her from her tortured, paralyzed body. Her face was aglow with softness that reflected a peaceful soul she had longed for in the physical realm. The agony she experienced should never happen to a human. Vennen carried oppression and a wounded soul to her death and possibly into a next life. One never celebrates a death, but in Vennen's case, I did. I grieved her absence. God parted the way, transitioning her from the physical to the spiritual. Knowing her faith was strong left me with a calm resolve. Vennen was home.

Vennen was my last reason to stay around Chester. Three weeks after her funeral, I am waiting for Chester as he walks into my house. I'm sitting with an armored attitude of steely-eyed defiance, rocking in place on my sofa with my elbows braced on my knees, my jaw clenched and my lips pursed. Sadie lies quietly beside me on her pillow as the past six years of my bottled-up resentment, bitterness, betrayal, and anger unwind and spew hatred at Chester.

"I will no longer tolerate your abuse or womanizing. Enough is enough. Your time is up. It's my time from now on. It's about me and Saxon. We're done! You can take your dogs and belongings and get the hell out of my house. Leave me and my dogs alone. Don't you dare set foot on my property, or the police will have you physically removed and handcuffed. It was always about your primal selfishness. One woman was never enough for you. You didn't have the balls to tell me you have another woman who is thirty-five and you have been screwing her. You disrespected me and hunted other women to stick your cock into. I was some handy object to have around. You vampire! You are a predator! I gave myself completely and endured beyond anyone's comprehension your sick emotional cruelty. You have drained me dry without a conscience. Admittedly, I let you. You have no idea what love is. It is time for me to live my life, and it won't be with you, even if I live alone the rest of my life. The betrayal and abuse you inflicted on your mother were atrocious. You need a taste of your own medicine. God will see fit to deliver to you what you deserve. Get out of my house, now! You're pathetic! You are repulsive to even look at you. You won't steal any more of my soul or heart. I may not have a penis, but I do have the balls to kick your sorry ass out for good. Take your shit and leave."

I am hopping mad and mean every word. Sadie keeps her head between her paws as she lays on her pillow. She has not seen that kind of anger out of me since Burt.

He is standing there astonished like Boo-Boo Bear slapped silly. He mutters a sniveling response. "I love you and was going to ask you to marry me."

"Oh, for God's sake man, that's crap. How dare you? Don't you even go there. In six-plus years, you could never say I love you. Do you really think I am stupid enough to stay with you? Your mother told me to never marry you. You're a bad seed. I'll take her word over yours."

Now I'm pacing and unhinged. "You severely victimized and used me, your dogs, and your mother. Anyone associated with you was nearly destroyed. The treatment of your daughter is unconscionable. You shunned her. You couldn't show her the love she hoped you had for her. The times she came to you, you turned your back on her. It cut her to the core. She walked away in painful silence. You didn't care. Very cold! You made her feel miserable and invisible. I know how that feels. I got the same treatment from my dad. So don't tell me rejection doesn't hurt. I'm done with you. You are poison. Enough is enough! Shove it up your whining ass. You're pathetic!"

I am liberated, but what part of me did this rise from? I have to check to see if this is really me talking, because it feels like an out-of-body experience.

What a catharsis. Empowerment, freedom, and a glimmer of divine enlightenment percolate within me. A personal moment of reckoning has arrived. It's time to stop the same merry-go-round patterns and face the root cause to deliver myself to new ones.

Fixing this man was never going to work, because he didn't want to be helped and saw no reason to change. Inviting in other's chaos and thinking I could help them change was a consistent pattern of mine. It allowed me to deflect from my issues.

He and his things were gone. But he lacked constraint to stalk my property. He made copies of my house keys and had the audacity to have funeral-size flower arrangements placed throughout the house when I walked in from work. How gauche, how depressing. In the garbage it all went, including the crystal vases. I felt violated and invaded. I had the locks changed, but he persisted in harassing me with phone calls and emails. I gave him zero response. He reminded me of a tomcat urinating to mark his territory. No restraining order would have made a difference for him. He's a copy of his father.

He lost his control of me. The more control he lost, the stronger my principles became, firing up in me a belligerent intolerance of him. I was adamant that no one would ever treat me like that again. Victim doesn't have to be my name. Nor do crybaby, pathetic, stupid, dummy, or fatty-fatty two by four.

His raging crazed state scares me. I worry he might resort to using a gun if his brain chatter ratchets up. It all hurls me to my therapist. I'm hoping she can help me understand my sinking into the same old patterns of emotional abuse and how to break free of the cycle.

"Ignore him, and never respond, not even once, or it starts all over and he wins. If he can wear you down and you give in, it creates hope of reconciliation. This is narcissistic abuse."

"What are the characteristic behaviors, so I don't keep falling into the same trap again?"

"Don't bargain with a person so they treat you well because then you reward them for their manipulation into complying with their agenda. Being treated well should be a prerequisite to an intimate relationship."

This is new information for me about what a relationship should be. Earning love was taught from childhood, an unreachable standard. It's no wonder my relationships never worked. I was thrown off course in childhood, an innocent girl believing what I was told and shown. It makes me fuming mad that I was cheated for so long. But through those rebounding years I built a resilient elastic self and survived the slap-downs. It's not the many times I fell, but the rising up and righting myself that matters, the courage to march back in and continue the fight for life.

My therapist gave me more to realize about those who would wrong me. "They create an image of fake reality to lure you into their world and take everything they can and destroy anything that gets in their way. A narcissist's world is completely external. There are no internalized emotions, bonding, caring, or loving. They create these scenarios because they want something from you, realizing you are a soft-hearted, giving, and trusting person."

"When they befriend you and you share your innermost secrets and vulnerabilities, they, in turn, twist, tweak, and distort them to use against you. The closer the connection, the more damage they do to their victims to satisfy their delusional needs. Keep in mind that there is no real person inside, but instead many personalities to cover up their dark side as they gain access into the lives of normal people and play the type of person designed for you so they can pull you into their psychopathy and abuse. A relationship with a narcissist is like being a cruel and demeaning emotional terrorist's prisoner of war. Love is not real to them, but a desperate pretense they lure you into believing." She painted the perfect picture of Chester and what I experienced with him.

"It is a web of magical charm they use drawing you into their world, to fulfill their needs. In reality, it is about control and power as they continue to devalue and prey upon you like a maggot feeding-frenzy."

"So I was the fly in the web, trapped and being eaten alive." That set me back in my seat. Yikes, I could be dead now never realizing the dangers I put myself in with him.

"Ignore him. Set your boundaries and hold your ground because he doesn't have regard for personal boundaries. Do not acknowledge him in any way. None! Walk away from this. He is dangerous."

My body hairs sprung up like spikes and blood pressure was booming in my head. She just pounded the fear of God in me. As I relived scenes of him in a drunken stupor, resorting to violence, a shotgun in hand, alone in his apartment, I realized my life could have ended in an instant when his mind snapped. Never thinking it could happen to me, I would have been found in a dumpster rotting in a plastic garbage bag.

She made it very clear I was not safe around him. Change the course or die. Develop your own self-respect. Do for yourself what you did for Saxon. Reformation for me was a process similar to the one that was succeeding for Saxon's behavior modification.

Not responding to Chester incited the monstrosity inside him, so much so that he made a spectacle of himself with Bill's clients. He showed up in the field, during a training session, bawling and wailing about our break-up in front of everybody. It was a disgusting drama, seeing this huge man carrying on about how he missed me and loved me and I was his only true love. He sobbed about missing Saxon and Sadie, assuming they were his property. When he was next to run his dogs, he dropped to his knees, weeping.

Bill pulled Chester aside and told him to knock it off, but it went flying over his head.

"Chester, you need to leave now!" He just sat there, pouting in his truck instead.

The Blind Retrieve

Leaving for three weeks of product training in Chicago, Bill assumes responsibility for Sadie's care.

Once I'm back from Chicago, it is another two months before the product launch. The company has us continuing online training, which allows me the afternoons to train privately with Bill.

In my absence, Saxon achieved a solid foundation of force-fetch, directional casting, and line to pile. Once Saxon was skillful responding to the casting drill and understood the separate skill of taking a straight line to the bumper pile, the two skills were combined and applied as one called line to pile. As he demonstrated proficiency with these skills, longer-distance challenges and various line configurations were added. Line to pile taught Saxon to take a true line and go straight out until whistled to stop. This is the foundation for incorporating the casting skills. The ultimate goal is to steer the dog remotely to a specific location to retrieve the hidden object. Teamwork, obedience, and leadership are key.

The casting drill teaches the directional hand signals. Using the configuration of a baseball diamond, the dog sits at the pitcher's mound facing the handler at home plate, waiting for the hand signal straight up to send him to second base, or perpendicular right or left to first or third base.

Bill is teaching me Saxon's line-to-pile drill. He faces me and shows the correct way to do a right and left back cast, so that my arm grazes past either ear straight up. Saxon is patiently waiting and watching me be instructed.

"Stand straight and keep your feet together," Bill says in his Marine voice. "Show me the left back cast." He corrects after I direct my arm in front of me rather than straight up.

"No! No! Because at one hundred yards, your arm disappears in your body. Try it again. Good. Give me a right back cast. Better. When you go home, practice that in front of a mirror."

"Now I'll show you a right and a left over cast to first and then to third base." He has me do the same.

"If you need to emphasize the cast more, take a right or left step toward Saxon for straight back, or sidestep right or left for some body English to exaggerate your casts.

"Now cast Saxon to the pile of bumpers behind him. Make sure he's watching you before you cast. Never shoot your arm up and cast too fast. Count to five, then cast. If he is not straight to the pile, blow the whistle and stop him so he turns and faces you."

I do that and Saxon takes the cast. Wow this is fun! I'm hooked.

"Whistle him into heel and have him hold the bumper."

"Nice improvement on his fetching and holding," I say.

"We've cleaned that up. Now send him from your side to the pile. Stand straight. You're bending over and crowding him. Stand up straight."

Bill teaches me how to line Saxon's spine at heel so he has a true line versus sitting cockeyed. If the dog sits crooked, he'll go in the direction the spine and eyes are pointing, which is considered a handling error.

"Make sure his eyes are looking at the pile before you send him." If not, that's another handling error. "Hold your hand sideways just above his muzzle and tell him 'Good!' when he's lined up. Tell him "Dead bird" so he knows his job is not retrieving a mark or thrown bird. When you send him, say, 'Back' and not his name."

I'm embarrassed that I am all thumbs trying to choreograph this. Saxon has it under control. He sits waiting for me to send him. I'm nervous and do not want to mess him up.

"Dead bird. Good! Right there. Back!"

Saxon speeds off the line aimed right of true course.

"Sit him. Sit him." I'm fumbling to get the whistle in my mouth. Bill corrects me. Saxon is way off the line to pile. I blow. He sits immediately. He is doing so well. Me? Let's just say, I have a ways to go.

"You're not fast enough with the whistle. Keep it in your mouth when you're handling. You gotta watch your dog and anticipate. Focus!"

This reminds me of my flight instructor when he told me to leave the day's buzz in my head outside the airplane. Fly the plane! Here, handle the dog.

"Okay! Okay!"

Never did Bill berate or belittle me, yet I was self-aware from an ingrained shrinking response when I made mistakes. Stupid is what I heard in my mind.

"Give him a straight left back."

Saxon spins straight back putting himself on true course to the bumpers, and he nails it.

Here, thinking on my feet is a split-second decision that's dependent on Saxon's response. It requires being in the moment, which is a new mode for me.

Strategy, art, problem solving, and seeing the bigger picture blossom from yard drills which become the separate pieces leading to a larger concept. Even more important is becoming one, working in concert.

Although the steps are rudimentary at the start, Bill teaches me how to fine-tune my handling for precision casting at ten-degree increments based upon angulation to land or water, wind direction, cover in the field, and obstacles. He expands my mind and Saxon's while we are in nature. That's where life excels and I begin to grow.

Saxon can now sit on the line, collarless and steady, having another dog next to him as he is either honored or honoring. The complexity of his drills is physically and mentally demanding. The more we ask, the more he delivers. The more advanced the skills, the quicker of a study Saxon becomes. Bill takes note of Saxon's sense of accepting challenges.

He'll sit calmly and slowly swishing his tail, kind of smug and confident with ears perked, smiling. It's like, *What else you got for me? That was easy.*

Saxon has a rapid uptake of concepts, combining skills with insightful anticipation while knowing what's next. Bill is bewildered how Saxon can know the configuration of the drill when he adds a new dimension and flabbergasted at Saxon's ability, unlike anything he's seen before in other dogs.

The deep-seated aggression was superficial compared to the true nature Bill recognizes in Saxon. Concepts that Bill pictures in his mind, Saxon sees. An enhanced belief in Saxon strengthens Bill's commitment and intensifies their bond.

Bill used Saxon's visualization capabilities to accelerate the more complex and counterintuitive training that goes against a dog's natural tendencies in field training. In other words, a dog will run around on land to get a mark in the water while a trained response will have him going straight to the bird. Or the dog will avoid a log en route to a mark, but with training will jump over the obstacle and go straight ahead. The trained response outsmarts natural intelligence.

A thinking dog is what Bill calls Saxon. He's a problem solver in the field. Those two are tuned in to one another. Bill always teaches a level above where the dog will compete and makes sure the required skills are internalized. He's training Saxon at the Master Hunter level to pass a Senior Hunter test.

"Put a picture in your mind showing the marks and a diagram of the concept. Saxon can visualize in his mind what is in yours. Picture your training." That technique helped me redirect the adrenaline rush I was accustomed to with Saxon's aggression and focus on being calm and one with him.

Often during my private lessons with Bill and Saxon, Chester would be lurking in the bushes like a peeping tom cat. But Bill caught him and told him to beat it.

"You are not allowed to be here when she and Saxon are training with me. You need to leave." Chester got ruffled and stomped off cussing under his breath.

Harassment from Chester continued with phone calls and emails, with him begging me to continue the relationship. He went so far as to accuse me of stealing Saxon and Sadie from him.

Against my therapist's counsel, I wrote him a letter summarizing his unscrupulous actions that outweighed the good in our relationship, although I did thank him for his dogs having been Saxon's bridge. Turns out the therapist was right. My fatal flaw. My letter only fueled his competitive nature and smoldering jealousy. His mind would trigger a scheme to restart the relationship.

Two months passed. I began flying for work five days a week with only seventy-two hours at home to be with my dogs. All too often, however, too much of that time I spent at my desk preparing for the coming week as they lay near me in my office.

When Sunday night comes, leaving the dogs with Bill is a heart tug. Usually, I sit beside Saxon's kennel in Bill's garage where the other client dogs sleep, telling him, "You have come so far from being an angry puppy. You're smart, courageous, and my great dog, I am proud of you, Saxon." Wrapping my arms around his broad shoulders, I kiss him. "Be a good dog this week. Listen to Bill. I'll see you every night in my dreams."

Saxon's body slumps in the crate with his ears down and his big, dark eyes mournfully looking at me. Sadie usually clings to me, showing me her love and letting me know she is all right and will wait for me, no matter how long it took. She is our glue and Saxon's support.

They were safe and cared for. They were still mine, not surrendered. Saxon had been given a second chance to grow.

The Act of Revenge

Across the winter months as Bill trained his client dogs, Chester shadowed Bill. He was nosy and prying, continually comparing Saxon's performance to his own dogs'. Red-flagging the situation, Spirit forewarned me of Chester's possible revenge.

"Bill, promise me you will lock Saxon's kennel door on your truck during training because Chester got my Dear John letter but thinks he owns me and my dogs."

Pretending to be a trustworthy friend, Chester is conniving to have Bill's wife, Joyce, side with him. He was digging around for information from her about Saxon and me, and in my opinion, he insinuated falsehoods to get her suspicious enough to get Saxon kicked out of training. Repeatedly whining about our break-up. He was a good liar. He underestimated her. With her background in criminology, she was building a profile on him and his narcissism. She was not a woman to mess with.

It is a Friday afternoon in mid-March. Finishing a long week of overnight travel across the Dakotas, I am waiting at the Fargo airport for my 1:00 p.m. flight home, excited to spend the next seventy-two hours with Sadie and Saxon. The flight is delayed due to freezing rain, frigid temperature, subzero wind chill, with snow blowing across the Midwest. I am eager to hear from Bill about Saxon's weekly progress. Bill has targeted the end of April for Saxon's first Senior Hunt test. My cell phone rings. It's Bill. I think this is strange because he knows I'll be home today. What could possibly be wrong? I cheerfully answer the phone as I stand between the double airport doors.

"Hello, Bill, what's up with you today?"

Bill is frantic and breathless. His words are choked.

"Saxon is gone! He is lost. He ran away. We've been searching for him for the last two hours, calling for him. My wife and I and Chester are trying to find him."

His words paralyze me, my breath leaves me, my body goes limp, and my heart sinks. I feel as though my entire world has collapsed. I am shattered and helpless knowing I am not there for Saxon. I let him down. I am sobbing and as frantic as Bill. There were 330 miles between Saxon and me. Filled with uncertainty, I realize there is nothing I can do until I get home and drive straight to Bill's farm.

"What do you mean, he's lost? Please don't joke with me. How can he be lost? How did this happen? Why did it happen? Why did he leave? What were you doing with him? Why is Chester involved in this? He had no business being around Saxon."

Bill told me the story. "I had Saxon out of the truck. He was running a two-hundred-yard blind across the pheasant field. Chester was sitting on the tailgate of my truck. I left the transmitter of the e-collar on the tailgate. I didn't have it in my hand. Saxon was halfway to the blind. He wasn't running very fast. I gave him a cast and then I heard him yelping as he bolted out of the field and did not stop. I think Chester grabbed the transmitter and shocked Saxon hard, causing him to bolt, shrieking in pain from the collar."

"What did you do after that?"

"I turned to Chester, asking what he'd done. He denied he did anything. I got in the truck and drove down the road into the field where we last saw Saxon. I started to track him until Chester let all his dogs out, destroying the track. I believe this was intentional on his part. I got Sadie out, hoping she could pick up Saxon's trail. The trail came to an abrupt halt. We've been calling and calling. I know that Chester reloaded his dogs and drove around the outer perimeter of the game farm."

"Where is Chester now?"

"He called, letting us know that he will continue driving around, looking for Saxon."

"Have you called the neighbors?"

"Yes, we gave them Saxon's description. We told them he is wearing two collars—a training collar and the other, an orange one with contact information. A neighbor two miles away thought he saw Saxon and that was when Chester left the farm."

"I will be there as soon as I can."

It is dusk when I arrive at the game farm. Chester, Bill, and his wife are standing there. I'm waiting to hear firsthand how his running away happened and about the last sighting. Dismissing Chester with a steely-eyed side glance, Bill brings me to the last place Saxon was seen. I feel like a mother who weeps for her dead child while being turned inside out from the stabbing pain of a branding knife. I drop to my knees, retching and sobbing at Saxon's disappearance. NO! This can't be real, never seeing him again. Saxon is my life. He's everything to me. Why? Why?

Invading my personal space, Chester intrudes, presuming he is offering comfort. He tries locking his arms around me. His touch is not welcome. I explode with rage. Both my fists slam into his chest and shove him away. I am screaming through my tears.

"Get away from me, you bastard. How dare you touch me or lay a hand on me. Where is your decency and respect? Let me have my privacy. You have no place here."

"I love you and want you to come back to me." Unbelievable!

What? Wait! How twisted was that! Saxon is missing, and he just made it about himself. It is always about him and satisfying his urges. Joyce, Bill's wife makes a mental note of his remark.

On the first night of Saxon's disappearance, Bill is a tower of strength. "I will stay here for the night if you want to stay in the dog truck and we will call for him tonight. Maybe hearing your voice will help him come back. We have to find him and we will do everything possible."

We were in for a long, cold night. Bill and I sat in his dog truck, calling Saxon's name. We thought if he would come for anyone, it would be for me. But there was empty silence in the night and in my heart. We heard an occasional eerie howl of the wolf pack and I feared for Saxon that he was being attacked and the howl was one of victory kill. I couldn't let my mind think the worst and kept hoping that he was an instinctual savvy survivor, despite being in the wild, wooded country so foreign to him. The combination of the subfreezing temperature, a dark, dreary night with sleet and snow seemed to make those moments even more dismal and distressing.

Saxon didn't have food or his medications. The Red Cedar River is about two miles away. The ice is thin and unpredictable. I kept imagining him falling through and drowning due to hyperthermia. His aggression left a greater vulnerability with stray dogs in the area. How would I find him?

I sat on his kennel blanket on the ground where he disappeared, waiting, and calling for him. Helplessly, weeping, knowing I might never see him again. The love of my life was gone and in peril.

Was this God's warning? God saying, "Listen or you will lose what is most precious to you." Was God tightening the vice to put pressure for that "Uncle" cry of full surrender to turn my eyes inside, instead of being that willful child on the run, letting fear rule over faith?

Lost Dog

Posters get distributed door to door from Eau Claire sixty miles north to Ladysmith, Wisconsin. A posse of friends tack them to bulletin boards in businesses and along roadways. Local TV and radio stations broadcast the message.

LOST DOG
REWARD OFFERED
SAXON is his name.

A big, blond male golden retriever, straight coat, is wearing two collars, a training collar with Bill's name and an orange collar with contact info. When tracking, his right rear foot will drag. He responds to "Here, Saxon," and food. He is approximately seventy-five pounds and seven years old.

I get on my knees and pray for Saxon's safety and the guidance finding him. While I can't help questioning if God hears me, I am certain He is showing me He is in charge, teaching the difference between knowing about faith and having a relationship with God, trusting faith to lead the way. Where do you start finding a dog in the wooded, wide-open country? The chances feel unlikely. We need a miracle. The next morning, the posse of friends, drive, searching the Sand Creek area, and go door to door with the missing dog posters. We call for Saxon as we drive. We contact the humane societies. Prayer chains are started and people come together, joining our search. I keep wanting to speak to him telepathically, but don't know how to do that form of extrasensory perception.

On the second night, Bill gets a call from a neighbor, saying a dog has been coming into their garage. We ask the neighbor if I could stay in the garage overnight in hopes it might be Saxon. I stay the night, calling and calling his name. Nothing!

I am distraught, knowing for two days he's been without food, alone, and possibly lying in a cold, mucky marsh or ravaged and devoured. My mind flees thinking the worst.

It is Sunday night. On Monday, I'm expected in North Dakota for appointments. Under the circumstances, my sales manager is compassionate and allows me to stay, searching for Saxon for another day. On Tuesday, work comes first, whether or not we find him.

It occurs to me what Bill told me about Saxon: "Put a picture in your mind and he can see it." Telepathy! I try to slow my breathing, be calm, focus, and picture Saxon in my mind. I call his name both mentally and physically the instant I visualize him.

"Saxon, Saxon, can you hear me? Show me where you are. Are you all right? Show me where you are." I repeat my chant over and over, setting my intentions by picturing his face and visualizing, looking into his eyes, in my mind, believing I will get an answer. I am feeling he is out there. I hold that image, keeping the space open during our search.

Monday's quest is unsuccessful. Chester calls me in the evening. "Does Saxon have a microchip?"

"Yes."

"M-M-M" is Chester's response. But why does he ask? This phone call raises my suspicion that he captured Saxon. Instinctually. If he did, what he is going to do with Saxon, sell him for revenge? Is Saxon the leverage he needs to blackmail me and get me back and reclaim his power?

But learning Saxon is microchipped, Chester realizes the chip tracks back to me and he'd be questioned. I'd bring immediate charges against him. His devious mind shifts since the angle of stealing Saxon didn't work, and he conjures another deceitful scheme. After hearing Saxon was microchipped, whatever his devious scheme was seemed to fall apart because he knew his subversive tactics would surface.

An image appears in my mind Monday night. It's Saxon showing me his location. My neck hairs stand. Saxon is sitting in Chester's hallway—the same hallway he was confined in while wearing the muzzle as a young dog. My suspicions are confirmed. The search plans change.

Jealousy fuels his mind games! It is normal to let the dogs loose out in his backyard together. But that isn't the case when I call his neighbor and ask if he sees Saxon in Chester's backyard among his dogs. The neighbor says Chester takes them in the front of his apartment, and he can't see them. I ask him to knock on his door, but he refuses to get involved. He fears Chester's rage too.

Saxon was dog-napped as a bargaining chip to force me to restore the relationship with Chester. His veiled attempts don't wash. He's pretending he cares by driving around the countryside day and night talking to people and placing posters, acting overtly communicative to gain trust and fool us. Once again, the narcissist that he is made it about himself, and his bragging and deceptive laughter are a dead giveaway.

Tuesday morning on the flight to Fargo, my heart is with Saxon and not on my work. Bill assured me his search for Saxon will remain relentless and he'd call if anything changes. I walk through my day heavy-hearted.

Joyce has a plan to trap Chester in his own scheme. She reaches me on my cell phone to give me my role in unmasking him.

"Call Chester and tell him you will do anything if he finds Saxon. Tell him you will love him forever and come back to him and marry him. We think he has Saxon because he won't open his truck so we can see his dogs. We think Saxon is in his truck. He is doing everything he can to get attention and he's too involved to find Saxon. He is within five miles of the farm, driving around. We keep asking his location. Bait him and see if he takes it."

"I will," I say and thank her.

I call Chester, feigning a voice of gratitude.

"Hi, Chester! Thank you for looking for Saxon. I know you love and miss him like I do. I want you to know if you ever find him, I will love you forever and will marry you. Please do everything you can to bring him back. I know if anybody can find Saxon, you can."

"I will find him." He takes the bait as I nearly vomit from speaking kindly to him, but this is about Saxon. Whatever it takes to get Saxon back is worth doing. Within two hours, Bill calls.

We have Saxon! He is safe in my truck. Sadie is in the kennel next to him. He is happy to see her and be with us. We got a call from the neighbors two miles down the road. The neighbors were walking their dogs. And they saw him lying in the ditch by their mailbox. He wasn't hurt or dirty. They called his name, Saxon. He happily came to them with their dogs. They walked him home as one of their own without issue."

I was proud of my boy. He handled himself like a gentleman.

All the behavioral training we've done worked. Saxon is near the other side of anger. Everything I wished for him, becoming whole and normal, was achieved. A second chance! I couldn't believe my ears. I rejoice and thank God for the miracle. Words were insufficient to express my deep gratitude. Trusting faith and prayer made me a stronger believer to trust God's ways and not mine. God never fails; we fail Him.

"What condition is Saxon in?"

"He hasn't been fed because he looks much thinner than when he was with me, but he is clean."

"How can a dog be lost in the country during the winter, in muddy fields and be clean?"

"We have more reason to believe Chester captured him."

"My wife called Chester ecstatic about Saxon's find. His response on the phone was somber." Any innocent normal person with true intentions who exercised extraordinary effort to find Saxon would rejoice. "It'd be too obvious for him to turn over Saxon after your phone call. He realized he was duped. He left here like a whipped puppy with his head down and tail between the legs." Bill chuckles. "We got him."

If his father could rip a live rabbit apart in front of his sister, Chester would stop at nothing to brutally kill Saxon to get even. I'm guessing he thought if he couldn't have me, then I couldn't have Saxon. Dangerous man!

"Bill, thank you for relentlessly searching for Sax. I know it has cost you a lot of time. I greatly appreciate everything you have done. Please guard Sax from Chester and lock his truck kennel any time Chester is around your truck. Chester doesn't have permission to be around Saxon at any time. Bill, promise me."

Flying home on a regional flight that seats ninety people, I stare out the jet's window, my mind is a whirlwind. The trauma of the last few days, of possibly never seeing Saxon again, imagining him drowning in an icy river, fighting off a wolf pack and being eaten alive, Chester's unconscionable mind games to regain control by attacking the innocence for blackmail, creates an unbelievable roller coaster of emotions.

Chester's mental terrorism matches the traits of a self-centered abuser who thrives on covert psychological and emotional abuse. He is void of any form of conscience. His pathology is rooted in subtle hidden aggression that brainwashes his victim to question their values, abilities, and self. He inflicts on other people what amounts to mental paralysis.

As quickly as the plane lands, I am off to Sand Creek to see Saxon, knowing he is safe in Bill's truck.

When I get there, Saxon catches my scent, hears my voice, barks, and starts diggin' to get out of his kennel. Bill unlatches the kennel door. Tucking Saxon's broad head under his arm, he lifts my dog out and puts him on the ground. Saxon spins in circles, inside out for joy, then jumps into my arms, slobbering kisses on my face with his tongue as his tail's velocity revs up close to the breaking point.

Sitting on the ground and holding his lion mane, I let joyful tears flow down my face. We are one enmeshed heart. I wrap my arms around his neck and hug him as he curls his head over my shoulder and neck feeling our synchronized heartbeats. Time stops. Our eyes meet. Our souls join. We know we have each other. My partner is back home and so is the part of me that was lost. That's all that matters. He is my heart dog. He completes me.

This is love, a love that transcends the real world and passing into a multiuniversal and Heavenly plane. God did answer my prayer, proving prayer is dependable if we believe. Saxon's return is the difference between intellectualizing prayer and praying from a believing heart.

Sadie is anxiously waiting her turn. She usually rides inside Bill's truck when BJ is not along. He opens his truck door, and she runs to me. She carries her head respectfully low and clings to my side just to be loved and petted. Her love is quiet, humble, and strong. I gently kneel to greet her as she extends her paw to me to be kissed. Calmly, I stroke her angelic head, lift it so we are eye to eye and see into each other's soul. We don't need words. We know the love we share.

Sadie has her partner. She and Saxon feel the freedom to play uninhibitedly. For all of us, God reveals His hand of faith and miracles that teach us they are on His terms, not ours. It's times like these that God reinforces faith, trust, love, and power. My pattern has been calling up to God in desperation, when I exhausted my options with wasted energy. Now I lean in faith's direction, not my own. This has been an amazing and difficult experience. One thing is certain, Saxon was God's chisel to open hearts, especially mine.

The bond formed with friends with pure intentions grows stronger. We collect ourselves now that the dog-napping is behind us. Training Saxon kicks in with six weeks to go before his first Senior Hunt test. A lot is at stake in earning this one ribbon: Bill's reputation that was belittled by hecklers, proving Saxon overcame his aggression, and displaying a righteous indignation to the people who wished him dead. Bill and I each have our reasons to accomplish using Saxon as our means to prove our point with hecklers and still help Saxon.

Saxon's training and high expectations often push him beyond his physical and emotional limits. Forging ahead, outdoing the next guy is engineered in us and projected onto Saxon. I am being myopic and outwardly focused. In my mind this is all about Saxon when, in fact, his achievements mean proving my self-worth at his expense. However, I don't see it that way then. Here's where Saxon and I were disconnected due to my consistent compartmentalizing. I tell myself Saxon needed to work and achieve, but I misread his pacing and whining as his need to be constantly active. As his restless behavior persists, I begin to open myself beyond the surface to see deeper into actions as to whether his field training is his real life purpose. What is he communicating that I am missing? Are his actions related to medical or matters of the heart? Saxon has my attention, but what is he showing me? The Holy Spirit is using Saxon to get my attention.

Achieving one ribbon will signify a triumphant breakthrough on Saxon's fear-aggression. We will see that these seven years of work with him were worth every hurdle. Saxon did the hard work of redefining himself. What is it about me that I continue to avoid the "heart work" when Saxon is trying hard to show me the matters of the heart?

One Ribbon, Please

Saxon's hunt test day is fast approaching. Bill is polishing and proofing Saxon's skills. He checks Saxon's body language around his dogs, reads him for any signs of aggression—including whale eye, forward posturing, direct stares, and a shift in his attitude—so he can stop the problem and redirect it before it escalates.

Everything in Saxon's past seven years culminates in this one hunt test. Bill reassures me he's prepared Saxon during the yard drills.

"All the client dogs, wearing e-collars, line up in a sit-stay on my front lawn. A bumper is thrown and they all stay. If they move, they get a collar correction for disobedience and are placed back in a sit. Next, the dog's name is randomly called, while the others stay and honor. Every dog gets a turn. Saxon sits steady until it is his turn and his name is called. He understands his job."

The way Bill trained and socialized him gives Saxon the confidence to hold his own in a hunt test. He retrained his repressed fear aggression and wakened Saxon's natural instincts.

On April 27 Bill headed to the West Allis Retriever Club with Saxon and his clients' dogs for the weekend. I was miles away working in the

Dakotas, unable to see Saxon run his test, but telepathically and hearts tethered, lifting Saxon up to God in prayer, believing God is with him during the test.

From Friday through Sunday afternoon, I waited for a phone call from Bill. Nothing! I worried something terrible had happened at the test. I got home Sunday evening just as Bill called. Finally!

"Meet me in the mall parking lot near the Mexican restaurant around nine tonight." His matter-of-fact monotone voice, shortness, and lack of emotion bothered me.

I drive into the parking lot where Bill is in his truck, leaning back in his seat and dozing with his cap over his face.

As I get out of my car, old fears mount in me. I have a gut feeling something really bad happened. It's my conditioning. Bill opens the truck door and slides out of his seat. He is quiet as he looks at the ground. Is he angry or terribly sad? Holding my silence is impossible. I feared what was coming next.

"Well, what happened?"

He gives me a sly smile just enough to show the gold edge of his front tooth as he looks over his glasses. Arms folded across his chest, he leans back against the truck, pauses, and slips the orange ribbon in front of him.

Then I hear two astonishing words I dreamed of.

"He passed!"

My knees go weak.

I nearly fainted. My breath left me. All that stored-up adrenaline was released as if a champagne cork blew off the bottle. The internal pressure subsided.

"He passed? Oh my God, he passed!"

"Yes, he passed." We both stood there jubilantly crying. All the hard work and perseverance shined through. I gave Bill a big hug for his dedication and for loving Saxon. He did it. All our hard work came together. Saxon's emotional reshaping resulted from his wanting to change and complying with the exacting physical and emotional discipline. That's what it takes to transcend from the past by giving one's all. He is a living example for me to follow in his steps. He accomplished the uncompromising job of facing the demon inside of him.

Our wildest dreams were real.

Before Saxon comes out of the truck, Bill gives me a play-by-play of how Saxon behaved and how he performed in the test.

"Saxon gave his all until he was exhausted. He never quit. He hunted tirelessly until he found the bird. He's a good dog, and he behaved on the line."

Bill describes the test's highlights.

"There were twenty-seven Senior entries. The weather and water were frigid. It seemed that whatever the circumstances, Saxon got the most difficult challenge in a test. Saxon's live flyer flew way out of the area of the fall, making him swim through muck and marsh much further than the other dogs. Saxon had heart and determination where other dogs quit. He pinpointed his marks. When he came back with the bird, physically depleted, he didn't have the strength to pull himself up onto the bank. The combination of the cold water and extreme distance, and his golden show coat, exhausted him. The judges nearly disqualified Saxon. He struggled and struggled to get up the bank. I asked the judges if I could help him and they allowed it since Saxon met all the requirements of the test."

The judges saw enough of Saxon's work that they were satisfied and felt they could pass him. A little compassion goes a long way. He achieved what we thought was unachievable. He led the way, proving old behavior patterns can change. Believing all things are possible girded our faith once again. Winning is a feather in Bill's cap.

"Do you want to see Sax?"

"Of course I do,"

Bill lifts Saxon from his dog truck. He comes galloping to me with every part of his body celebrating his victory. He wiggles and wriggles, and his tail wags his whole body. Proudly holding his head high, he jumps into my arms, greeting me with elation and doggie kisses. Saxon sees Bill holding out the ribbon for him, leaps, and fetches it in his mouth, looking like a champion. Funny boy, he's running proudly through the empty lit parking lot, galloping like a bucking stallion. I am belly laughing, watching Saxon celebrate. He holds the spotlight, and I am thrilled for him, remembering his puppyhood and how he peeled away the unhealthy layers of anger one at a time, and replaced them with joy and purpose.

Bill pauses. There is that determined stare as he points his finger at me. "We did it, Saxon did it." I know exactly the inference in his remark. The verbal jabs are aimed at his peers and those wanting Saxon dead. He is sneering at those believed Saxon was not worth the time and effort. Bill and Saxon express their ridicule of those who were wrong.

Saxon proved to himself and to us that where you come from in life isn't where you have to stay. Bill made a difference. Underneath the pressures of training was the heart of a champion and a kind of love we never expected to share.

"Are you quitting now?" Bill asks me.

I give it a fleeting thought and ask him, "Is it possible that Saxon could achieve a Senior title?" That would require four passes. My question attests to how limited my confidence and thinking are. Bill looks at me and issues an ultimatum.

"There is one condition that he gets a Senior title. You have to handle him in the tests. I got the first ribbon, you finish him. You will never appreciate the title unless you do it. He's your dog. Sax manifested he can do the work, can you do it together?" Never then did I realize the dual meaning his words held.

Tables turned, my throat locks up. I wasn't expecting that I would have to actually take full responsibility for my dog's test of his success. Pushing it off on others always worked before, not this time.

My face flushes and fear wells up in me, knowing I lack the confidence. I worry that my fears could trigger Saxon's aggression.

"Saxon is a lot of dog!"

"Listen, you want to take him as far as he can go. This is your chance to finish well. It's not just Saxon's responsibility, it's yours. He's come a long way. The two of you have to do this together as a team, working from the inside out. Face your fears together and do it on the test line. He did, why can't you?" Bill is right, I know, but I'm ashamed to admit it.

Here's where the challenge to go inside and begin my own recovery begins. No longer passing this off onto others, I feel my feet are being held to the fire. It's time to own my stuff.

"Would you try to put one more ribbon on him and give me more time to work with him?"

"I will agree to mentor you, but you have to run Saxon. He's a well-trained bird dog and he has heart." From that point on, every possible free moment Bill mentored me in the art of handling Saxon through a senior hunt test.

From April through June, Saxon runs seven senior hunt tests out of nine entered to finish three more ribbons.

Saxon is entered in the May 5 Blackhawk Retriever test, along with twenty-six other dogs. He is sick and we're not sure why. The vets couldn't find anything conclusive. They recommend the typical protocol of rest and antibiotics. Stress was a large factor for Saxon, more than a normal dog could sustain. Stress was never considered in the equation. We are forced to take his name from the entries.

Whatever is brewing inside him certainly affects his performance. When he recovers, the training marathon will resume. So much of how I lived my life under pressure I have imposed on him. Looking back at his training, I see how I disrespected his feelings and needs and just pressed forward. I didn't listen to what Saxon required as I should have, which has made me feel even guiltier than before.

The regimentation and training that Bill acquired in the Marines gets incorporated into gearing up his dog training and winning at all costs. Our mindset chasing the Senior title is who we were during this period and doesn't excuse what we did.

On May 20, Saxon fails the Rice Creek test. We didn't realize how hard we were pushing him physically and emotionally. Saxon trained all week and competed on the weekends. He was giving his all seven days a week. This was a test of perseverance, stamina, mental toughness, focus, and tenacity, and he did it all without complaint.

On May 26 he failed at the Duluth Retriever Club. But we passed the Northern Flight test in Minnesota on June 3. And having passed at West Allis, that's two down!

This was a memorable test because a dogfight nearly ensued. Saxon and I finished the landmarks and honoring off-lead directly in front of the holding blind of the next working dog. He was a high-strung, intact, black male Lab in the blind behind us. The Lab lives to possess birds and fight if another dog tries to take it. His handler was waiting for his number to be called, trying to calm the dog down, "Quiet! Quiet! Sit! Sit! Heel! Stay!" The dog was jumping uncontrollably, leaping up behind the camouflage holding blind, crawling under the blind, and the handler was yanking the dog back. He was barking incessantly and mindlessly out of control. His hyperactivity was upsetting Saxon, and my anxiety was building. Saxon was off-lead and collarless. The rules say you can't restrain your dog when honoring. I heard Saxon's low growl and saw his whale-eye as his head slowly turned toward the lab. Sensing my fear rising, I firmly, but quietly said, "Sit, Saxon, sit." When the Lab's number was called, the dog barked and shot out of the blind, leaping and spinning in midair off-lead, ahead of his handler, passing directly in front of Saxon within inches of his face. Rattled and riled, Saxon began to break his sit, so I quickly placed my foot in front of him while grabbing his ear. He retracted and, fortunately, the judges missed my touch of Saxon. However, it did not go unseen. Doug, a gunner in the field, saw my reaction. Holding my breath, I just needed Saxon to sit through the two marks until the Lab was released for the first bird.

Saxon properly stayed and the Lab passed within inches of him for his first retrieve. The judge released us from the honor position. Whew! We passed the land test! I leashed Saxon behind the second judge, praised him, and ruffled his coat as a reward. All the behavioral protocols, sit-stay obedience, and impulse control built the foundation for this moment and it paid off.

"You did it. Good boy." He knew a piece of hamburger was waiting in his kennel when he completed his tests.

As the water series finishes, the judges collaborated which dogs qualified. Even though we completed both series, passing with an average score of seven is required across the criteria of marking, style, perseverance, and trainability. All the handlers gathered in the award tent waiting anxiously for the judges' decision. Doug winked at me, leaned over, and whispered, "You know, you can't touch your dog during the test." He understood Saxon's reactivity and cut me some slack. I thanked him and justified my touch by saying I just wanted to prevent a dogfight and maintain safety. Doug has a soft heart for goldens, since he owns a few himself.

Sadie usually rides in the back kennel while Saxon's kennel is positioned right behind my driver's seat. Second fiddle is where Sadie ranked. Dogs understand the top dog is closest to the pack leader. Although I'm guilty for lowering her pack status, which is unfair to her, in her heart she knows I love her.

As she rests solemnly in her kennel, her body shows her feelings and reveals stacked layers of depression and her unworthiness. She lumbers heavy-burdened much like my inner feelings, mirroring my heart. Yet I am unaware of the signs.

Sadie never complained or sought attention. She was ever grateful for any attention and affection she got. But it was only a token and a superficial pat on the head because I was so wrapped up in my own world. I glazed over her, chasing corporate quotas and hunt-test ribbons.

Her dim gaze told the sadness in her heart. Returning the look, I told her, "I'm sorry, Sadie, but this is all I have to give, and Saxon is taking it all right now. I do love you very much. Just know that for now." It hurt me to have to do that to her.

Each time I took Saxon from his kennel and prepared to take him to the hunt test line, I opened the back of my van for her to see the test. Sadie looked at me out of the corners of her eyes, without lifting her head, shifting her body away from me, in a heap, resting her golden head on her paws, feeling unimportant. That action told me her message of *Just go do your thing and when you have time, I'll be here waiting.* The dismissal summoned similar feelings from my childhood. Maybe it was supposed to have that effect because the Holy Spirit was prodding me and using the dogs.

Our third pass was on June 9, in Virginia, Minnesota. Absolutely unbelievably, we were three down, one to go!

The test in Central Minnesota on June 17 brought to mind another memorable and mystical moment from a person watching us from the gallery. Saxon and I were coming off the water series test line when one of the participants stopped by and said, "When I watch you and Saxon walk to the line, it is magical and surreal. You belong together. He does this for you."

The man was right because that's how Saxon and I feel in our hearts about each other, bonded. I loved Saxon for Saxon, regardless of what he could do for me. His big-hearted regal presence made me feel royal. Looking back, I see he did do it for me and I wonder now how much it was for him versus him wanting so badly to please. He was very obedient, but I was not sure if this was what he truly loved to do. Sensing his pure aura had me questioning his purpose. It once again gave me an inner pause to rethink his purpose. It's interesting how God's timing presents reminders to jog my memory and plants people strategically to rouse my heart. There are no coincidences.

Since we failed the water test, the next test to finish the title was June 30 at the Chippewa Valley Retriever Club. Bill strategized on which side to heel Saxon and how to give him the best advantage at the line.

Four for four, and Saxon titled. With his title ribbon in hand, Bill and I hug, wet-faced with joy. Our hearts overflowing with gratitude and pride. Saxon got a great tummy rub and fur ruffle. He and I tease each other while I ask him to speak and he *Whoofs* back. Thumbs and paws up, it was the silly game we play to celebrate,

Saxon fetched the ribbon, and his frisky joyfulness took to running with reckless abandon. Proud boy! Saxon's success bonded the three of us through faith and believing the impossible is possible. Faith's reality was our rock to success.

Aggression will always be in Saxon, but it no longer defines him. He raises his Ebenezer. That is, with God's help he arrives safely and is resurrected into a new life.

My time chasing the Senior Hunter title is when Bill qualifies for the Master Nationals with BJ to be held at Remington, Maryland, later in the fall.

Flooded with gratitude, I convey in a note to Bill my realization of how God challenges every part of our lives and stretches us to grow richly in faith and never be fearful of setting high goals. Spirit sends visions that He can open doors, no man can, and uses a dog as His instrument to waken a hibernating human soul. God implants talents in our DNA at birth. By believing in faith, it is our earthly responsibility to disentangle and apply God's plan and purpose with which we were born to use helping others find their way.

Saxon accomplished in nine months what a normal healthy dog would in a year of hard training. After finishing another group training session, I find myself by the tailgate of Bill's truck discussing what's next for Saxon. Chester is eavesdropping from the back side of Bill's dog truck, threatened by our discussion of advancing Saxon.

"A Master Hunter?"

"Bill, are you crazy? He's eight years old and has health issues. We accomplished our goals and more. This already was a marathon for Saxon."

"Yes, the training is physically demanding and the tests are long, but he already has the concepts. Do you still want to take him as far as he can go?"

Well, he had me choking my words. I felt if I didn't say yes, I had failed Saxon and disappointed Bill. Winning was everything to Bill. That's the Marine he is!

"Listen, you're either on the bus or you're not. Which is it? Go big or go home!"

Bill calls my bluff putting it to me to weasel out or be brave and take the chance.

I was pinned. Was it right for Saxon? We surpassed one of our wildest dreams for him.

Master Hunter stakes to me represented an elite group of accomplished handlers, which left me out of their league, feeling intimidated. I thought I would get my butt kicked and would shame Saxon by pushing the handling off to Bill and putting the stress on Saxon since the concepts were beyond my understanding.

Master Hunter tests are designed to demonstrate teamwork and a trained, precision response to complex, counterintuitive concepts compared to how an untrained dog would respond. It's geometry for the dog and handler against natural forces and topography. A finished hunter! Complete focus on the test line.

"You need to handle Saxon in the master tests," Bill told me. "You will never understand or have the memories with him if I do this for you. The journey is about memories. You need to do this for Saxon. You both are a team now. You promised to take him as far as he could go. Keep your promise to him. I know I can do it for him. You need to know you can do it for him and win. It's your journey together."

It was about memories, a deeper bond, stronger faith, and unmeasurable love between Saxon and me. Bill understood the journey with BJ and wanted the same for me, knowing the amazing capacity of a dog's love and what it can do to a human heart.

Bill's wife affirmed that needed commitment. "You have to do this for Sax. It's important." I didn't then realize how important this was and that there was a deeper meaning attached.

"Would you get Saxon's first Master ribbon if I finish the other four for his Master title? The Master concepts and seeing the test in the test is where I need your help." Strategy!

Bill agreed to run Saxon's first Master test.

Knowing how hard Saxon was going to be pressured to perform, a vet check was done to determine his health and stamina before he embarked on the challenge. No red flags came up, with the exception of his bad hips and allergies. But the tick disease had never been resolved and it was chewing on his gut. Plus, stress during the tests exacerbates diarrhea.

Looking on the surface and overlooking his emotional well-being, I knew he'd have to reach down into himself farther and deny his feelings for a title. He'd endured eight years of bottled stress and no opportunity to down-regulate. Now we were demanding even more of him.

Bill suggested we wait with his training because the required skills demanded an enormous effort on everyone's part. But we had momentum, and if we were to stop now, I'd cheat him of the chance to go as far as he could.

Intuition told me we might not have another year to do this. I took that to mean his physical body. My core was trying to warn me of the seriousness of his health and how the pressure of training would exacerbate his emotional and physical deficits. But my reckless head said press on.

Being caught up in Bill's excitement and his pursuit of winning another Master National ribbon ginned me up and caused me to overlook Saxon's health.

Two conversations existed between Bill and me: the spoken and the unspoken. The unspoken was the heart connection we shared bonding our friendship.

Feeling intimidated, which came out of an old pattern of not being able to say no, led to winning at all costs. Clouded by chasing ribbons, self-ambition overruled the heart. My wanting to make a difference rebounded to the superficial. The old nature rose up and won.

Thinking this was in Saxon's best interest, I grind on. He became a performance tool and a crutch supporting my egotistical expectations, bolstering my self-worth and identity, filling and frosting my hollowness to satisfy my longings. I tell myself I exist because he exists; without him I am nothing; life is meaningless; I'm not good enough. So my pattern of overachieving with Saxon resurfaces, and all common sense is lost trying to climb over my shame. All the while, Saxon pays the price.

Second Wind

Rise up we do. There are lofty visions of earning the Master Hunter title and qualifying for Master Nationals. Figuratively, it's a straight vertical pitch up a steep grade. Failure isn't a given a thought or consideration. We believe in the depths of our souls the Master Hunter title and qualifying for the Master National Retriever Championship are possible.

We stand head-first facing the risks and challenges, our bootstraps hiked-up, our fears released. We forge courageously into the headwinds.

Bill is striving for vindication. His animosity spikes, having the opportunity to stick it in his naysayers' face. We dig in with a fierce determination, more in our heads than our hearts.

I am laser-focused to show Saxon can hold his own with the unbeatable Master dogs. At all costs, Saxon is put under enormous mental and physical pressure to train and perform at the highest levels to satisfy our expectations and uphold our reputations. Always on, always wired, his internal juices flowing, he has to be self-contained about his aggression.

There is a fierce and tenacious pattern within me, which I inflict on Saxon, to be always strong, to never let my guard down, to never show failure or weakness, to remain unwavering, and to execute the plan.

From the moment Saxon rises in the morning until he sleeps at night, his paws hit the ground running through his grueling field training. He is a mirror of me and my workday. Head down and on a mission.

The Master Hunter title requires qualifying five times. Each qualification has three test scenarios. The first test is land, where judges expect the dog to mark and remember three fallen birds, make a blind retrieve, and do a walk-up to the line, testing steadiness on a surprise bird and honoring another working dog after his turn. The second is a combination of land-water marks with blinds. The third is a triple on water. The dog must qualify with an average score of seven across all series. That's one Master test.

I pause to think, Could Saxon physically, mentally, and emotionally bear up under this? This was exhausting for any athletically healthy dog.

Qualifying for the Master National offers two options: passing five of seven tests or a total of eight.

I ask Bill to run Saxon and get one pass. He agrees. Bill handles Saxon in Bemidji, Minnesota, on July 21. Standing out of sight, I watch from a distance, praying and visualizing the mark, hoping for the impossible, believing it is possible. Saxon passes his first Master Hunter test because of Bill's experienced handling.

But in August, impetuously, I put Saxon in a Master test in Northern Iowa. Bill warns me not to do this because we might not be ready as I hastily think we are.

"You're destroying your chances to pass the five of seven tests you need to qualify for Master Nationals."

Impulsive and bullheaded, I am not listening to his advice. I think I know better. It's my fatal flaw.

A few weeks prior to the test Saxon is hacking. It's something I heard before and dismissed it for eating grass. But this sounds different. He has a persistent and deep retching cough in combination with vomiting and diarrhea. The vet rules out kennel cough, and his vital signs are normal. He suggests doing a blood panel soon. Trusting the doctor's advice, I go to Iowa.

The overcast, rainy morning creates a penetrating damp chill. Pulling into the test site at seven are multiple dog trucks full of dogs barking with excitement, mostly Labradors. Kennel doors sling open as they air the dogs. Professional handlers bring as many as twenty dogs on their rig.

They huddle nervously near the test line, rubbernecking to get a glimpse of how the judges set up the test and analyze the best way to handle their dogs.

"All handlers! Come to the test line!" The judges have the test set up and are ready to explain the test and their expectations. Behind the first holding blind is a black Lab, the test dog, and his handler is ready to do the test demonstration for the group. The judge calls the configuration a "five-bird pickup." I have never heard that term before. He defines it as a triple with two blind retrieves, between the marks, a walk-up, and an honor. This first series is loaded up-front to eliminate dogs. Right away, I feel I am going to be one of them. Fear rattles through me like a jackhammer breaking concrete.

Surmising the setup, the more experienced people quickly see the challenges in the test and strategically know how they are going to handle their dog through this first series. I, on the other hand, don't. Bill was right. It's my own fault for having made such a shameful decision. My irresponsible prideful act is yet another in my pattern of foolishness that backfires.

Simply standing with the professionals, I feel both inadequate and intimidated. My balloon deflates. Now is my chance to leave and save face, but no. My pride kicks in and puts Saxon in a compromising situation.

We wait for our number to be called. As I stand angst-ridden in the holding blind, conflicted about the test and Saxon's behavior, I try to conceal my emotions. But that is impossible with Saxon. He dials in and smells the fear in my breath. His aggressive propensities never left me because fear has dug itself into my muscle memory. The slightest low growl fires me up.

It's our turn. The judges sense my rigid posture and deliberate movement.

"First Master test?" one of them asks.

"Yes." He doesn't have a clue as to what my greatest concern is.

"Breathe," he advises me.

Saxon watches the marks fall. I am ready to send him. My heart sinks as the honoring dog breaks his sit, running hell-bent after the flyer right past Saxon's nose. Saxon stays and resists a confrontation. Gasping and nearly coming undone, I hold my breath.

After that fracas, handling Saxon to the marks is my next step, and my handling is a mess. At first, he doesn't take my casts. Then when he does, he turns the wrong way, showing the judges insufficient trainability and teamwork. Poor grades in three of the four categories. Not good!

The judges are in a huddle, a bad sign. I see them fold my judging sheet over. We failed. There's no callback to the second or third series. Kicking myself, I know I failed Saxon. I shamefully leave the test line. But I am proud of Saxon. I pet and praise him for his restraint and for having achieved something greater than a ribbon.

At the truck, Sadie looks at me as if to say, *Well, what happened up there?*

I give her a side glance. "Don't ask!" is my reply.

She looks back at me to let me know, *That's what I thought.*

Dang, there it is again. I imagine a disgusting head shake like my father did.

The blood panels are in. The results show his liver enzymes are up, and the vet has no explanation. Being under constant medical observation and treatment coincides with his up-and-down field performance. Exhausted, unable to collect himself mentally and physically, he caves under all the pressure to perform. His health maladies haunt me.

Saxon's same, deep, retching cough resurfaces in December. After more tests and diagnostic procedures, there's still no diagnosis. We monitor his condition. My gut senses something serious is coming.

Telepathically, he conveys to me git-r-done, as if he knows the future. His propensity to please drives his determination to finish the Master Hunter title. With Bill's individualized training, Saxon forms a unique ability to see the test as a broad concept while understanding all the moving parts. Standing on the line, his look says, *That was easy. What else ya got for me?*

Inside Saxon, the Master Hunter dog is an old soul with an abounding wisdom, intuitive understanding, and unexplainable foresight. Others see him only as a dog. Bill knows differently. Bill gets it.

Within me a small voice whispers, "Ten years, you have ten years." Ten years for what? I erase the omen from my mind. Off and on, the voice's persistent frequency and raised volume. Inside Saxon is an urgency I don't understand, so we press forward to our goal.

At the beginning of April, Saxon's liver enzymes increase and his white cell count is at the low end of normal. His pulse jumps from sixty-eight beats per minute to one hundred twelve. Heart rate is in normal range, so the vet isn't concerned. Reluctantly, we trust the findings, deciding we can continue his training and testing. But the change of liver and white count results shows a negative trend that is nagging at me.

By the end of April, he is back at the vet. His body is going haywire inside and out. His cough is worse. He is sick and depleted. His blood panel has wide swings outside normal ranges. Aside from his illness, arthritis shots are required twice a week. On May 2, a Saturday, he has to get his shot, Saxon is unable to run his Master test in Gilmanton, Wisconsin. I'm volunteering for the retriever club. Bill is there with his other client dogs. His wife is taking Saxon to the vet.

At the test, Bill's truck is bouncing and barreling across the field toward me. Bill waves from the truck for me to get over to him immediately. He is fuming mad, and his angry look paralyzes me. He is aiming the blame at me.

"My wife called. She's hysterical. Saxon attacked the neighbors' dog. The dachshund is in critical condition, fighting for his life. Saxon ripped him up pretty good. A death blow to the chest. Both dogs are at the clinic now. Saxon is in quarantine and possibly being euthanized. You better get up to the clinic right now and pray that dog doesn't die or Saxon will."

Euthanized! No, this can't be happening. I feel Saxon being stripped from my arms. Not now! The vision of Saxon being a Master Hunter gone. My core values were now being tested as to what held the greatest priority and created the internal conflict, Saxon's ribbon achievement or choosing to listen to God's guidance.

"Go and take care of Saxon and get to the clinic as fast as you can."

The message screaming in my head: "Is chasing ribbons worth risking Saxon's life?"

Through my tears, I drive to the clinic. God is waiting in the wings wondering if He'll hear from me. My relationship with God has been on a will-call basis. I define God in a way most comfortable to me and what I want Him to be. The pressure is ramping up. I turn to God.

"Please, God, give Saxon and me more time. Please don't let this happen to him. Please heal the dachshund's body and restore him to full health. Help us find a resolution for everyone so anger doesn't exist. Help us understand why this is happening so we can reach a peaceful resolution. What do I need to learn from this? Show us your miracles, dear God. I know you are with me. Your presence surrounds me as I pray. In Jesus' name, Amen."

The vet meets me at the clinic door. Remorsefully, I enter and long to see Saxon first, but the priority hanging in the balance is the life of the dachshund named Casey.

"His skin is badly ripped. It's remarkable, Saxon missed his spinal cord and jugular vein. The dog is in intensive care on life support. He is barely holding on. He's on pain medication and antibiotics. We hope he doesn't become septic."

"Can I see the dog?"

"I shouldn't do this, but I understand how you feel. You can't touch him, but you can look at him." She places her hand on my shoulder. It's as if the Holy Spirit flows through her touch in an emotionally difficult moment.

She takes me to intensive care and allows me a few moments alone. Seeing the damage, I weep and pray over him, not knowing if he will live or die. A premonition comes over me as I connect heart-to-heart seeing Casey healed. The Holy Spirit is present.

"Casey, Casey, I hope you can hear me. I am so sorry for what has happened to you. You can make it. You will live. Please fight for your life. We all love you, and you are in God's hands. He can heal you. Believe that. Please fight! You have to fight! You have purpose. Your owners need you. This is not your time." The vision disappears when the vet's hand touches my shoulder. It is time to leave.

The vet takes me to Saxon's cage. He mournfully looks at me. He knows he is in real trouble. His body hangs low and he belly-crawls slowly to me in deep remorse. Sitting on the floor with him, I hug him, letting him know he is loved and I need him. Quitting on him is not optional. Screaming and yelling at him would be a disservice. Instead, I assure him, this will be history and we will go forward. From his puppy days to now, what has happened is not his fault.

Saxon's rage exploded from constant torment and suppression when his puppy memories resurfaced through the aggressive neighbor dogs. The dachshund taunted Saxon, running back and forth along Bill's fence barking and growling. Saxon couldn't take it anymore. I understand his rage.

Furiously attacking and punishing Saxon for his actions would only do severe damage. He needs a safe harbor, love, and support, what I wanted as a child but was withheld. Anger is not welcome here. Healing is.

"Saxon, you're a good dog, but you know you did a bad thing and we have to hope Casey lives. Please tell him he has to live. Tell Casey you are sorry." I have shoved blame his way when it was mine to own.

Saxon surrenders his full trust to me, pushing his big head into my chest as I hold him. He was sick, alone, rejected, and frightened from the stress. Trembling, he realizes this might be goodbye. Now all we have is each other. It is a cherished time, based on love, trust, and faith that move us forward. I kiss him before the vet closes the door. I hold a space of hope. I believe God has this under control, which teaches me that I don't.

Saxon is in quarantine until Casey's outcome is determined. Everything is on the line and in the hands of the vet to do her best for Casey to survive. She assures me she'll be beside Casey through the night.

Ribbons don't matter now. The lives of these two dogs do. Setbacks, uphill struggles, and downward slides were the norm for Saxon and me in our fight to survive. Nothing came easy for us, ever. Pain and ridicule were on the path we walked through life while always hoping for something different. We rise up more resilient each time, one rung higher, and wiser with a stronger wholeheartedness.

Facing Bill and his wife brings an onslaught of blame, finger-pointing, and anger that fractured our relationship. Trust is compromised. Being yelled at was normal for me to accept. I'm standing in their kitchen, taking the verbal whipping. I stay strong in Saxon's defense, but I accept personal responsibility. I must listen more and be careful when picking my words. There is no need to fuel the anger.

God jerks me, a reminder to take the high road. A financial agreement is made to pay all of Casey's medical expenses to prevent a future lawsuit against Bill and Joyce, making all things right, with a cooling-off period.

I visualize Casey alive, hoping he sees my vision. Over the next seventy-two hours, his condition improves. He is out of intensive care and sent home a week later to continue his recovery. Saxon is spared. God comes through again, and faith's mystery prevails.

The dogfight changes our relationship. Bill and me are at a defining moment, questioning whether to quit or continue our quest for Master Hunter and Master Nationals. Can we go on or are we going to let the fight break us?

Standing beside his dog truck outside his home, Bill backs off the pressure to press on and with great reservation asks, "Is it wise to continue training and qualify for the Master Nationals? You need to realize how far you've both come. Can you be happy with that and walk away?"

His question leans compassionately toward Saxon's well-being.

With Saxon sitting at heel, I pause and hearing Spirit's inner voice, "Ten years, you have ten years." Saxon is nine years old. Either decision is a gamble.

I still need Bill's help when I work. I rationalize that as long as he is caring for Saxon, we need to finish the Master title. At his age, this is our last chance, our last year to try. From there Saxon could retire and be my companion the rest of his life. That is very self-serving, but I don't sense Saxon wanting to give up either. Looking into his eyes, I feel a sense of urgency to press forward, but Saxon's reasons are different from mine. Saxon has a soul purpose and very little hullabaloo about ribbons. Reluctantly, Bill is all in.

July 31 is the cutoff to qualify for the Master Nationals. We'd earned two Master passes in June. Our fourth pass is on the Fourth of July weekend in Minot, North Dakota. We are halfway to passing eight tests with four for four! There are three weekends left to qualify for the Nationals and the last weekend is a doubleheader.

The Minot Master test took stamina and fortitude. With temperatures in the high nineties and high humidity, I risked heat exhaustion for Saxon, Sadie, and myself. We were dog number seven of fifty to run.

I lift us in prayer that God lays His hand on our work. The Fourth this year is a day to remember. I am nervous and flustered, forgetting my whistle in the truck, walking with Saxon to the test line without it. The judge notices my frantic frustration. He generously pulls a whistle from his bag and reminds me to breathe. He's Bill's friend and a man of faith. Faith and grace are necessary today.

The test is a five bird pick-up. Usually, Saxon's weakness is remembering the middle memory bird. If I aim him to the area of the fall, he trusts me to handle him to the bird. As he returns from his second bird, I line him for the middle memory bird and send him on his name. He slowly trots out with his ears cocked backward, listening for a command and scanning the field for duck scent. The rules allow me to handle him once across the three series of tests, I am about to blow the whistle. Saxon crosses a dirt road on his way to the bird. A sparrow flew directly in front of Saxon and directly in line with the fallen bird. I know it is hard to believe, but it's almost as if God sent the sparrow to jog Saxon's memory. The other judge laughs as Saxon speeds up.

"Prayer works and God does answer prayers at just the right time," I say. Smiling, he puts his head down and writes the score on the test sheet.

The next morning, Saxon and I finish the second and third series. We both lie in the shade while being treated for heat exhaustion. Sadie is in her kennel, panting from the intense heat and watching with worry for both Saxon and me in distress. We are all she has.

We passed! One more pass and Saxon has a Master Hunter title. We were on a roll. The Master National is a long shot.

Blending my goal with faith, I actively trust God's grace to carry us through. His way works. Learning a believer's life is a daily walk of faith and obedience to His will. Even while I am predominantly chasing ribbons and titles, my faith and prayer life are growing in small steps as I let God's voice direct the way.

Prayer is part of our routine preparation before each test. We're in Burlington, Wisconsin, the next weekend. I'm sitting by Saxon's car kennel, holding his front paw. Our hearts are united as one in prayer, asking God's grace for a pass and God's Helper to run alongside Saxon.

Our prayer is answered! Title. Master Hunter. We passed, jumping another hurdle. This was a huge moment for us. We achieved in under than two years, starting at the age of seven, what was almost inconceivable with Saxon's aggression. He learned to put anger aside, breaking through the aggression that once controlled him.

Three to go. Master Nationals don't seem impossible. I am stoked. We really have a shot. Saxon senses my joy. Spinning and barking in circles, he is proud to be with me, being my partner, and pleasing me. Our bond increases. He is happy.

Number six test is passed in Bemidji, Minnesota. Unbelievable, six in a row!

The last chance to qualify before the cutoff was in Duluth, Minnesota. There the club offers a double master, with the event running Friday through Sunday.

On Saturday, Saxon earns his seventh pass. Exceptional for any dog, but even more so with the aggression issues challenging him. And never a dogfight at any test.

Sunday morning is the final stretch and last test. Here we go! Being careful not to be overconfident and ruin our progress, I focus on him retrieving each bird as I count down from twelve to zero. I'm not going to let my head wander into victory. Staying in the moment is crucial.

When the judges call the handlers to explain the test and their expectations, I'm half listening. It all seems pretty routine for a Master test. The curve ball comes, however, when they explain the test line rules and arrangement of the dogs in relation to the position to the handlers. This is a remote send for the working dog and sit-stay for the honoring dog.

This is a configuration Bill warned me about, having experienced it at the Master Nationals. It's something we didn't train for. Preoccupied, I focus on the idea the handler stays behind the blind when sending the dog, and I didn't hear that I could step out once the marks were down and then send from heel position. That's atypical and confuses me. I'm feeling the pressure to pass.

Normally, each handler stands alongside their working dog and the honoring dog at the line. This time it's different. The test line has two camouflage holding blinds positioned side by side. The handlers stand behind those blinds while the dogs remain in front of their blind. The standard rules require we handle a gun with each mark as if it is a real bird hunt. The judges steepen the standards, testing control and steadiness under pressure, needed to become a finished Master Hunter.

It is our turn. My adrenaline surges. My heart pounds. This our final shot at the Nationals. The honoring dog is a muscular, athletic black Lab who shows an unsteady propensity to break a sit-stay to claim the birds. His front paws pitter-patter in place waiting and watching as each mark is thrown, hearing first the duck call, then the thrown bird and gunshot report. The Lab head-swings, anxiously eyeing Saxon as we come out of the blind. Tensions rise.

When the judge calls my number asking if I am ready, fear fizzes inside me and the pressure builds in my head as I stand in the holding blind. Hyperventilating, I have a death grip on Saxon's lead. Slowly, I methodically remove his choke chain. My breath reeks of fear and Saxon knows it. Is this the moment I dreaded all along on our path through hunt tests? Is this how it will end with the dogfight of all dogfights? The vision grips my mind so much that I'm not paying attention to the judge's instructions for what we are to do at the test line.

"Dog to the line," the judge announces. Off-lead and at heel, Saxon and I walk to the test line from the holding blind. The judge instructs me to put Saxon in front of the blind. I step back into the holding blind as he sits alone. It rattles us both. Confused, Saxon doesn't understand why I am behind him. I'm always at his side. He glances at the black Lab ready to bolt off the line as the Lab lowers his head, staring at Saxon and ready to race him. Saxon sees the Lab's challenge. His hackles lift when they exchange body language. Tensions mushroom.

The judge asks me to give him a hand signal when Saxon is lined up and ready to start. I give Saxon time to settle, see the concept, and focus. I signal the judge. He signals the gunners. Once all the marks are down, the judges pause before calling "Dog!" to see if either dog breaks their sit-stay. The Lab stayed. Whew!

Saxon is sent from behind the blind. He turns and looks perplexed. His eyes ask why I am not standing beside him. I feel stupid that the judge had said I could step out from the blind and send him. Given that second chance, I do that now and resend him. Strike two. He goes partway off the line, then turns toward the Lab. Here we go, a dogfight. That is my first thought. His attack growl immobilizes me and fear's muscular memory ignites. I have to think fast. Snapping my fingers, I quickly reposition Saxon in heel, redirecting his focus on the marks. He repeats the same confusion on a third send. We're done. The test rules require Saxon to run the mark, because the honoring dog needs to demonstrate steadiness when Saxon leaves the line to retrieve. Saxon composes himself. He runs the triple clean without handles and lines the blind retrieve as a finished Master Hunter should. Huge handler error on my part!

Saxon is on lead honoring the next dog. Our dreams of qualifying for Master Nationals are squashed. Humbly we walk off the line with honor and gratitude to be here. We did our best. Many of the handlers congratulate me for my fortitude and guts in getting Saxon this far. Very few, if any, would have done what I did for Saxon. I never expected the recognition and applause. It told me that people were watching us give it our all, right to the finish line. We never quit, regardless of the challenges we faced.

Proud is an understatement of my regard for Saxon and the transformation he made. In less than two years of training, his quick mind hurtled him from an untrained hunter to a titled Master Hunter while passing six consecutive Master tests. This was considered exceptional.

He proved he could put his learned aggression behind and move forward. Yet I didn't relate that to myself.

Many doubted we'd make it. But we did. Tears roll down my face as I walk back to my truck. It's over. Now what? I hug Saxon thanking him for all his relentless determination and hard work. Even when he didn't have the strength, he came through, rising above adversity. Saxon is my champion and inspiration. Never having a dogfight during a test was in itself remarkable. It changed Saxon's life. He left his angry history behind and found joy in hunting. Over nine years, inch by inch, layer by layer, peeling back the imposed anger that controlled much of his life, he evolved into his true loving self, secure in who he has become. Yet something didn't strike me about turning my eyes inward because it was always about Saxon. It was always out there versus in myself.

Nearing my truck with Saxon, John Blackbird, the regional vice president for Master Nationals, is getting ready to run the test with his Lab. He was one of my judges in Minot. I wish him the very best in finishing for Master Nationals. It's just good sportsmanship. I shake his hand and turn to put Saxon in his kennel.

He's a friend of Bill's and knows Saxon's backstory. John followed Saxon's progress from the day Bill agreed to train him for one Senior ribbon. John is a private, respectful person who carries himself with authority and operates by the book. He's a man of faith and the '60s culture, but he has a fieryfiery tongue and, if pushed, could lower you to a gnat. His tests were fair and tough. The old saying was, "If you passed one of John's tests, you earned it." John didn't hand out gimme passes, and Saxon passed under his test. I'm taken completely off-guard by what he says next.

"Would you and Saxon like to be the test dog team for Master Nationals?"

That floors me. I'm speechless and breathless, but manage to recover, and the words roll off my tongue as if someone else answers for me.

"Yes, we would be honored."

I'm extremely emotional as I hug Saxon. I'm grateful he is such a tremendous partner who has righted his self-worth.

Holy crap, I'm in over my head again, but what the heck, go for it. Most times we operated as trial by fire, feeling our way through never anticipating what would hit us.

Another seat of pants we'd figure out. It dawns on me that a test dog's responsibility is setting the example for the other qualifying dogs. He'll be doing that in Hibbing, Minnesota. The 290 dogs are divided and grouped into two division flights. Saxon is slated for Flight B.

What a stunning honor! John recognized Saxon's ability passing six consecutive master tests. The Master Nationals meant running a double Master over the course of seven days. Passing wasn't important. Meeting elite standards was. We would demonstrate one new test every day.

Never considering Saxon and the marathon he had just been through, I am selfishly asking more of him, again, pushing him to an even higher performance standard with reputations on the line. As before, my caving to others' expectations precedes Saxon's well-being.

Faith's mysterious stronghold continues to evolve because Bill wants me to experience struggle, handling Saxon through the tests. Without doing that, I'd have ribbons and never appreciate the unconditional love and bond that Saxon and I could gain. Faith and prayer carried us to the finish line. God gifted us with an impossible dream.

The hair-raising responsibility I just accepted is frightening. It magnifies the impact of Saxon's training. I call Bill to inform him.

"We failed the last test but were invited to be the test dog for Flight B at the Master Nationals."

His voice quivers as he and I both begin to cry. "Remarkable," is all he could say until he recovers his composure.

"Now do you understand why you needed to run Saxon in the test and not me? It's your journey and your memory. You are a team, an A-team. You did it together. No one can take that from you."

Through our struggles we grow our faith.

Bill is vindicated. "We got 'em didn't we?"

"Yup the naysayers can eat crow."

I'll never know if Bill had a hand in this decision, but intuitively I felt he did. Or was it God? The latter is where I lean, proving once more who's in control, and standing beside me. Ever proving I should trust him.

Finding our second wind translates into increased training demands for Saxon. We had six weeks to perfect his training before the Nationals. Bill and I strategize how to fast-track Saxon.

For Saxon, this is canine geometry, testing a trained response. It will show the culmination of a truly finished hunting dog operating at top efficiency.

Bill's heart feels into Saxon, sensing he's more than just another dog to train. He's a dog who inspires humans to dig out their destructive mental and emotional conditioning in life. Saxon reaches into that part of Bill, softening his anger and heart. For me, that's still not the case. I'm holding out, and staying busy, living in denial.

Master Nationals

My prayer before going to the test line: "God grant us the ability to be our best and the strength to see this through with excellence. Walk beside us today and may we be a blessing for those watching our work. Carry us through and keep us safe. You've brought us this far and we trust you will carry us to the end. God grant your grace and mercy on us. Amen."

Each time I said that prayer, I envisioned Saxon and me on the line in a warm light of love and an aura of blue light. God was with us and I felt it. An ethereal presence appeared at times and I heard it. We were one with God on the line, coming from a place of divine love. Sadie heard our prayer and usually I'd walk back to her kennel and hug her for being our support.

We're here in Virginia, Minnesota, getting ready to kick off the first test of the week. The weather is dreary as it continues to drizzle.

I put on my hunt test attire—a black handler's jacket, a lanyard with my whistle, cap, and the TEST DOG cape. This is Saxon's time to ready himself and focus. He's excited as he leaps from his kennel. As soon as his paws hit the ground, he runs leaping and spinning in circles. He's delighted to get to retrieve birds. That is style. Comical boy! Heart dog!

Waiting in the holding blind, he sits at heel with his head and body calmly leaning into me, soaking me in. He is safe and loved. Fear is gone.

It isn't the weather giving me chills, it's standing in the holding blind hearing our names announced through a bullhorn: "Amberac Saxon Surfin Safari MH handled by Bonnie Wright." The words reverberate across the test grounds, penetrating through me in rippling waves down through my feet,

Unbelievably, were it not for Saxon and the emotional, physical, and mental challenges he scaled, we wouldn't be here. His accomplishments are amazing. He did all the hard work, facing his fears. I am both humbled and proud to be standing beside him. Faith replaces fear, knowing we are a loving team in one another's eyes.

"Handlers to the line." The judges explain the test.

"Guns up. Test dog to the line."

Saxon knows right away it is our turn. I slowly remove his slip lead. Walking to the side of the blind, Saxon stays facing out from the blind, until I call him to heel. Usually, I pause, giving him time to look over the field concept, picking out the gun stations. He heels in perfect lock-step like Velcro to the line. We walk as one. Saxon feels my pride for him, prancing confidently beside me with upraised eyes and a smile.

This is a triple on land set into a crosswind. The flyer is on the left seventy yards from the line. The right bird is a retired mark (the gunners were out of sight) and the middle gun station is the memory money bird. The flyer crates are in the crosswind, blowing duck scent into the test and across the middle memory mark that tests marking or a dog following his instinct, not his eyes. The middle bird was Saxon's nemesis. I handle on the middle bird, but the handle is what the judges want the handlers to recognize as the test's challenge. The purpose of a test dog is to identify the pitfalls and to show how a dog will overcome his natural tendencies versus trained response.

Saxon wins the judges' hearts because he is happy working. His style score increased dramatically as he freed himself from anger. He carries his duck proudly, holding his body confidently and his tail high, prancing into heel with a bounce in his step. There is not the slightest inkling of fear or aggression. His obedience at the line is perfect.

I relax when asked to honor on lead.

Once released from the honor, I toss my cap for Saxon as we run free in the field together. He retrieves it. He frolics, exuberantly rolling in the wet grass, pushing his paws to the rainy sky, celebrating our time together.

I look at Saxon and wonder about our future together. With deep sincerity, his dark eyes tell me our time together is short after this is over. How bittersweet? My heart is raining.

"Ten years. You can have him for ten years." The words haunt me.

The second test is a land-and-water test. The location is named the horse pasture. Demonstrating this test brings a smile to everyone's face. It's fun. Saxon's true self surfaces. He's a strutting showman. Retrieving the bird to my hand, he's high steppin' like a Tennessee walker. He saunters into a heel position, making certain everyone sees him holding his prize.

"Looks like he's shopping for a new handler," Lyle, one of the handlers, says, and the gallery erupts into laughter. Lyle nicknames Saxon Mr. Happy Feet. Saxon's comedic nature touches hearts that grow fonder of him each day. We are accepted and we belong.

One day, Saxon, Sadie, and I are sightseeing at the Hibbing minefields. Saxon and I share a private moment alone on the tower. He's holding his head down in a solemn demeanor. Silently, I look at him. He looks in my eyes and expresses deep sadness. Stoically, he holds the weight of the world on him. No words are said, but our hearts understand that a life-changing event is coming. It is unbearable for me to know now. The timing is wrong. There are two more test demonstrations before we head home.

The concept of the water test is an interrupted double, testing memory, perseverance, left brain logic, control, endurance, precision, and aptitude. This is the most challenging and rewarding of all tests. For the handlers, it's an eliminator test.

"All master handlers, we are running the test dog," the judges call for the gunners. "Guns up." Saxon and I come out of the blind. The handlers surround us on the mound overlooking technical water.

Saxon is given a minute to look at the landscape and the test concept. I visualize the layout in my mind, telepathically, like countless times before. Saxon gets it, as it clicks inside me. I take a long breath, before cueing the judge.

Standing on the hill with him as he looks across the water at the orange blind retrieve ribbon, his tail swishes side to side. I know he knows. He understands the big picture facing him. He knows all the moving parts of this test. His eyes lock with mine, almost winking as if to say, *I got this, Mom, you're along for the ride. Just send me.* Such confidence!

The test proceeds. A cold blind retrieve was first, meaning a blind was run before the marks, which is out of order of a normal test sequence, then retrieving the first mark, followed by the second blind and the second mark, an interrupted double. This tests the dog's memory.

I send him down the slope to the water. He pauses, turns, and looks back at me. But why? He dives into the water. Did my voice sound too harsh? My heart skips a beat and maybe his did too. What instantly changed for him?

Using hand signals, I steer him across the one hundred eighteen yards of water and land transitions. It takes three casts to direct him straight to the blind. Cheers from the gallery laud his excellent performance. Whistles blare and thunderous applause erupts. The crowd knows how many moving parts in this tough test came together with a laser focus for perfect execution. Handle the dog!

After the last handler has finished the test, the judges tell me Saxon's demonstration of the first blind was one of the best performances among the handlers. It's a pleasure to hear this, knowing he is good at what he does and earned those skills honestly.

Thinking to myself, I marvel that the dog who once was devalued is now held in high esteem with the nation's best dogs. Professional and amateur handlers and judges respect him. He is the star for Flight B, having worked with 150 qualified dogs entered. He is my boy and the joie de vivre. His life is changed and he is changing mine.

The final test is September 27, a Saturday morning. Cold, damp weather lingers all week. It's bone-chilling. That and the demonstrations tests our mettle. We persevere, holding high standards. But before we demonstrate the test, I ask the announcer to allow me to extend my gratitude and thanks. He does and I say over the loudspeaker: "Saxon and I are honored to serve here this week with everyone. This is a unique family of great dog people."

Finishing the test, I raise my hat, give a wave, and salute everyone leaving the line. Tears of joy flow. I am overwhelmed by the special memories, heartwarming experiences, and supportive friends we gained throughout the week. This is an once-in-a-lifetime event that I never thought possible. And here we were enjoying our victory dance because we believed, we did the hard work together forming a strong performance. Thanks to Bill, we are here.

Saxon received an encore. One of the Master National judges comes off the line to congratulate us and give Saxon a big hug. The gallery sees his joy as his tail whips side to side. Offline, I toss my hat one last time, releasing his inhibitions. He is proud to be by my side, as I am by his. Freed from his past aggression, he is now where joy replaces fear and joy is not a stranger.

Most people never understood our greater accomplishment in overcoming aggression. For those who did, they felt compassionate and individually in private came to congratulate me for seeing Saxon through. I want to believe that we made a difference and taught people to look at dogs in a different light than just an animal to train. There's heart and soul under each coat and a will to serve with unconditional love. Dogs lead us down paths to find a better part of ourselves. They're honest. They teach us about integrity. They have no conception of evil or jealousy or discontent. They know love, harmony, and peace, and hoping to inspire us to seek that in ourselves if we can look beyond our selfish ambitions. When chaos, anger, and hostility enter their lives it creates confusion and they have to find an outlet and his was fear that caused modeled anger. It was opposite of who he was built to be.

Saxon pioneered the way for trainers and handlers rooted in a militaristic approach to change. Training a dog according to their individual temperament kept the dog's true nature alive, preventing it from being crushed.

Sadie waits patiently in the truck. Her solid presence is always comforting, each time we finish a test. Arriving home, we are emotionally and physically spent. We have met our goals. Now what? Training daily identifies who I am. It's the drumbeat giving me self-worth and purpose. What is our purpose now that we have accomplished the highest goal in field work? The need for rigorous training is gone. We took Saxon as far as we could. And he did it. Saxon can relax. But I can't. I'm restless, pacing back and forth on the inside.

The Earth Quakes

A month later, on a Monday afternoon of training, I pull into my garage at six thirty. I open Saxon's kennel door. He is unable to move or stand. His breathing is labored. His gums are gray. His life force is leaving. Adrenaline skyrockets in me. I am frantically calling vet clinics. Only one is open, and it closes at 7:00 p.m. I explain my emergency. They are prepared to meet me. Saxon is dying. Now is not the time to collapse. God's voice speaks to me. "Keep a cool, logical head, focus, move thoughtfully and deliberately. Think, you must think straight. Fall apart later." It's the airplane stall all over again.

Dr. Kevin Landorf and his assistant meet me at the hospital door. They rush Saxon in on a backboard. They draw blood to analyze a comprehensive blood screening. They check his heart and take X-rays. Anxiously, I wait in the exam room for the results, trying to remain positive. Shocked to my core as the blood pressure in my head soars, I feel guilty. I caused this for Saxon.

"Were all the ribbons worth it? Who was this really for? Did I do this to him? Wasn't this my fault? Did I push him beyond his capabilities? Why? What was I missing that I should have seen? How and why is this happening, after everything we faced? Did life's brakes have to be slammed this hard for me to be wakened?" I am lightheaded. The room starts to spin. My life is in limbo.

All the warning signs were there and I chose not to heed them.

Dr. Landorf enters the exam room. He is somber. Gritting my teeth, I wait to hear if Saxon survives.

"He's alive, but he has an aggressive blood cancer called hemangiosarcoma. It's the first case we've seen in the area. This is a sarcoma arising from the lining of blood vessels where the cells lose their competency and cancer erodes them, leading to internal hemorrhage. Saxon's X-ray shows an enlarged heart and a tumor in the right atrium."

I'm relieved he is alive and dodged a bullet, for now.

"Cancer?" Ma's demise and now Saxon's.

"My options are what?"

"Drive Saxon to the University of Minnesota, possibly losing him on the way, or agree to a pericardial effusion, which I have never done."

"Do the procedure."

Saxon's heart rate is in tamponade at one hundred sixty-nine beats per minute and with rapid respiration. He is fighting to live. There isn't time for sedation, which is too risky anyway.

The care team allows me to be in during the procedure. I am reassuring Saxon he's not alone. I am holding his broad head in my hands, but losing him.

"Saxon, stay with me, stay with me."

For his sake, I visualize us running free, full tilt through the pheasant fields, laughing together, showing hope of having a stress-free life. He's cracking the core inside me.

Fortunately, a cardiovascular tech from University of Minnesota is in the room. It's no random act, but an orchestration of God. She instructs Dr. Landorf. Steady-handed and methodically visualizing, he counts the ribs and feels exactly where the fourteen-gauge needle needs to be inserted. A six-inch catheter pierces his rib cage, passing through the chest wall into the pericardium. Saxon never flinches. Dr. Landorf visualizes the exact needle placement. Saxon sees his mental image, understanding the delicateness of piercing the heart and setting the needle precisely just inside the pericardium. The catheter was perfectly placed. Out came ninety milliliters of fluid from his pericardium. He is given oxygen. Amazingly, he stabilizes and walks out of the clinic wagging his tail in gratitude. A miracle!

I gave him to you and I can take him from you. Was this my conscience or God's warning I hear about trusting faith? I can't bear the idea of being without him. It haunted me.

At the University of Minnesota, Saxon is placed in the ICU. An echocardiogram is scheduled for the next morning. My staying the night is not permitted. I feel a piercing pain in my chest as he was ripped from my arms.

All the times he built me up and supported me, now it is me being his Gibraltar. Before leaving him, I cup my hands on his broad head, looking eye to eye and soul to soul. "I'll see you tomorrow, so wait for me. You're safe here. They will be with you and help you. I love you, Saxon. You have my promise I'll be right here waiting for you in the morning."

Kissing his black nose, patting his broad chest, and caressing his head and back, I assure him of my unwavering love. One last hug and the tech whisks him away. I watch his pigeon-toed gait and his beautiful golden tail swish more right than left. His aggression never crosses my mind as he enters a world of strange, sick dogs.

It is mystical watching him walk with certainty through the ICU door. Calmness and warm light envelop him as if he's walking through Heaven's gate. He is at peace and on his way to the other side. His life's purpose is on the cusp of coming true.

The door closes. I am limp and uncertain if I will see him alive again. I am helpless. This was out of my control. I cry all the way home. Half of me is in the ICU. He is my life, grown into my heart, giving me a reason to live and a cause bigger than myself.

Sadie knows the seriousness of my coming home without Saxon. Her low body, lowered ears, and sad eyes tell me when I enter the house. At a loss to help me, she lays her head on me in solemn silence, supporting and being near me.

God rounded me up and corralled me. Having no other place to hide, I look up to God. Kneeling in bed, at His mercy, raising my arms and hands to Heaven, I wail and plead for a miracle, believing in and expecting one. I envision God's greatness and myself as that willful, unruly, naughty child, straying but now so desperate, speaking from the heart versus the head. I have nowhere to run, except to put my trust in God.

In His spotlight, naked before Him with hands to my heart, I feel God's love, mercy, and grace pour down as my wet eyes and open heart look up, pleading with this prayer: "Dear God, please don't take him. Please, dear God, give us more time together."

In my tears and prayers, my Sadie beside me, comforting me and licking my tears, she is my strength, my rock. It's who she is, my therapy dog sharing my pain, assuming my heartache. She was designed for moments like this.

The next morning, I wait outside the ICU door, holding my breath, wondering if Saxon is alive. The door opens, he and the tech walk out. Saxon greets me as if nothing is wrong and he is overjoyed to see me. He's alive! I am overcome with gratitude that God has delivered another miracle and that prayer is a dependable resource. Trust, it's about trusting and believing that God has this under His control.

We wait in a cubicle for the cardiologist to take Saxon in for his procedure. When the echo is done, the cardiologist brings me to Saxon. Dr. Chris Stauthammer, DVM, shows me the tumor in his heart. Awful news. He confirms Dr. Landorf's diagnosis, hemangiosarcoma, adding that Saxon has eleven days to live. Stunned, I look into Saxon's death door, and tearfully ask the doctor, "What do I do with eleven days? How will I know the right time to help Saxon?" I couldn't believe those words came out of my mouth.

"Make the best of the time you have together. If he needs a second procedure, euthanize him then." That's all he could offer in consolation. I am paralyzed.

Saxon is not disposable. My emotions are erratic. The word euthanize pulsates through me. Anger rises in me. Then shifting from an irrational state of mind to a resolved resilience, I buck up and the will to fight grips me—my normal reaction when the odds seem impossible. Together, Saxon and I are warriors when faced with adversity.

Our eyes lock, like a deer staring wide-eyed into headlights. Fear instantly strikes both of us. Living in denial sucks me into the present. I am acutely aware of every second and breath. Live life now!

Saxon has been living in the present all along. Saxon understands the severity of his diagnosis. His breathing evaporates and he realizes his life's purpose is barely begun. Eleven days isn't a long enough time to teach me how to transform my heart.

This is my time to rally and relieve him of the pressures of training. Coping and facing Saxon's death gives us two choices: going home to die, or living with the cancer and doing what he loves, hunting birds. We are born risk-takers and at times reckless. Envisioning him enjoying a stress-free life as a healthy, strong, playful dog could give him hope and peace

Saxon sees my vision as a burst of energy wells up and showers him. His tail swishes. He stands strong and forward with direct eye contact. I am willing to gamble. If he dies in the field, happy and free, joyfully hunting pheasants to his last breath, I would feel alright. And I'd be there, sacredly holding and loving him to his last breath. He understands.

Together, we walk out of the hospital in faith, determined. After all, there's a chance the doctor is wrong and he lives beyond eleven days. Bold? Yes! Risky? For sure! But why not try?

Bill gets my phone call. "Will you plant some pheasants in the field for Saxon?"

"You bet I will." Very obliging was his tone; suspecting why is not an issue.

Arriving in the field, Bill gets the news about Saxon, a blow to the chest that crushes him. Bill walks Saxon to his dog truck, sliding down the side of his truck to the ground, hugging him and crying. The two of them shared a miraculous experience together. Saxon taught Bill to walk in the dogs' paws, treating them as individuals. Saxon is Bill's heart dog. Together, we discovered Saxon to be more than a dog winning ribbons; we recognized his pure heart.

On the four-wheeler, Bill speeds out in the field, hiding a pheasant for Saxon. Here, in the field, Saxon comes alive. The puppy in him bursts through the surface. Hunting and nosing out a pheasant nestled in the grass, hearing a rooster cackle, an airborne pounce, the drumming of wings, and the gunshot during a flush exhilarate his chase to retrieve. Joyful rush! This beats waiting to die!

Chasing the bird, he collapses, gasping for air. We carry him to the van and rush home. Is this our last day together? Only God knew that. I am believing it is not.

Bill offers a burial place for him in the high country overlooking the training fields of his game farm. This is gracious but doesn't feel right. I feel Saxon's wishes bidding to be near me, home, safe in my arms when he dies, and Saxon gets to choose his resting place.

We are huddled in the privacy and quiet of my living room. Saxon is wrapped in a blanket. He and Sadie lie beside each other on their pillows. Sadie comforts Saxon. Here, we are the peaceful pack of three, linking hearts, praying, while a river of love flows free.

My mother's image comes to mind. I see us gathered to hear the scriptures and pray at the beginning and ending of our day. So it is here. Short of a medical miracle, faith is our fortress for an outside chance of recovery. All things are possible if we only believe. Handing over the trust to God is growing in me.

Thinking the doctor's diagnosis is wrong, I seek a second opinion from the University Of Wisconsin Veterinary School Of Medicine. The results are the same. Eleven days. My eleven days are now eighteen—more time and that's what mattered. It's still a tough pill to swallow, but the doctor relieves my guilt, letting me know he isn't in pain. Hunting birds hadn't hastened his death, so he was free to be himself and not suffer.

Every miracle and answer to prayer have built my trust to follow God's ways. While physically alone, I am lovingly supported by the Holy Spirit's guidance. We are together as a loving family, caring for and doing our part to support one another, the way it is supposed to be.

Sadie amazes me. She is loyal to Saxon. Each day when I come home from work, she is by his side. Telepathically, she tells me, *Mom, I supported him today.* She loves Saxon like he is her son and expresses such tender compassion and love. She gently licks Saxon's mouth. He returns the affection in kind. Heart to heart, eye to eye, with an honest transparency, they share their love. What a beautiful relationship, designed from a pure heart. This is love in its truest sense. It is a model for me to see and feel what a loving, respectful relationship is versus the division and chaos in my upbringing and adult relationships.

Saxon needs a second pericardial effusion. I ask Dr. Landorf, "Is it possible to do this a third time, rather than euthanizing Saxon?" Choking on the "E" word, I am not ready to lose him.

"Let's wait to see how he recovers. If he rebounds, there no reason to rush this." Such insight and compassion! Dr. Landorf understands our bond and our remarkable trek.

With every day that ticks off, my actions and thinking center inside to exam my heart. This is a lesson about understanding love, as my heart tunes into God's Helper calling and fear is silenced.

Believing love heals all, I bring Saxon to my pastor. We lay our hands on him, praying over him, blessing him in the church sanctuary. He is lifted in prayer as he is surrendered to God's will.

Going through the motions, I decide to meet with the University of Minnesota oncologist and listen, all the while discerning the quality of life for Saxon on his terms. The doctor offers chemo and surgery. The prognosis is death on the operating table. With chemo, his final days would be suffering from drugs. Neither is an acceptable option. The doctor leaves the room to let us decide privately.

Saxon heard the doctor's words. He bravely walks over to my side, placing his head on my thigh. His eyes are soft as he looks to me. I hear his thoughts. *I will do whatever you think is best, Mom. I trust you.* So wise!

I look at him and ask, "Do you want the medicine or do you want a quality of life as long as you can do what you love?" He gets to choose this time.

His upraised eyes reflect what his soul feels: Quality of life is more important than suffering through medical procedures. His last days are to be self-directed, holding beautiful earth memories.

With the time and life remaining, pheasant hunts, two to three times a week, are planned.

Together, we play. We are silly and it doesn't matter. He loves to tug, so while tugging we resemble an Irish jig. He'll have a death grip on the toy and I'll alternate side to side tapping his front feet. Then I hear his play growl as he plants his back feet jerking backward with all his might. When I stop and whisper, "Out," he gently releases and folds into a down stay, wagging his tail with a happy grin. Silly boy!

I wasn't expecting it, but in the midst of Saxon dying, I was learning to laugh, love, and play again. I toss toys and tennis balls down the hallway of my house so he and Sadie can play. Backing up his butt to me to be scratched as he wiggles side-stepping to and fro, he lets me know what makes him feel good. *Oh yes, right there, that's the spot that itches.* We laugh. Holding a toy in my mouth, I look at him and indicate he can have it. He is soft-mouthed, taking and giving it back to me on the slightest whisper. We are backstage performers, frolicking and free from judgment.

Understanding one another is a special part of our relationship. We are mirrors of each other. We get it. He more than I. Our entire life, we have felt others didn't understand us. The sideliners. The misfits. The oddballs. But we are God's characters he uses to teach others.

On a night in November before the pack settles in bed, Saxon and I sit on the floor beside the bed. Cupping my hands under his head, I speak to him from my soul's depths. "Saxon, I love you. I will always be here every step of the way. Your life's legacy, won't be forgotten, I promise. I am sensing you don't want to leave me. You're mentally wrestling whether to stay, and over time, your body won't let you. Your safety, dignity, and respect are protected, and the rest of your days are your choice. If you are suffering, I will help you transition. I promise to deliver you in prayer to God, when the time is right."

The tone in my voice tells him his time is near. I am asking a full surrender and trust of his life to me as I trust faith to lead us through this valley. We embrace, wrapping his broad head and neck around my shoulder, pressing hearts together. His long, sloppy, tender licks wipe away my tears. I'm crying as he courageously faces death, reassuring me it will be all right. It's as if he sees the future.

We connected telepathically, and in this moment, his thoughts tell me, "Seek a higher realm of mindfulness through visualization. When my body is gone, we can meet spiritually in cosmic dreams. I will be beside you." This is startling and a revelation to my once clueless mind.

During our time together, Saxon's life and mine had many matching pieces. It was as if in God's plan he hand-picked Saxon to walk in tandem with the Holy Spirit alongside me, watching over, teaching and directing me, and in the process delivering divine love unconditionally, sacrificing and serving a purpose greater than himself. The progress of my spiritual growth hadn't deepened to Saxon's. Because in my mind the will and realization to go beyond the surface were unimportant. He's able to penetrate my superficiality and sees my soul cry.

As December begins, Bill's wife calls. "Spirit just died in my arms." Bill is heartbroken at the loss of his high strung two-year-old Lab. She was ear-marked to follow in BJ's steps in the Nationals.

Bill buries her that same day in the high hills overlooking the pheasant field.

I meet him in the field. We are old dog-friends sitting together on his tailgate, dangling our legs, and drinking a pop in his outside office. This time, I am consoling him and reminiscing about Spirit's antics. Like the day she belligerently turned her back and looked over her right shoulder to him doing a blind retrieve, and he was torqued about her deliberate disobedience. Our conversation swings to Saxon's passage, and how Spirit helped him become socialized. Both of us are spilling tears.

Slyly, just as he had slipped out Saxon's first Senior Hunter ribbon, he reaches behind him and presents me with his handmade wooden war cross for Saxon. The moment is bittersweet, spiritually symbolic, one soldier to another. Stand where you walk and go forward with integrity.

We share a remembrance of a labor of love that produced victory over Saxon's emotional battles and the honor he earned. Whatever differences we had from the past are forgiven. Gratitude blankets the past. Words escape me for Bill's compassion and kindness. Ours is a loving, enduring heartfelt friendship unlike any I've ever known with another human and one that would have never happened without Saxon. It is a rite of passage that would have been lost had we quit.

"Pay it forward," Bill says as he winks looking over his glasses.

"I will as often as I can. For Saxon, for the rest of my life, I promise."

In Free Fall

Searching for palliative care and quality-of-life options for Saxon leads me to a holistic canine chiropractic assistant named Rosie. Her highly intuitive energy reminds me of the medium visit many years ago. Rosie's focus is treating both animals' and humans' physical, spiritual, and energy imbalances. This modality is a care treatment which is unfamiliar to me.

Rosie's blunt summation is aimed personally at me. Very little is about Saxon.

"It's you who is filled with trauma. It's you who needs to heal. Your solar plexus is blocked." The solar plexus is the seat of how we relate to ourselves and the world. It is the core of our personality, our identity, our ego, and our willpower. It is where self-confidence, self-esteem, and self-discipline reside.

"Hogwash!" I do not want to hear it. "Can't be, this is about Saxon. You must be wrong."

Rosie didn't budge. "You've locked away and carried childhood trauma and refuse to face it. It's been festering all your life. Eventually it will debilitate you or kill you." I didn't connect Saxon's health condition to myself.

I am fear-stricken, but my mind does not grasp why. "But this is about fixing Saxon and giving him quality of life, that's why I am here. I don't need fixing."

"Journal, you need to journal and bring it in at every appointment. Write down your feelings."

How foolish, I thought, but, okay. I will play her silly game. Pen in hand, my mind is blank, nothing! Then the words, anger, fear, alone, sad, sorrow, and depressed spill onto the paper as she works on Saxon.

In Rosie's vision, Saxon sees his lifeless body and the stark vision of reality strikes his essence. He's running out of time to complete his physical purpose.

That evening we are sitting on the floor pillows when he looks up at the ceiling, then instinctively lowers his head. He gazes in my eyes, and I know his time is near. Holding him close, I comfort him through his fears. Inevitably, I know I have to let him go.

I assure Saxon, he need not be afraid, "I've surrendered you to God's care. You are in the best hands possible. I won't hold you back, Saxon. You are free to go when you are ready. You are God's creation. You have blessed me beyond measure."

I plead with God not to break his heart, to spare him. His heart knows enough pain. My mind is horrified. I imagine his heart bursting and hemorrhaging from the growing tumor.

We head out of town to the Careyville bike trail for our daily walk. A virgin snowfall blankets the still pathway. I let the dogs out of the truck. Saxon is exuberant, spinning in circles, He and Sadie play tag and race each other.

Periodically along our walk he freezes like a statue. He cocks his head sideways with perked ears and nose buried in the snow, Dig! Dig! Dig! Dig! Wham! Upward he springs. Then he dives head first into the snow, trying to catch a mole, all the while making sure I am watching. I hear the critter skitter under the snow. Saxon hears it too, which elicits a higher prey drive in him. Tag and the mole is it. Saxon is a riot to watch. He's that way intentionally, to make me laugh and laugh. His frisky actions channel a higher symbolic purpose. Seeing is believing. The roles of trainer and student reverse. His breaking ground is meant to be my first symbolic lesson toward unearthing the unconscious shame.

Further down the trail, he is mischievously diggin' another hole. For sure there must be a bone in there and he must find it. He digs to where his head and shoulders are submerged beneath the snow. Going still deeper, his rear end points to the sky as his tail snaps side to side. The snow stings his belly, which is shaved after numerous ultrasounds. Snow is flying out between his back legs like a snow blower. He stops, pops up his head, panting with a wild-eyed gleam, and checks to see if I am still watching him. I am. Good! Dive back in and dig. Pop up and watch. Then dig some more. I'm belly laughing and nearly rolling in the snow, which eggs him on to dig harder. Step two in his uprooting lessons is hitting pay dirt. Watch, this is how it's done.

Driving his point home, he pantomimes how I am to heal my past. He instigates a dig, burrowing a good twenty feet along the trail's edge, leaving a lasting mark and lesson for me to think about and act upon: Keep diggin' through the dirty layers until you get to the core, to determine the root causes, even if it takes the rest of your life.

From then on, every walk is a strong reminder to unearth life's destructive patterns.

A long, hard doggie shake symbolizes the Old Saxon being extracted from the surface as the snow flies around him like chaff. Salvaging his puppyhood for the rest of the walk, he starts doing doggie angels in the snow, wriggling on his back and barking. Sadie and I join him. We chase one another and roll in the snow. They're barking, I'm laughing, silly, giggly, and reckless. Saxon's real soul surfaces. It's mischievous, witty, comical, a tenderhearted, humble temperament that cares deeply and loves unmeasurably. He pours out so much joy in his dying.

Look, Mom, I'm normal. His essence tells me I can be the same. Just keep diggin' to piece your heart back together.

This is Saxon's third procedural visit with Dr. Landorf. It's a Friday, he sticks up Saxon's X-rays against the light table. Saxon is sitting on the exam table. His head is inquisitively cocked, ears perked, and neck stretched as he listens to the doctor.

"The good news is the fluid in Saxon's heart is gone and so is the tumor in the right atrium of his heart. Saxon's pulse is normal. His bloating shows no fluid in his abdomen."

Saxon swishes his tail on the table like he understands, giving himself a paw up high five. He's cleared and symbolizes that he rid himself of his past life.

"How does that happen that the tumor is gone?"

Dr. Landorf shrugs and is speechless. He hadn't seen this before. Not only is my faith girded, so is his.

Eye to eye, I say, "It was God!"

God shows me how faith and prayer work, confirming all things are possible if we believe. Seeing the miracle that even the sickest heart can heal is a message to me. But the prognosis remains grave. Though his heart is spared, the cancer peppers his liver.

It's Sunday, after the morning church service. Back at home, Saxon is standing in front of me, eyes locked. I have a vision of him retrieving bumpers.

"Oh, you want fun bumpers?"

Giddy, he spins and barks. *Yes! yes!* He wants me to throw some bumpers so he can retrieve them and stand by my side as a team before his Heavenly transition.

I go out to my truck and grab three orange bumpers as we head into the snowy backyard. Pretending we are standing at the hunt test line watching the marks go down, I throw his bumper only ten yards. He waits for me to send him. He retrieves the bumper for the last time and sits at heel, waiting with eyes fixed upward for me to take the bumper from his mouth. It is our final walk together.

I hum *Silent Night* as I rock him in my arms. A sacred time, dying in the privacy of his family, where he is safe, loved, and warm.

In this precious moment I come to realize the depths of his love teaching me the importance of living life from the heart and not the mind. Coming into his world, I respectfully place myself in his paws, overtaken by his unselfish sacrifice for me. His love is pure and freely given. It is nothing like I had ever known before.

"Saxon, I love you like no other. I am so sorry for being such a poor pack leader when you were a puppy. I'm guilty for planting a seed of anger in you and causing you to acquire aggressive behaviors." His soft eyes thank me. His heart forgives me.

Then worry washes over his face, concerned if I will be alright when he leaves?

A somber silence penetrates the house. Expecting at any moment his last breath, I wrap him in a blanket. As his body shuts down, he shivers, holding back pain. Sadie snuggles beside him, giving him a lick on his nose. I am teetering, blocking, trying to be strong. Grief is hovering in the shadows waiting to latch on and control me.

Saxon stands up, stumbles, gasping. Hunching over, I catch him, hold him, caress his head, and lay him down, rocking and humming to him, lulling him into a peaceful sleep. Only his head is exposed through the warm blanket. "You are free to go to Heaven. Your work here on earth is done. Dear God, take Saxon to Heaven. Wrap him in your loving arms and restore him. God, from my hands to your hands, I give you this precious soul, Saxon. He is your creation. He gave his all for me."

Just before his last breath, I ask Saxon, "Will you come back to me and live a life full of harmony, peace, and play while serving others? I promise I will help other dogs, and people will remember you. I will write a book in your honor. I will forever miss you."

I kiss him goodbye. As his soul ascends, he shares with me a remarkable vision. Our essences comingle as we rise together into the warm, opulent light and narrow tunnel called Heaven. Saxon turns, raises his paw, and stops me. He has permission to cross over and I don't. He's home.

I will wait for you and keep an eye on you. I will always be with you, in your heart. I will return when I am healed. You will see me again when your heart is healed. Sadie needs you now, she thinks I am sleeping. I never told her how sick I was.

I have a premonition. I see myself being peaceful and harmonious while supporting and advancing other people's lives with a dog's comfort and unconditional love.

Sobbing inconsolably by his body, I see God's plan to break me. Grief is God's healing mechanism and tears wash away the pain. Ahead of me is a long road of healing. Saxon has given me hope for my future.

Sadie is sleeping unaware he died and I lie there holding him. Stillness saturates the house. Two of my favorite songs, "You Raise Me Up" and "Thank You," play softly.

Dawn arrives. I call a friend asking his help to take Saxon to Dr. Landorf to be cremated. He walks in my house carrying a black duffel bag. I'm numb. My power to function mentally and emotionally is gone.

My neighbors come to help me with Sadie. As Saxon's body is carried past Sadie, she howls and tears come from her eyes as she watches Saxon pass through the door. She is wailing as a mother weeps for her dead child. I cry for Sadie's loss. The psychic pain crushes us both. Now thirteen years old, Sadie comforts me. The pack order changes.

Dr. Landorf meets us at the clinic's back door. Seeing my grief pour out, he consoles me with a hug. He understands our tumultuous undertaking. "Saxon was a teacher for you. He was a very special dog. He was comical, with a big heart, and who relished life."

Saxon touched many lives that went unnoticed to me. He gave Dr. Landorf the opportunity to learn pericardial effusion and help other dogs diagnosed with hemangiosarcoma so those who loved them could have more time with them.

Dr. Landorf promises me that Saxon's body will receive an individual cremation and be treated with the utmost respect. There will be a handmade, sealed-oak urn for Saxon's ashes. He recognizes Saxon's spiritual aspect—a portion I need to realize within myself.

"You seem to have a great understanding of the spiritual nature and the soul of the dog," I say. He simply smiles.

Saxon was of God's making and His messenger. They worked in tandem to waken my blinded mind.

Beneath a tattered pine I place his war cross and a solar star light in the deep snow of my backyard.

Telling Rosie that Saxon passed is uncomfortable. Intellectually, I know she is right when she told me previously that it was I who needed to heal my past and now I feel ashamed to admit it. I send her an email and she graciously replies.

"We can always ask what we may have missed. We will always miss something. What I know is that Saxon was working hard in healing mode. I also know that healing looks scary, uncomfortable. He was using all his resources doing what he had to. He was not sick, but would have looked that way to others. He fulfilled what his soul needed and left clear while he walked beside you, helping you discover what your soul needed. He was wise and was a teacher and master guide for you. Now the question comes back to you. Can you hold your self-worth as high as he held it to continue your healing work? You deserve so much more. We offer you a safe place where we can help you with this and more.

"I know you must be hurting. Saxon was one of the greatest. His life was a miracle and surrendering to Divine wisdom is very hard. He struggled making that decision. My prayer is that you continue to feel his presence and know he loved you."

Learning of his death, Bill and Joyce sent this email:

"We were so sorry to hear about our beloved Saxon passing tonight. You have to be proud of Saxon and yourself as a team for all your accomplishments. If you stop and think about it, just for him to sit and honor and watch another dog go after the bird was an amazing accomplishment for him. WOW! Achieving all his master passes was incredible! He was so proud. I'll never forget when he received his titles. He seemed to know how extra special they were. But most of all was the love that he had for his master. His love and trust were for you. Anyone that was truly watching you run him knew he dearly loved you and, in return, that love was mutual. I'm so glad you have the memories of walking up to the lines at all the different hunt tests including Master National. No one can ever take those away from you. Sax was so happy to have you at his side. God bless you and Sadie at this time."

Hopelessness, despair, and monumental grief consume me. Family is nonexistent. A few very close friends, a neighbor, and members of the business community offer their support. Yet, I go it alone, suffering, not wanting to burden them.

Spirit in the Sky

Saxon spirit calls me. It's pulling me toward his training fields on Christmas Eve. "Watch for the first brightest star and you will see me."

It is near midnight as I arrive. Stepping out of my car, I can see my breath, hear the glittering snow crunch under my feet, and feel the icy air on my face as my tears nearly freeze. The night is peaceful and still. Darkness surrounds me. A shooting star rockets past Sirius, the brightest star in the sky, known as the Great Dog Star.

"It's three days since you passed. Your presence surrounds me. My heart is listening and eyes are watching." The star energy tethers us. Saxon shows me that all I needed to do was step out away from home's distractions and sit with him in prayer, so we can talk. This is his first lesson of proof from the other side as I feel him beside me. It gives me comfort that he is with me through my spiritual crisis.

Paw print by invisible paw print, Saxon leads the way to my heart's enlightenment—just as he demonstrated on his final day. His job is unearthing my fears and old beliefs, across a lifetime. God's Spirit beside me, supporting me in love but I don't realize his presence as I am so taken by losing Saxon.

His death is percolating in me. The silent roar of his absence makes me fragile. I am rocking on the brink of a mental breakdown. There is no life without him. Every day is riddled with mood swings, foggy head, illogical behavior, and panic attacks, mental instability, and gloom. The earth that once supported me quakes beneath my feet, leaving me as dust. Every time I think about Saxon, I collapse, sobbing. Nights are the worst because suicide tests me as I face a dingy bottomless hole. Saxon gave me purpose, a reason to live. Never has my heart ached as now. I consider suicide as I sit where he died. With only a lit candle and a knife in hand, I am ready to slit my wrists, when Sadie comes. She puts her head and paw on my lap and her pleading eyes say, *Stop. Mom, I need you.* She saves me. But that's how bad I wanted to be with Saxon. Life here is unbearable with the reality of facing my demons and feeling so alone.

But killing myself would be a betrayal to Saxon, a shameful cop-out. He brought me as far as he could. It is my role to do my own difficult heart work, as he did his. I must be responsible to myself.

Faced with surrendering the in-here sense of self and the lived experiences of the out-there embattles my mind. It means going deep-in—surrendering completely to God's will, trusting, and giving up myself by choosing to walk by faith. It takes guts and letting go. Full surrender and complete faith are what Saxon demonstrated when he put his life in my hands. It's my turn now with God.

I'm beginning a long, messy, grueling, painful uprooting of trauma in order to recover. This is unfair to Sadie, expecting her to carry my grief and hers. Yet she unconditionally sacrifices for me. Selflessly assuming the burden of my depression and grief is toxic for her. It's who she is, a therapy dog, giving generously from her heart.

Trying to find meaning in Saxon's death remains balled in my head. On every flight to the Dakotas, I sit by a window staring out and weeping. Our lives flash before me, like a movie reeling fast forward before the end of a life. I visualize Saxon in my arms when he died. I go back in time to the sassy puppy face at four weeks old, the vicious dogfights, the behavior modification protocols practiced in my basement, our last day with the bumpers, peeing on the bird, his hug. I see the compassion he showed after losing Jule and Bill's tenderness when he sat by his truck and hugged Saxon. I remember Saxon's own pride when he pranced with his duck at the Master Nationals where he got the nickname Mr. Happy Feet. I replay my agony on the day of his diagnosis and his releasing of frustration by digging on the bike trail. I sense the comingling of our spirits and his immense love for me. So much more! What did this all mean and how is it supposed to fit together? How does this relate to me? Guilt and the quandary of unanswered questions about his life weigh heavy on my mind.

The hour-long flight is my time to journal, when I can pour my heart out through the pen, filling page after page. My writing can't keep pace with my thoughts. I am lost in words I didn't know existed inside me. Then I read what I wrote and discover my emotions in lockdown, pretending the hurt away, as if it never happened. But it did happen, trigger-stacking trauma upon trauma, layered over a lifetime.

The plane is at capacity. My thoughts are zoned, in my own world, as if no one else exists on the plane. I hide my tears and try to keep from being seen sobbing. When we land, I pull myself together, buck up, and pack-up my grief.

Meeting my clients takes all the emotional strength I have. When they ask about Saxon, tears flow and hugs come my way. Saxon's death affected them as it did me and we have grown closer as people, not just as clients, bridging into belonging and being loved, feelings I've wanted all my life. But grief is still stalking me. It has glommed onto me as a relentless companion I didn't want.

Through numerous late-night phone conversations, Karla, a colleague and friend from corporate, reenters my life. We talk into the morning hours about our animals, comforting and holding each other up discussing the loss of our animals. Mostly, I listen and learn from her.

For the last two years anguish has overpowered her. Her life was slammed with the death of two beloved German shepherds to hemangiosarcoma and two horses, plus a divorce and had to take early retirement after she had a heart attack, all of which inflicted emotional shock and forced her to the brink of a mental breakdown.

Her acquaintance with grief and the loss of unconditional love elevated her third eye to an ultrahigh spiritual frequency melding as one with the universe becoming one and universally aligned with nature and God. Now coyotes and foxes come to sit with her in the fields as she thinks about them. Deer meander next to her. She has achieved the ability to speak and visualize with animals across the veil. Hearing about her skill intrigues me. My craving and curiosity kick into high drive for my own potential for communicating with Saxon. It's what Saxon was trying to tell me about developing my third eye. I explained Saxon's passing to Karla. She then shared her own connection to it.

"I know because he came to me and showed me where he is. He showed me that he is free and healed and wanted you to know."

Bristling, I wondered why he came to her? Why didn't he come to me? That didn't feel right. So I asked her.

"Why did Saxon come to you and not me?"

"You were too close, and your heart is blocked, your mind is cluttered and noisy. There is a good chance he will come to you in your dreams." That's how I saw him. He showed me he was alone, trotting a gravel road. He was lighthearted and peaceful. The road was lined with tall trees swaying gently in the wind. Beside the road, rolling fields were illuminated with a palette of wildflowers. Mountains on the horizon expanded the vast landscape beneath an azure sky that hosted soft, rolling, white clouds and brilliant sunshine that warmed his face. He lilted along the trail carefree. His tail reflected a joyful heart. A glow of blue-green light surrounded him. Musical notes chimed out of his heart. The rain was gone. He was glorious!

At a later conversation I told Karla about my dream.

"OMG! He came showing me the same image he showed you."

My curiosity intensified. Saxon is orchestrating through the veil. His soul lives on. Mind-boggling as a myriad of marvels evolve. Motivated, I need to know more about the spiritual nature of things.

"What happens to a dog's soul when he dies?" I asked.

"The dog's spirit leaves the body, soon after the heart stops. The brain no longer functions. A lifeless body remains. However, the spirit has the option to come back and help those they were closest to and help them heal or resolve their own unfinished business."

Uncovering piece by piece I am awakening to my soul path just as Saxon did.

"Music assists the spirit's communication. The music lifts their spirit. You will feel his tingling presence beside you, and you will know it is Saxon."

She confirms the sensation I feel. I am more aware of his energy.

She lit in me a spiritual quest to educate myself about animal communication, spiritualists, and shamans. My goal was seeking these people.

A Pierced Heart

There are many things I hate about my grief. No rules. No schedule. Can't fix anything. Not sure what needs fixing. Embarrassing. Losing self-control. Crying and thinking I can't cry more and then I do. Exhausted. Broken. Friends who say, "Just get over it" and "It's just a dog." Wanting to sucker punch them.

Blocking, denying, and burying my emotions by never expressing feelings is what I learned during childhood. This is what needed now to come undone and detonated. Until then, I'm not understanding the resurfacing and am thrown off-kilter. I'm unhinged, spinning, and going crazy as my nervous system is going haywire. Where is this attack coming from? I just want it to stop, like an addict going through withdrawal during recovery. Please make it stop!

Blindsided by my chaotic neurosis, the survival mechanisms of avoidance, denial, deception, and lies aren't working. Facing the truth? Never. Peace is an arm's length away. Reaching for help is unnatural. I'm conditioned to shut up, buck up, and hunker down. My mind tells me I'll be labeled a weakling or dummy.

God's Spirit anchors me, as grief's chisel jackhammers my heart, breaking bedrock to uncover the truth. Grief wrestles me down and relentlessly demands my attention—until I cry, "Uncle."

Three weeks after Saxon's passing, his spirit is heavy on my mind to find comfort and relief. I hear "You Raise Me Up" on the car radio daily. Tears blur my vision. Many mornings, I walk into my accounts red-eyed, and then I'll be stumbling in a mental fog through the day. Saxon speaks to me through this song, hoping the words will tell me in my despair to reach out to God for reassurance. I visualize the night he died in my arms. But I'm stalled. My mind is cemented by grief and emotional pain that Saxon is unable to penetrate.

Spirit whispers about self-care. This is a new first step for me after having always put others first. It leads me to a holistic masseuse named Karin, whose deep-tissue work provides grounding and relaxation for my mind and body. During the massage, I'm in a deep sleep when a vision appears, startling my inner senses. I wake up gasping. My eyes spring wide open. Karin is alarmed and wants to know what happened. I see Saxon's eyes, though not his face, but the rush of his black, piercing, telescoping eyes quickly vanishes. The fiery eyes resemble a leopard. I am unsure what to make of this.

"Are you sure it was Saxon's eye and not the leopard's?" Karin asks.

"I want to believe it was Saxon, but it looked like a leopard,"

"Saxon sent you a message from an animal spirit guide."

An animal spirit guide, what's that? Does this revelation that an animal spirit world exists reduce my human importance?

Being torn to believe in the animal spirit world again challenges my belief system. Is this demonic? Giving it consideration could inspire me to be open to the spiritual significance. Investigating further, I learn the leopard signifies a rebirth period after suffering and death. The cat is a healer of deep wounds, bringing up old issues and redeeming one's power once lost during wounding.

I'm outwardly focused, so my humanness doesn't comprehend this relationship. This is divine guidance. Telepathically, Saxon's presence is beside me, supporting, prompting, and leading me forward. The feeling is strange. Why Saxon is giving the best part of himself for me? Why do I deserve this? I'm conditioned to control everything on my own. I'm frustrated that he's driving my recovery.

Keep on diggin' is his message.

Karin tells me of a spiritual reading she did that helped her through an emotionally difficult time. Then it hits me. That's where I am. A realization begins by my admitting and succumbing to the fact I have emotional issues. Am I nuts?

My childhood default was: Never admit emotional instability because then you will be keyholed as a mental case, a weakling, which compounds your self-condemnation. Hide. Bury it. Buck up. Be tough! My willingness to come out of hiding is reaching for help and breaking a powerless mold. I needed help.

Karin gives me Grace Angel's contact information so I can make the call.

I make the call and schedule to meet Grace for a spiritual reading. With my ingrained pattern of destructive self-containment, stepping outside my comfort zone by going to a complete stranger clashes with my family culture and traditional Christian upbringing. I am vulnerable. In exposing a raw, bleeding heart to a stranger, I summon the courage to trust myself, believing this is the right step toward healing.

Saxon trusted me. Now it was my turn. I drive to the meeting. On arrival, Sadie rests in the car. Grace welcomes me into her home with open arms. She offers tea and a seat at her kitchen table. As I enter, my body appears broken and downhearted. Her loving, outstretched hand touches mine as we sit. I am safe. We share the bond of love and triumph as it wells up and spills out of my heart.

"He's gone and my life is in shambles."

Grace holds me, silently waiting for my tears to subside. It feels good to be held.

"Are you ready?" she asks quietly.

Reverently, she compassionately guides me into her healing room. The shades are drawn. Aromatics and a lit candle establish a calming atmosphere.

I am wary of mental seduction, having heard tales about séances and Ouija boards. I wonder if I am bringing evil into my life. I hear my mother's scolding voice, which evokes fear, guilt, and shame that I am disobedient, a sinner worshipping false gods.

A greater desire to heal overpowers my fear of remaining a strangled victim of the past. My way isn't working. As we sit quietly, Grace slowly turns her palms upward and invites my hands to blend our energies. Surrendering, I extend mine, palm to palm with hers. We take three deep breaths and become heart-centered.

I bow my head. Grace prays, asking the presence of the Holy Spirit that this healing serve the highest good and that it ground us. My fear of evil dissolves. I trust the process as her prayer calms me. She begins a meditation, welcoming those of the highest vibration to step forward. The room fills with essences. I sense Saxon on the outskirts, supervising. It is eerie but safe. I feel a reassuring, unseen hand on my shoulder. As she feverishly writes their information, divine messages flow through Grace like crystal spring water pouring through a vessel.

She reveals a shocking discovery. My energy conveys devastation, tremendous sadness, and anger at God. Anger? What anger? I am not an angry person!

Grace strikes a nerve. The traumatic maltreatment experiences I deny reliving are blocked and locked away. An unrecognizable anger instantly swells within me. Rejecting anger, I try to justify and redirect my reasons for coming here. It's about finding answers for Saxon!

In her vision, Grace sees my father step forward. Shrinking, defeated, and pulling inward, he is very sad. Sharing her vision with me, Grace sees in the background my healed ma and her parents standing clustered amid the soul group. Ma is luminous. Dad is ashamed of his ruthless behavior affecting my life and wants me to know the remorse he feels for me. But I don't appreciate what I see as his sniveling and crawling. My crimson rage and rebellion fuel my anger toward him. The nerve this struck didn't prepare me to want to listen to what he has to say.

Grace establishes a two-way communication between my father and me. "What would you like to tell your father?"

Finally, after all these years of hiding and being silenced as a victim, I am freed to have a voice, and my vengeful words backhand him like he did to me.

"You hurt me. You never told me you loved me. You rejected and dismissed me. You violated me and made me feel worthless. I am not ready to forgive you. Why did you hurt me? You were supposed to be my protector. Most of all, why did you make me bury the puppies alive? Why? I still hear their innocent cries."

There it is, unexpectedly, my recall of burying the live puppies. My amygdala recorded it all. The horror strikes me like internal shrapnel. A revelation out of the blue jolts me. I am reliving a day when I was five years old, a little girl exercising normal separation behavior, testing boundaries. But I am misunderstood as a willful child who needed to be crushed for the sake of conformity and maintaining the generational norms. Better to blow off the child's feelings, she has none. Strike her fiercely to prove your authority. And Dad did.

My body's cellular memory flashes on his cold, sacrificial emotional abandonment. Mostly what embroils me is his unemotional attack on the innocent, myself included. How could he?

Grace communicates that his response is silence and his body language is deep remorse with his head down, eyes averted, and hunched over in shame. His soul is not at peace because he is working through his generational sins and unable to forgive himself until he is forgiven. That takes full surrender to God.

Before the session ends, I try interjecting questions about Saxon, but they are minimized and deflected. Feeling set up, I don't like the outcome of the session. I am frustrated and torqued at not having my way. In a sense, I have been tricked. It was the only way to bring me to Grace.

Grace ends our session with prayer. It wasn't what I expected but what I needed. The painful truth. Saxon and Grace team up orchestrating my new reality. Together they are assisting my soul's growth. I am disappointed that I learned nothing more about Saxon. Yet I didn't want anger to be my identity.

Closing the door behind me, I am puzzled. Why am I angry? What caused my anger? What was this all about? More questions than answers keep the "why-child" in me diggin'.

Sadie is sitting up in the car with ears perked. Her sweet face looks out from the steamed-up driver's-side window like a Miss Daisy. She lovingly waits to receive me. My anger fades and my heart opens, smiling at her.

Talk to the Animals

The possibility of speaking to the animal spirit world fascinates me. Longing to speak directly with Saxon spurs me to learn. Yet why the spiritualists could have a two-way conversation with Saxon and I can't perplexes me.

After doing a little research, I enroll in an introductory animal-communication seminar through the Gurney Institute of Animal Communication to be held in Texas during March. Diggin' further, I come across a recorded meditation titled "Heart Talk." The main idea was to visualize a traumatized heart contrasted with one that is emotionally healed. Visual imagery is familiar to me from Saxon's field training. I order the CD, which arrives in the mail a few days later.

Setting the tone for healing, my bedroom is darkened. Only the flame of the lavender-scented candle penetrates the darkness. The flame's flicker welcomes Saxon's presence. Sadie and I lie on the bed. I shut my eyes and rest my hands on my heart, visualizing Saxon's presence. I feel him near me. It seems like old times when peace and love prevailed as the pack of three slept contentedly together. Soft, soothing flute music, drumbeat and an angelic woman's voice speaking instructions begin. Becoming relaxed and openly heart-centered allows my mind to clear and visualize. The soft-spoken voice establishes a visual, anatomic cross-section of the heart. I envision myself and Saxon paired at the inside opening of the heart's right atrium, symbolizing the location of his past tumor and the old blood, his past aggression. He sits at heel, looks up at me, telling me he is ready to proceed. I am humbled. The stark contrast of him healed, living a cleansed life, and serving, while I am suffering, weighted down by hidden, stored-up emotions awakens me, bringing me to my precipice, seeing his transformation.

He led by example, showing me that when the heart frees the darkness a life can change, and assuring me to have trust as the outer self wastes away and the inner self renews day by day. Saxon allows me the space to open up and hear me out.

Returning my gaze, his wisdom knows that the truth cannot be changed, but it can change me and sanctify the lies woven in my nature. Our heart walk begins. It's time to face the truth. Reverently and prayerful, in the safety of two trusted, old dog friends sharing the most intimate parts of ourselves, he listens to my heart speak.

"You've seen my shame, felt my guilt, and shown me yours strapped in a muzzle. My pain and heartache were transparent in your eyes but not in mine. I chose not to see it. Your death both wakens and breaks me. My human faults are overlooked because you accept and love me as I am. Like Christ, you steadfastly walk beside me in love and remain in my heart, your being speaking and guiding, when I am open to listen.

"Saxon, you understand that my way of learning is to see and experience before I can shed the past. Your physical life is a living example, mirroring a broken body. Your sacrifice for me is intended to be my human lesson, recognizing and symbolizing that my life needs to change, reinforcing that where I came from doesn't mean I have to stay there. I get it now. I'm sorry I didn't then, yet so grateful. Life doesn't have to come from a place of pain. I can come from love.

"Love wasn't taught to me. You showed me pure love. You are a physical representation of faith to feel and hold, giving me hope to press on."

As oxygenated blood leaves the left ventricle of the heart, that's where Saxon and I stand, viewing a new circulatory system of life. The old blood is recirculating and regenerating beat by beat, visualizing a vibrant, sunlit horizon that warms us and is a peace that passes all human understanding that reigns in our hearts. Saxon shows me what my future can be like. *See, you can do this,* his thoughts convey.

Tasting peace strengthens my desire to heal. Healing requires full surrender and living by faith. First one must trust and believe in the possibility.

The meditation ends. I turn and face Saxon and express my gratitude. "Words are not sufficient to describe the profound effect you had on my life. I am honored to have the privilege to be with you and share the partnership we had here on earth. I loved you like no other. In my humanness, I didn't see God, so He gave me you to touch, hold, and defend, and to feel love through you. Though you are not here, you are with me, helping me grow in the grace of God. Your love is amazing. I miss you. I love you deeply and know the feelings are mutual."

He vanishes.

Sadie moves from the middle of the bed and snuggles alongside of me, licking the tears rolling down my sobbing face. In this moment, she put aside her grief to comfort me, giving me the best of herself.

Saxon likes to mess with my head, proving he is around. Al's braid of sweet grass is kept atop the TV. Coming home after work, I discover it knocked down and think, that's odd; Sadie's been with Sue all day. I replace it, thinking nothing more. Waking the next morning, it's knocked down again. I replace it, but I'm confused about why it keeps falling because Sadie slept with me. One more time, it's knocked down again, and Saxon appears in my mind, chuckling as if his paw is covering his mouth, keeping a secret. I realize this is him showing up, letting me know he is watching over me as promised. Cool dog.

"Oh, it's you, you silly boy,"

Made you laugh. Jokester.

The Bridge

Sue cares for Sadie during my workweek. She takes her to the vet clinic while grooming dogs and kennels her until I come home.

In February, two months after Saxon's death, I stop by to pick up Sadie. Sue has rescued a five-year-old female golden with a stark resemblance to Saxon and the mannerisms of Sadie. Jazzamine is a brood bitch, having produced four litters, and the owner couldn't keep her.

Sue sees my interest in Jazz. "Would you take Jazz?"

"Yes, but not right now. It's not fair to Sadie."

Sue wants coownership so she can have one litter of puppies from Jazz. Because my hopes for Saxon's reincarnation are high, I make the assumption his rebirth is imminent with Jazz. We barter my dog training skills to complete the training of her younger golden retriever, Robin, in achieving the Senior Hunter title. Field training is my avoidance tool to distract me from facing grief and the inner truths. The agreement is done. The remaining part of winter, I pour myself into training Robin.

Sadie is due for her annual physical and blood work with Dr. Landorf. Something is wrong. She fusses over her food and is eating less and less. The estrogen dosages are increasing for incontinence. Her body develops benign lipomas. Her urine is cloudy dark with crystals, and her lymph system is wacky. Her other blood results show abnormalities outside the normal range. The outliers in the blood panel indicate that her immune system is struggling to hold a balance. I'm worried.

In March, I fly to San Antonio, Texas, to attend the animal communication class, bringing a photograph of my dogs. Sadie is with Sue while I am gone. On arrival at the site, the attendees are greeted by the receptionist who has us sign in and gives us our information packet. In a half hour, all nine of us gather in a circle. The group leader, Carol Gurney, introduces herself and gives a brief background of her experience, how she began this work, and why it is her passion. She asks us to introduce ourselves, share a little of our experience, and express our purpose in attending. She begins to explain why we aren't able to communicate with our own animals.

"We're too closely connected to them. Our hearts and minds are a muddled mess. The mind needs silence. As children we are open to listen, but as we grow into adulthood, we shut down and don't trust our intuition and visions sent to us. The lack of use makes it difficult to bring it to the surface and use our instinct. We discount messages and aren't aware of our animals' reaching out to us telepathically, or disbelieving, we tune them out. Other times, we aren't grounded and there's interference in our energy field, so the reception is poor. Humans discount an animal's ability to communicate and feel, but their souls live in our world and absorb our unbalanced nature. We are the ones disconnected from the universe as we choose to perceive ourselves superior."

The session begins with a meditation, teaching us to silence our mind. We are going learn to be grounded, open our heart's, listening, and set the intentions to communicate. Slowing down and leaving my grief and work on the other side of the door will be a challenge.

Carol asks us to visualize our animal and hold their picture in our mind. We are paired, exchanging our photographs. My memory escapes me now about the story of this woman's dog. I do recall it as a small breed and the devastation she feels about his loss. Her dog comes to me and she knows I am speaking to her dog. She breaks into tears when she hears the answers to her questions.

I am amazed. I did it! I can visualize, energetically and telepathically connect, and emotionally sense this person's animal and deliver the right information that gives relief and comfort.

We switch to a new partner. The roles are reversed. Same thing happens. My partner is given two pieces of information, Saxon's name and the fact that he died in December. I visualize him and am shaken. She identifies details in his life, including the Master National events and his final days, which confirm his presence. Saxon tells her, *I am so sorry I could not let you know sooner that I was sick. I am sorry I could not tell Sadie either, but that was the soul contract designed for me. I miss you, Mom, and love you very much. I will always be with you. I am healing. My body no longer hurts. Thank you for helping me through my aggression. It was a physical process I was meant to live. So I could heal my past. Now it is your turn. I will be by your side, helping you. You will know and feel me by you, so you, too, can heal like I did.*

I weep, hearing his response and become a believer that I will be able to communicate with him.

Coming home, I realize I am losing Sadie. She continues pulling away, seeking solitude. We take to our separate corners in the house and the loneliness speaks volumes. She needs consoling because I've emotionally abandoned her. A life pattern done to me is unfortunately passed along. I sense she is making a life-death decision. I arrange a meeting with Grace. Grace does Sadie's reading.

"Sadie is a very happy dog. She is a joy. She is very sad about Saxon. You've kept her involved, but she is very concerned about you and feels it is her responsibility to care for you. She feels a bit overwhelmed. She knows you love her, but you are still in a lot of pain, and she is too. She tries very hard to make you happy and laugh. She is going to be okay, especially if you are okay. She loves a ball, and she always wants to play."

My sorrow increases. My grief is draining her. Helping myself is difficult. Guilt sets in. I feel this is my fault. What could I have done differently for her?

Dr. Landorf examines her monthly. I suspect cancer, so I request an ultrasound. It shows a benign splenic nodule and an enlarged lymph node. She struggles to eat a half a cup of food a day. The medical results are real and I deny them. I can't accept losing her too.

Again, I meet with Grace for another reading of Sadie. Grace asks to be alone with Sadie. When Grace finishes, she tells me Sadie's message: "You have a huge fear of being alone. The grieving is getting in the way of being in the moment. You are addressing birth and death and what that is on a higher sense. You are struggling with staying in body form. Your soul wants to leave." was Grace's response.

Sadie tells Grace her wishes, *I want to go, I am happy to go when it is okay with you. I don't want you to be alone. I will stay until you are ready to let me go.*

My intuition is right. Our time together is short. How can this be happening? How can I survive the loss of my two soulmates within months of each other? How much pain can this heart take? As angry as I wanted to be with God, I tempered my anger, knowing in my heart that He had a greater purpose and plan. Because of my running away from the truth, God is standing in the wings, hoping for me to reach out my hand to His in faith.

Grace's reading ends with hope as she directs her conclusion about me saying, "You will have freedom in a new space and essential opening into a new life. Training and assisting the unfortunate animals will bring more love here with these animals than you ever imagined. Make compassion your passion."

Sadie goes through additional medical tests both with Dr. Landorf and at the University of Minnesota. The university diagnoses her with inoperable spindle cell carcinoma that weaved its way in and through her peritoneum. There it is, two dogs with cancer just months apart.

During the summer, Sadie is always with me. For all the times of taking the shadows, this is time for her to be in the limelight of my life. Our remaining time together is special. She envisions reuniting with Saxon. I can tell she is ready to leave anytime, knowing I will be all right. Her decision is made and she is at peace. She reminisces about the three of us walking together on the bike trail. Those were cherished walks. She had such a lovely saunter, reminding me of an elegant, French aristocratic lady carrying a vintage lace parasol, casually strolling along the Seine in Paris, pausing to savor spring's beauty, teaching me to do the same.

Through the tumultuous life she lived with me, she has managed to stay interconnected and grounded in nature. Sadie is my calming force. Every evening, comforting one another, she and I share a prayer before we fall asleep as I hold her in my arms. Intuitively I know, Sadie is struggling, in deciding to leave or stay because she knows I am not ready to let her go. She asks divine wisdom for more time, and she gets it.

In July, Sadie, Robin, Sue, and I are at a hunt test in southern Wisconsin where I handle Sue's golden retriever, Robin. This is Sadie's last trip to a hunt test. Robin earns her Senior Hunter title. My obligation to Sue is complete except for Jazz producing a litter.

Kneeling on the ground beside Sadie, looking eye to eye, seeing the love and truth that connected our hearts leaves a lasting image in my mind. Sadie's beauty and heart epitomize the nature of a golden retriever as gentle, loving, forgiving, self-sacrificing, passionate, joyful, and gentle.

She's angelic. There's a glowing white aura around her. Death is near. She has a pure heart and has always celebrated nature's beauty. Her actions teach me an appreciation for the oneness of nature and its stillness.

It is the end of July. In my house, Jazz comes for a brief visit and is introduced to Sadie. In no uncertain terms, with hackles raised and tall posturing, Sadie lets Jazz know this is her home. Sadie's boundaries let Jazz know she is welcome to stay, but Sadie is still here and alpha. Indirectly, I offer Sadie permission to leave when she is ready and not rushed. I let her know I can manage her loss through having Jazz.

A week later, we go to one of the field training sites, where Saxon and Robin practiced for hunt tests. Sadie wants to play and chase the bumpers. A rain shower begins and behind her on the hill a beautiful rainbow appears. I take her picture as a sweet memory of this angel. It is Sadie's gift to me to enjoy the beauty and know there will be hope for all animals. Her legacy is about service to others and learning to just be.

Soon her body refuses sustenance. Dr. Landorf finds the cancer is spreading. In a private room he suggests to not put her through anymore. It is time to let her go. The fight in me is gone. I concede.

He understands I need to spend the afternoon with her. He agrees to come to the house that evening bringing an angel bag, a royal-blue body bag. We spend the August afternoon walking slowly through grassy fields. She rolls in the grass under the sunny skies. It's our last walk together. The pose that sticks in my mind is seeing her on the brow of the hill, standing strong and determined as she looks back one last time.

We sit side by side overlooking the rolling hills and valleys. I wrap my arm around her back and talk about how she was my rock. Holding her close, caressing her, I want her to know how very much she means to me and how much I love her. I am grateful for her patience and for her leadership when I didn't understand leadership. I recognize the quiet beauty that flows from her heart for others' well-being and comfort. I feel it's important to tell her the difference she makes in my life and how she is valued.

She wakes in me the truth that serving others for the greater good holds higher value than the pursuit of ribbons. I realize how upside down my values are and how I resist changing. On this day she moves me closer into my true self.

As we sit quietly, my mind hears, *don't worry, Mom, be happy.*

I buy her a helium balloon with a sunflower and smiley face that sings, "Don't Worry, Be Happy." The balloon makes me chuckle and that's the way Sadie wants it: Release the things that drag your heart down; keep an open heart.

I wish I could stop time. Dr. Landorf arrives. It's a beautiful August summer evening. The sun is setting just over the trees of my backyard. The western sky glows, encasing a rich magenta range, streaks of papal purple, gold accents with warm amber, and fiery reds. Sadie and I walk outside. We sit on the top deck step facing the sunset one last time. I gently put my arm around her back and we talk. This is a sacred time for us. I need God's presence near.

"In just a little while, you will be on the other side of that glorious sunset, in Heaven, romping and dancing in fields of flowers with Saxon. Your wishes will come true. He is waiting for you. I will always love you and look for you when it is my turn to cross over. The three of us will dance and celebrate. Send me a sign and surprise me occasionally, letting me know you are around."

As I choke back tears, my mind hears, *Yes.*

Sadie is ready to leave. That's it. I give her a hug and kisses. She stands up and dismisses me. Pragmatically, she walks back into the house, leaving me alone on the step. I find her lying in the hallway to the bedrooms with her paws crossed and her head resting on them. I sit on the couch and silently watch her moment of peace. I walk to her and cup my hands under her chin, lifting her head so our eyes meet one last time. I whisper in her ear.

"It's time, my sweet baby. I need to let you go. I will be okay. I need to give you to God now."

On her own, she rises and walks into the Angel Bag as if to say, *Mom, I'm ready.* She bravely faces death, as a transition to eternal life as the soul lives on. I sit on the floor beside her, softly caressing her head, letting her know she is safe. I place her favorite soft, yellow toy duck under her chin, for her head to rest comfortably. She loved that duck and carried it everywhere.

In her radiance, I see a peaceful angel waiting to see a dear friend on Heaven's edge. Saxon is expecting her. He is beside her. It's her time.

From the puppy I held in my arms at Flo's property, an overwhelming power of responsibility and love passed through me. Over thirteen years I learned how special Sadie is. Her lineage is from performance champions stacked with accolades, but her unpretentious heart was destined for serving and providing comfort—a lesson intended for my understanding.

Dr. Landorf gives her the first injection, making her sleepy. Immediately, I question if I am taking her life too soon. But it is right for her to not suffer. She's ready. It's her wish.

Before Dr. Landorf gives the injection to stop her heart, I kiss her good-bye on her forehead and tell her I love her. Sadie takes her last breath. Her soul jets from the room like a shooting star in the constellation of Perseus.

I stay with her body through the night, feeling her essence around me. For a brief moment, Saxon sits beside us, comforting and supporting. He knows how difficult this is for me.

I envision Saxon taking her paw, escorting her into Heaven. They are reunited. She is home and free, not limited to a physical body.

At 3:00 a.m., I open my drapes seeing the planet Venus as a large, luminous white light hovering low over my neighbor's house across the street. It is supernatural, an indication Sadie crossed over and she's at peace. I hear her whisper.

I'm here, Mom, and I am okay. I am with Saxon. We are dancing and celebrating Heaven together. Smile and be happy for us. Don't worry about us, be happy."

I walk onto my back deck. The balloon soars in the sky as the music plays, "Don't worry be happy." She is gone.

The reality of her absence opens a gaping hole in an empty house. Sadie and Saxon are both gone and I am alone to face myself. They were my family. Now I realize the value of Sadie's quiet presence, one I took for granted. A part of me dies this day from the lonely ache I feel deep in my core.

In the morning, I close her angel bag with her peacefully lying there. I ask a friend to help me transport her to Dr. Landorf so he can arrange a private cremation for her. He realizes how difficult this is, losing two dogs in eight months.

Sadie's urn is a beautiful white marble urn with a cupid angel sitting on the second step, blowing a kiss from her hand. Sadie is on the other side of the sunset, blowing angel kisses my way. Every once in while I feel a butterfly kiss and I smile remembering the times she tenderly licked my tears and opened my heart.

Under my old pine tree, in the backyard, a solar star light shines and an angel figurine with wind chimes inside a harp accompanies the wooden war cross. As the wind moves through the chimes, I feel Sadie wishing me peace and healing.

It is time for Jazz to come home. I still have the obligation for Jazz to produce a litter before I own her. Entering her kennel, I slide down the kennel panel to the floor, sobbing as I hold her beside me. Jazz knows instantly of Sadie's passing. The mother in Jazz immediately presses her lovely head in my chest, compassionately hugging me. She becomes my support, licking my tears as Sadie did for thirteen years. Together, we somberly step out of her kennel and go home.

As I am laden with grief, my concern of smothering and depleting Jazz's energy surfaces. I am aware of the toll it took on Sadie. Jazzy lacks the sense of belonging. She has been a kennel dog used for breeding purposes, now abandoned by her owner and moved around like property. Her maltreatment feels akin to mine. We need one another.

Sadie's surprises start happening. It isn't more than a day later and every day that follows that I hear on the radio "Beautiful in My Eyes," Joshua Kadison's song from his album *Painted Desert Serenade*. Another song that reminds me of our walks along the bike trail is *"Come Saturday Morning"* It's a message from Sadie, letting me know she is near and thinking of me as I am of her. To this day, the frequency is different, but it still happens. As I think about her, I turn on the radio and I hear those songs play.

Out in the field teaching Jazzy to retrieve the dummy from the launcher as Sadie did, there in the bottom of my bumper bag I find a feather, which signifies a kiss from an angel. The feathers will continue appearing numerous times, along my paths, waking me of her presence. Each feather bears a message from its bird's spirit. Hawks and eagles are flying over the fields as I train, which before was uncommon. Eagle medicine means rising above the momentary to spiritual eternity. A circle of twelve eagles soars high as a faith symbol and a connection to the divine indicating to me a message of a renewed life. The message of the red-tailed hawk feather symbolizes family, friends, and community where our insecurities of being abandoned, left alone, and humiliated are formed. It's in the family unit where we acquire a sense of belonging, and learn love, anger, and passion.

Spectacular double rainbows grab my attention. I know they have meaning, but I am not in tune with it. They pique my curiosity to learn their significance and correlate it to my life. Back home, I learn they symbolize transformations in life. The first rainbow represents the material world. The second rainbow is the Heavenly world.

Each night Jazz and I sit outside on the back step. I focus on the angel and the war cross, waiting for the solar light to illuminate the night and assure me of Sadie's and Saxon's presence, which I rely on for comfort. Jazzy's lesson for me is about learning to separate myself from the mental noise: *Just be and sit in silence.* It's a characteristic I have noticed in each dog.

I feel Sadie urging me to call Karla. When I do, Karla tells me about a long conversation she had with Sadie.

"She is deciding her next mission of whether to reincarnate with you or go elsewhere. She needs to know if she comes back to you, how she will live versus how she wants to live. Based on her experience, being a beautiful, second-fiddle golden retriever is not her choice. The outside beauty is irrelevant compared to the beauty from within. If she becomes a stray, would you judge her unfairly?"

Sadie is testing any change in my moral fiber, and there isn't one yet. I am still locked on ribbons and her morality is about service. We still clash, and it won't work. It is my loss. She has her answer. I am sad pushing her away again while holding tight to my habitual ways. She turns to her new life calling, but reminds me to keep my heart open and know that anytime I think of her she's near. I feel left behind as she moves forward, while I'm stuck in my old ways.

Karla and I discuss Saxon's reincarnation. Saxon's prediction is eighteen months, but his requirement remains for me to heal from my grief. Harboring grief muddies a new beginning.

My assumption is Saxon is returning in Jazzy's upcoming litter. But after two failed attempts to artificially inseminate her, the breeder of the sire has a litter coming in April of the following year. That litter becomes my hope.

Dumping my grief is Saxon's first demand and now is the time get on it. Haunting me is my concern for Jazz assuming my heavy heart, which leads me to contacting Rosie. She is absolutely irate about my lack of commitment and unwillingness to do my own heart work. She tells me what I need to do emotionally for myself during Saxon's visits. I realize I dropped the ball, procrastinated because it wasn't important to me, and wasted her time. Rosie, stepping into my personal space, points her index finger in my face.

"When it came time for you to step up and take personal responsibility for your care, you bailed. Not on me, but on yourself. I believe this is a common pattern, especially for women. I don't have the luxury of hiding behind a professional cloak. What you see is what you get. My hugs, my prayers, my heart are all mine. They are not part of some professional status I get to put on in the morning and take off at the end of the day. Should you choose to stop the pattern of trauma for you and your animals, I will continue to be available. I wish it could happen with sunshine and chocolates, but only hard work, commitment, and courage will bring it to pass. Saxon did his hard heart work. Now do yours. Bolting is not the answer to healing. Where's your personal integrity?"

I've just been blindsided. My intention coming here was about Jazz and turns out to be about me again, as it was taking Saxon to Grace Angel. Both dogs worked on my behalf to dig out the root causes. Both were a bridge for me to release the sublayers. All I do is resist their help, brush it off, thinking I don't need help.

Jarring me to pay close attention to the same love-hate relational pattern imposed on Sadie and now with Jazz makes me question why I act the way I do. I am feeling conflicted and intellectually know it's not right.

Jazzy is extremely sensitive. Hers is a wide-open heart. Often, I try appeasing her with a fleeting love pat to her head but am really dismissing her entirely, and she slinks off to hide in a corner, disconnected. I am zeroed in on my computer, strategizing about corporate sales goals to avoid dealing with my inner emotional condition. I persist to avoid grief at all costs. It eats at me, bothers me like an unrelenting insect buzzing in my face whispering, *I'm here let's talk. Can you hear me now?* I want to block it out and try to smash it because it swarms me until I fly off the handle, crying, "Uncle!"

Grief is cyclical. It's back, hunting me down. The harder I resist facing it, the more I am barraged. Dismissal, denial, and compartmentalizing, these tools are crumbling under the pressure of emotions heaving to the surface like a looming volcanic eruption.

Rosie is right. Healing takes courage and hard work. Finally reaching a point where my need to heal crushes the need to run away, I begin to succumb. Facing the suffering I've encountered along a road of self-destructive patterns, listening to the inner-critic loop, lies, and confronting the consequences of habituating tell me it's time to change.

Is it better for me to consult a therapist who can prescribe antidepressants or to take the faith's path? Drugs numb the problem. The roots remain tied tight. Taking the path of faith, I must face the unaltered truth. It is a rough and tumble road diggin' up the past, but it yields peace and drugs don't.

My true self is gaining ground over the false self as I find a nondenominational church for help. Their slogan is etched in the foyer: "Wherever you are on your journey of life, we will meet you there and accept you as you are to help you find Jesus."

Walking in broken, cautious, and alone, exposing my vulnerability, I am threatened by fear's voices that warn me about reaching out for help. I choose a seat in the far back corner by the door so I can bolt in an instant. I hope no one sees my disheveled condition as I cry through the service. The old gospel songs bring the vision of me and my mother at the piano together. I cry harder.

I feel a sense of belonging in a place that offers safe harbor and solace to my aching heart, an atmosphere of unconditional love. The Holy Spirit fills this place. Each time I leave I feel spiritually fed. I have found a place to disentangle myself.

Attending the Saturday evening services, I gather that God designs messages aimed to remodel my heart. The message series focuses on self-destructive behaviors including matters of the heart and how it is physically affected by harboring anger, shame, resentment, jealousy, guilt, rejection, contempt, revenge, betrayal, and grief—all the behaviors attached to unforgiveness and emotional abuse.

It's in Pastor's messages that I reach a new realization, as he addresses futile survival mechanisms, which he refers to as our lizard brain, certainly a good description of how I am living most of my life. Pastor calls it emotional abuse. It never occurs to me, as someone raised in an emotionally abusive home. Living that way seemed normal. The behaviors and role models were to be accepted, never questioned. The confluence induced codependency. So why should I have considered myself abused even though the traumas I experienced emotionally derailed me across my life? Finally it has a name. My body remembers but my mind is amnestic to the traumatic events.

Finding out the root causes sets me back, asking why I was born into an abusive family and stirring up many victimizing moments. I learn that my grief isn't primarily about losing Saxon and Sadie. They are instead catalysts to opening a deeper hole inside me. Every time I think it is about someone else, I'm spun around to face myself in the mirror.

In the two years since my dogs died, I've been a recluse, feeling hopeless and lost. Grief stares directly in my face. My life is murky, foggy, and complicated. Most times, it is full of self-orchestrated chaos for the sake of being busy and in motion. Fear takes over. I am bolting and hiding from the truth, disconnecting and powering through pain.

Grief is God's pressure cooker. How one bears up under external pressures depends upon the amount of faith stored within. A person, like a clay jar, will crack if left empty.

Drawing a mental picture of my animal angels sitting together, watching me from above and waiting, I hear them say, *Lordy, Lordy, why is she prolonging the pain in her heart? Why does she complicate everything? Her denial blocks a greater plan.* Animals have a different understanding of dying than humans. For them death is another dimension of existence and interconnectedness. The transition is much easier for animals than it is for humans, who, in our small-mindedness, struggle to let go.

Diggin' Through Rubble

A friend once said to me as I was struggling to find a soul purpose. "The answers to your questions are within. Only you know those answers." As a child brainwashed to distrust my own thoughts and rely on others' opinions, everybody else was right, I was wrong, and my thoughts didn't count. To this day, trusting myself is a dubious proposition that dismantles my confidence.

Rosie was my catalyst to pick up the pen and discover who I am.

"Journal," she said.

The first time sitting with pen and paper produced nothing. Writing was always an embarrassing academic handicap.

But at this point in my life, I had to try and I did. My first crack at it was confusing and jostled the "me" inside. It reflected how disjointed my life was. What I wrote, just like my thinking, was scattered, illogical, off-kilter, and fragmented. Nothing flowed. Wide mood swings and a feeling of hopelessness overwhelmed my ability to express what I wanted to say. That's how broken I was. It proved easier to go on living a super-ficial illusion, skimming the surface, and skirting the real issues rather than facing the truth. There it was like vomit, in front of me, on paper and I wrote it. Writing dredged up what was in my heart, unraveled the abnormal life I lived and the hidden trauma layered beneath the surface was now becoming real. Diggin' up stuff set off a chain reaction of more questions than answers, more whys, hows, and what ifs. It left me lost and more messed up.

The emotional upheavals over a lifetime affected my physical heart. During an annual checkup, I was diagnosed with early-stage hypertension, which alarmed me because I know it can cause heart disease, a stroke, and a host of other maladies. The medical pronouncement was a spiritual warning that I have heart work to do. As I likened Saxon's tumor to my unhealthy condition, I realized the depths he went to in showing me through his illness my own. Bolting was not going to heal this wounded heart; I needed a heart overhaul.

Nothing was off limits. I would be diggin' into faith. All complementary esoteric healing methods and spiritual paths, including the church, were potential resources.

My exploration began with a shaman teacher, Mary Stoffel, from Isanti, Minnesota, who led group classes on past-life readings. Shamanism first originated in Siberia and is practiced in many ancient cultures. There's a belief of animism, that every living thing has a spirit. Shamans connect to an upper spirit world to raise the conscious. Shamans are visionary healers. Because the soul escapes to the spirit world, a shaman's ability is required to retrieve soul parts. I enrolled in a couple of her classes and had a private session on discovering my past-life connections with Saxon and Sadie.

She explained that both Saxon and Sadie have been with me through multiple generations. Saxon is part of my soul group, helping all in the group lift their souls' vibration and consciousness as we attempt to resolve accumulated, unfinished business of our past lives. He is a master teacher, operating on both sides of the veil. He walks beside me in body and spirit. Souls both human and animal, good and bad were in my life, and served a particular purpose to kick start my spiritual growth.

Being both enlightened and confused, again, led to more questions than answers. Curiosity inspires an intense searching.

Learning that Mary had just published her book about shamanism inspired me to tell my story. She put me in touch with the woman who assisted her, Montana Grey.

I called Montana to introduce myself and the basis for giving structure to my journaling. Montana lived in Loveland, Colorado, so our working relationship was done by phone. We talked and I quickly understood her to be a spiritually elevated life coach and a skilled seer past the veil of her own experience, psychic trauma, and soul loss. Anger raged inside her still. She spoke openly of her verbal berating, shaming, and having been sexually abused. The more I listened, the more I saw how her story resembled mine. Like me, she had a father who shunned her and abused her animals. It's the nature of two abused people to bond with one another. We developed a friendship of trust and a professional relationship. It was Montana who shot me onto a higher spiritual plane to resolve my grief and heal.

Her reading of Saxon smacked me against the wall. What Saxon said about me was a gut punch.

She doesn't have time for me anymore. I can't get through to her. She's scattered and in constant motion. She can't be still. I don't matter to her. I'm knocking and nobody is answering.

My guilt and shame flared up. I covered my face with my hands. I accused Saxon of having the wrong perspective on me as I deflected responsibility and blamed him. My actions and rationalization inflicted emotional pain on him. Even though in my mind, he was my complete focus, I was just not listening. Being consumed by immense grief smothered the voices of God and Saxon.

When Saxon identified how blocking was second nature to me and how my restlessness was self-destructive, I was rattled by his message but could no longer deny what he was trying to convey to me was true. It shifted me into gear to learn another animal communication modality. I found an organization called Healing Touch for Animals®, offering classes for energy healing of animals. I signed up for a weekend seminar in Chicago. Jazzy came along.

I soon learned how to balance and clear off a negative energy field and restore positive energy to the body. I also learned how to evaluate a dog's energy by using a pendulum. By deep breathing techniques, I was able to become centered. I came to understand what Sadie and Jazz had been trying to teach me about being still and quiet. One of my classmates was a woman named Linda who attended with Angel, her huskie. We were paired in an exercise to sense each other's aura, the distance our electromagnetic field extended.

"Wow! Six feet," Linda said. The normal was three. Well, that was fun and interesting, but I wasn't sure how useful it could be and where in my life this would apply. The rest of the weekend we were taught about a dog's chakras—centers of spiritual power in Hindu and Buddhist tradition—and the use of a pendulum to determine their functionality. This new insight distracted me away from my grief and planted an awareness in me of how a toxic environment and human emotions affect our dogs. Maybe that's all it was supposed to do then. A purpose was served that would advance my soul's growth.

Even as my manufactured distractions and excuses faded, grief brush-blocked me at every step saying, "Hello, can you hear me now? I'm not leaving until you do something to flush me out." Such an annoyance.

Grief has stalked me like wolf's prey, until I buckle. I'm overwhelmed. How do I hurdle the death of my two dogs? How do I go back through an entire childhood and relive abuse and find healing? How do I lay all this out for the world to see and not be judged? Where does the courage to begin come from? While I built walls around me, I never learned how to construct safe boundaries. Life has rules, protocols, cultural mores, and conditions. I get jumbled and wonder how I can walk through each day, appearing normal and performing normally to earn a living while I am emotionally defective and spiritually bankrupt? It is agonizing to be communicating spiritually with God and Saxon in search of a middle ground for my internal grief while functioning in a corporate world where my moral compass and core values are tested daily. I feel like Rodney Atkins is advising me when he sings, "When you're going through hell, keep on going." I have a choice to stay stuck or move through it. "Survival," my mind tells me.

Change is scary. The voices from the past chatter, "Don't do it." I worry if I ask for help I must be a stupid, deranged weakling. I struggle spiritually, feeling threatened, keeping God at arm's length, never allowing Him to come closer. My finite mind is my stumbling block. Despite what God sees in my heart and the number of times He has delivered faith through prayer and miracles, so much is still intangible and maybe even a figment of my imagination. My difficulty is surrendering to an unseen entity, believing His way is better than mine, and having enough faith and belief to know it is real and stronger than me.

I am ashamed of my small-mindedness. I admit I am at the end of myself. My pigheadedness envisions Christ and me standing on the edge of the cliff with a gorge between us. My mind is unable to see the bridge, but Christ's outstretched, compassionate hand offers the bridge to eternal life if I trust and believe. The decision to walk across it or stay where I am tests my faith. Do I trust Him?

"Come take my hand." God assures me it is safe to trust.

"Lord, I fear falling to the depths."

"I will catch you or teach you to fly. Trust my words. Fix your eyes on me and cross over. Leave the past behind. On this side you will find healing, forgiveness, and peace like no other." Recalling the times I was at life's edge, He caught me just before the fall.

Premonitions of my future light up during my dreams. God understands my human nature, my need for tangibility, and the "what's in it for me" factor in my decision. My dreams are multidimensional. I can foresee my soul's longing fulfilled when I will no longer be living a life of selfish ambition. I weigh the risks, have hope, and am assured the hard heart and emotional work is worth it. But the first step is the biggest, and it's one I'm not quite ready to take as fear holds me back.

I'm a "to-do list" person. I put priorities in chronological order. My top priority is locking in Saxon's reincarnation. Farther down the list is dealing with my childhood trauma and grief. Sitting on the step of the back deck of my home, I look up at the sky and my eyes lock on the brightest, pulsating star, Sirius. I use the techniques taught in the animal-communication class to quiet and center myself. I look inside to feel my heart's emotions. I'm leaning toward trusting faith.

Saxon is larger in spirit than in life. I begin my conversation with him like a prayer, intent on serving the highest good and not my will. Sitting reverently in silence, my heart asks Saxon to be with me. I bow my head and tears flow. I see Saxon at the edge of Heaven's tunnel, looking down on me, lying with his paws crossed, ears perked. He is listening like a counselor and best friend. My first words to him are, "Saxon, I miss you and I love you." His silence continues. I tremble and weep. He is compassionate and patient. I am calm. Being together and feeling the other's presence brings contentment. We both realize how much we miss one another

I close my quiet time with Saxon, praying, "Thank you, God, for giving me more than nine years with Saxon. Thank you for showing me your great love and mercy through him. If it is your will to renew his life with me, please bring him back and show us your purpose in a new life together again. Amen."

Coming into the house, I find Jazzy lying by the back door, patiently waiting. She understands what just happened outside. I know she knows it instinctively. Yielding and walking through grief, knowing I am safe, and not alone, I empty my eyes and heart to Saxon and pray to God. My lamentations continue until I am physically limp. A layer of grief is lifted. Spiritual support allows me to slowly heal.

The clock is ticking down on eighteen months before Saxon's reincarnation. So it means speeding up the healing process. Grief doesn't meet deadlines or bend to my demands. It will take its time and have its way. Saxon's impatience demands I spread his ashes before he reveals himself in the April litter. He drives a hard bargain.

Our conversations are banter.

"Can't let you go."

You must.

"I can't just open your urn and throw you to the wind. This feels wrong." Intellectually, I know he is right. But where is the right resting place?

I don't belong locked up and preserved. You are holding me back and preventing me from helping you eliminate unconscious generational behaviors that hold you back. Is that what you really want? I can't help you if you can't help yourself.

Crying, flailing my arms, and pacing around, I tell him, "There is so much I never said to you that I need to say now. Your death shattered my foundation. My life is in fragments. Brain fog and mental malfunction prevent me from hearing you. My heart is blocked. Expecting me to have a clear mind in the midst of tragedy is unrealistic . . ." But he interrupts me.

Since you realize all of this, why can't you let go to have a better life? Maybe your old thinking tells you that you don't deserve a better life.

He's right, yet I deflect his remark. I twist it as being sarcastic. This is a common trait of abuse is to hang onto the artificial, manufactured barriers that justify actions.

Wanting to have it my way reflects childish belligerence, anger, and resistant reaction. I shift away the subject of our conversation, in my favor.

"Saxon, I've been in contact with a breeder in Tennessee. I trust you will be there. Please help me decide who you are in the litter."

You will know me when you see me. I will not show you until you release my ashes and my spirit from the urn. There it was again. No wiggle room.

"You are asking the impossible. The act of releasing your ashes is symbolic to completely opening a wounded heart and letting years of heartache spill out."

That is exactly my point for you. I'm glad you've come to that conclusion, finally.

"This could destroy me or completely free me of my demons. It's a painful decision. I am not sure my faith is strong enough to sustain stirring up those traumatic events and let it all go. It's so much of who I am."

What have you got to lose? Helping you is the reason I chose you. Remember, it is about the greater good and being spiritually elevated. You have heart work. It is up to you now to serve your purpose in this life. I'm not bending until you comply.

It's been more than sixty years since I sat in the old pine tree as a child, wondering what my life's purpose was. That question remains unanswered. But Saxon gives me his advice.

Strength and blessing will come. Trust this.

The pressure on me to open and release his ashes creates a conundrum. I keep thinking how broken I am, and the unraveling is just beginning.

After the puppies are born, the breeder sends pictures on a weekly basis, showing three males and three females. Even though it's customary for a breeder to get first pick, I ask for it. But my request is denied. The breeder marks the males orange, black, and blue-green. As the puppies grow from week to week, she keeps asking me which one I want. There was time to think, but not much.

Coming to Terms

When I was a child, my mother read the scriptures to us daily. We memorized them in Sunday school. Those verses come to me now. I hear my mother say, "Lay your burdens at the cross and be healed." That message is where my heart and soul have led me. I remember Ma playing gospel songs on the piano and singing, "At the cross, at the cross where I first saw the light, all the burdens of my heart rolled away. It was there by faith, I received my sight, and now I am happy all my days." The words describe a regenerative life, a life of self-initiation.

In Eau Claire, three crosses stand on a rugged hillside near the Calvary church on a dead-end road. It is dusk on Good Friday. I drive to the three crosses that eerily occupy the hill. The wind howls mysteriously as it swirls between the crosses and pushes rolling, gray clouds in the overcast sky above. Holding the oak urn, I walk to the foot of the crosses. I stand before them and feel the Holy Spirit's presence. I drop to my knees in humble brokenness and weep. The mist dampens my face, mingling with my tears. Wind gusts flatten the prairie grass around the crosses and press my mind to give all this to God. The site bears the feel of the crucifixion and causes my heart to bleed. I am humble and emotionally naked in Christ's sight. I gain strength and courage, trusting that I will be liberated. I kneel before the cross, face to face with God. Here, there are no lies, no dogma, and no excuses or blaming, just honesty as God sees all. Honesty is what Saxon was demanding of me. I bow my head and feel Christ's hand touching me and God's angels surrounding me. I am supported in love. Submissively as a dog belly-crawls on all fours, I say, "Your child is here, God."

In the distance stands the essence of my parents, jointly cheering me on to find forgiveness and to heal from the inside out. Surfacing and accepting that I have a wounded heart, sorrow wells up in my throat and pours out of my eyes.

I reach for help. The word "weakling" can no longer inflict pain on me. I look up at the crosses and pray, "God, I am here. I am listening. I'm damaged and broken and at the end of myself. You've brought me to my knees. Help me through this. Thank you for your gift of life, the mercy, the patience, and grace you show me daily, even in my unwillingness to listen. God, I know you know this: Were it not for my dogs and their unconditional love, I never would have understood the meaning of love and survived. Through their gift, dear God, you showed me a sampling of your great love and the great sacrifice Christ made. I might not have come here today were it not for your Spirit bidding. You've proved over and again to trust you."

I feel the presence of Saxon and Sadie holding a space of love for me. "Saxon, I am here with God and in prayer surrendering because of you. You lived a life teaching by example."

Layer by layer my truth becomes visible. I am now intentionally leaning into the truth and starting to let go even as I still cling to Saxon's ashes. It's a fierce internal struggle to transcend old beliefs. The fearful mind incarcerates us. It holds us to what is familiar and shackles us from stepping away.

"Dear God, give me strength to open and empty this sorrowful, guilty heart, setting both Saxon and me free." Then I hear Saxon.

I love you and I am always with you as God is with you.

A sampling of peace enters my heart. What a strange contrast to chaos. Pure love. Sitting for a few more minutes, I reflect on what just happened and the depth of this experience. I marvel how great a God we have and how we are a speck in comparison. Why do we think we can control anything and have the results that God produces?

Heading back to the car, I pause, and look back at the crosses. I say to Saxon, "If I release your ashes, I fear losing you completely."

There is more to this than the physical. It is a spiritual love that transcends any love known to humanity. It requires forgiveness.

"But my heart needs more time before I can come to terms with your request."

You have some time, but you need to act or your opportunity is lost.

The Broken Seal

In a darkened living room lit by a candle, I am seated, rocking in a chair, with Jazz at my feet. I stare at Saxon's picture on the hearth, contemplating opening the urn to release his ashes. His eyes stare back at me.

"I know being sealed in a wooden box is not where you want to be. You are free and want the same for me."

As I say this, I realize how much I need to have control. But I am building up gumption and coming to terms with opening his urn, regardless of how excruciating it will be. I put Jazzy in the bedroom for her emotional protection and my privacy.

Broken and shattered, now sitting lotus-style on the floor, in anguish and in tears, I place his urn directly in front of me. His essence materializes. There he lies, confidently facing me. His eyes and glowing golden coat form a commanding presence in the room. My hands wrap around his urn as I hold it close to my heart. The urn tingles from his energy. His essence presses my conscience, pleading to be released.

Let me go!

My heart bleeds red with each turn of the screw. Trembling, I am hardly able to hold the screwdriver. Tears splash on the plastic bag inside that contains his ashes.

"Please, Saxon, come sit beside me. I can't do this without you."

I pray for God's strength. This is more than opening an urn. I am aware of the symbolism of uprooting a lifetime of wounds stored throughout my body. I recognize the learned survival behaviors that fed my false self. This needs to be done, but not all tonight.

"I will spread a few of your ashes by the war cross in my backyard. Then I will find the final place where you will have complete peace and interconnectedness with nature, and the rest will be released."

Saxon agrees to that. Kneeling in front of the war cross, I take a pinch of his ashes and scatter them. It's a first step toward healing.

Wiping tears from my face, I feel another presence. I look back at the house. Jazzy is sitting there. She has an uncanny ability to open doors using her nose and paw. Her wisdom far exceeds mine. I realize no walls can separate us. Her compassionate stare and deep resolve indicate she completely understands this moment. She is there for me. It's just who she is, my beautiful bridge.

One more week before picking my puppy. How do I decide the right one? My answers come using the pendulum, learned from my energy-healing class. Clockwise means yes and counterclockwise means no. Testing this before I start, I hold the pendulum over Saxon's ashes. Circling clockwise validates that his energy is present in the urn.

Astonished, I put his ashes in my hand. I feel prickly sparks. I cannot believe this is possible. Again, I hold the pendulum over his ashes and the same clockwise centrifugal force circles. Saxon's presence is undeniable and leaves me breathless. This is no coincidence. It broadens my understanding of the vast spiritual world.

In my bedroom, with his ashes in my hand, I visualize us sitting on the floor as I held Saxon before he died. I lean into his energy to feel that same energy in the litter. I am honored that he considered coming back to me.

"How will I know which puppy you are?" I ask repeatedly. The pendulum above his urn circles clockwise. Instantly "blue-green" comes to mind.

"His name?"

After the brightest blue star.

"Sirius."

The pendulum stops and hangs still. He disappears.

Sirius

Saxon was right. I know him when I see him. During the temperament test, he is the only puppy who looks up to the ceiling. I instantly know Saxon is in the room. That is the final confirmation and thumbs-up. His call name is Sirius (Siri). His registered name is Passion's All Star's He's a High Flyer.

After the test is complete, Sirius is carried outside the building and set on the ground. I stand back in awe of him. I watch him sit quietly as he surmises the huge world and calmly watches birds flying high in the sky. He sits there, as if put on a new stage, ready to embark on a grand adventure. I feel his inner strength and wisdom. He is grounded, confident, independent, and well-balanced. This is a new start in a big world, and to me the moment is surreal.

Siri gazes to the heavens as his earthly assignment is delivered. This new life is not about stacking up ribbons; it's about continuing my regeneration, harmony, and serving the greater good.

I'm not there yet. I'm still stuck in my old nature, and I see Siri as a great prospect for a triple-performance champion in show, obedience, and field. I'm bending to the breeder's influence, just as I did with Sadie as I again listen to other people's wishes. Siri gets a rocky start. Breaking his moment of silence, he comes to me in a very sensible wise manner, looking me in the eye, implying, *I am ready. Let's go.* Respect is apparent.

We arrive home and alone. Jazzy is with Sue, so Siri can acquaint himself to his new surroundings. Well, he needs no introduction to the house. After I take him out of his in-flight Sherpa bag, he has his bearings immediately. He scampers down the hallway, runs into my office, and comes tearing back to me. Sitting front and center at my feet, he looks directly into my eyes. In his mouth, he holds a single playing card from a standard deck, the king of hearts. I didn't realize there were any playing cards in my office. How did he know about them? His message flies right over my head. It had to be something about the heart. He was the next teacher sent to help me finish healing my heart.

Not accepting him for who he is, I've imposed Saxon's persona on Siri. Sue strongly suggests I have his heart checked at eight weeks of age by a board-certified cardiologist. The concern is over a possible heart murmur. I have him checked, and a slight grade one or two is found. Even though it could be common at this age, I am more tuned-in now than before to matters of the heart. It is God's reminder about finishing my heart work. If I don't, I'm going to have another ill dog.

There was no escaping my promise to Saxon, but the thought crossed my mind now that I've obtained the puppy with minimal output. I could weasel out and not spread Saxon's ashes. Then guilt sets in at the thought of a breached contract. Saxon would know. He expected honesty. What would be the consequences for my unfaithfulness? There'd be nowhere to hide because he follows me. God would know too. From that moment on, my level of integrity changed. I made a conscious first step to resist the temptation of any embellishments, fibs to others and myself, and be accountable for my thoughts and actions. Truth matters.

Love is what Saxon taught me. He supported me. I got what I prayed for, yet I'm having an awful time letting go of habits that hold me back. Fear is more familiar than joy. Am I worth the effort? Do I deserve to be loved? What does joy feel like? What do I do with joy?

Letting go means more than releasing Saxon and Sadie. It is a transcendence. It involves rewiring the mental and emotional triggers that tell me I am not worthy and do not deserve respect or love. I hear in my mind my sister's voice echoing, "You're pathetic. You deserve to be alone the rest of your life." Her shaming words make me shrink and feel invisible.

Siri isn't allowed to be Siri. He's overshadowed, constantly compared to Saxon. Expecting higher standards from him out of the gate, I drive him to be perfect. With Siri, I'm beginning where I left off with Saxon's hard-driving Master Hunter training. In doing that, I'm renouncing Siri's true self for what I want him to be. As a result, his confidence suffers. Insecurities take over, which compromises our bond. He's being pulled down emotionally and forced to live a false self as a direct reflection of me. My old nature gets passed along to the next generation of dogs.

Siri comes from an excellent pedigree of show dogs. He is handsomely structured. The breeder's strong influence swayed me into putting him in the show ring at seven months old. My conscience nags me to back off, but I disregard it. He earns his first obedience title in rally, a preliminary to the novice class of obedience.

But Siri displays disruptive, unruly, and rude behavior. He resists. I think he is testing my leadership but, really, he's teaching me to face my inner fears and see my truth. He wants me to recognize that his love is sitting at my feet and doesn't have to be earned. The concept is foreign to me. I dismiss his message and ramp up the pressure to perform. He doesn't want to be pushed into the conformation ring to earn ribbons.

While chasing birds is instinctive, he is expected to do Master Hunter marks going straight in and out from the water. The force-fetch process is done. He is collar-conditioned. Performance! Performance! Performance! It's all about me and my identity.

Saxon reminds me that my grieving needs to stop now that I have Siri. But I'm stuck in my rut, so Saxon finds another way to make his point. In a dog-training program I'm watching on TV, the trainer explains that carrying over grief of your deceased animals and projecting onto the present animal is unfair, will cause problems with your relationship, and lead to chaos. Dogs view your ongoing grief as lack of leadership and a weakness in the pack. If no one leads they will. Hmmmm, Siri's unruliness.

This suggests that healing the past strengthens a relationship and builds confidence in the pack. Animals view grief differently than humans. They know when to move on. Being anchored in grief threatens their existence. If they detach from the interconnectedness of the world, death is certain. Animals live interdependently. They can let go and move on. Humans drag it out. They may never let go. For dogs, life is transitional and about heart. Humans are encased in a stiff-necked, resistant hard-wired mind, living separate from an interconnected world.

The trainer calls my attention to exactly what I am doing to Siri and Jazz. This needs to stop. They aren't the problem. I am. They, in their own ways, are showing me an image of myself.

Siri's ridiculous, erratic behavior escalates. It pokes at my irritations. His growling, pacing, whining, and physically charging me reflect my erratic frenzy. On a dime, he turns tail to chase butterflies, which has the effect of making me go from anger to laughter. Manic episodes. Silly smart dog!

It's wrong to isolate and carry the burdens alone. I ask for help in order to break learned childhood patterns. I hear God's voice from within. "Let go of your grief." The choice to reach out and accept His help is mine.

"Walking Through Grief" is Pastor's message series. He speaks about the importance of belonging and support from small groups and community, which is vital to healing. It is as if God is sitting in the back row with folded arms across His chest, eyes on my back, watching my reactions, and providing the opportunity for me to take a next step toward healing. This is my chance to move away from destructive thinking, to stop resisting.

This is the prayer from Pastor's sermon: "Holy Spirit, Jesus sent you to walk with me and speak with me. You are the great giver of perspective and clarity. Create in me the mind of Christ that I may see things clearly as Christ sees them. Give me His eyes and the courage to look at and understand things as they really are, especially in me. Give me a proper focus and healthy attitude. In Jesus' name, Amen."

There it is again: living in the present. The message captures my attention. My mind turns on, opening instead of bolting. And I listen. Pastor hammers home the importance of sharing your pain with others. It is time to concede that if I share my pain in a room full of strangers, new doors can open and healing can happen. I want that in my life.

The many years of hearing the messages of turning my faith to God and letting Him guide my life hit home. It isn't a doctrine or dogma; it is a meaningful way to live differently. Grief is part of the healing process. It exercises a faith discipline through prayer. This is where I form healthy boundaries and solid morals, values, and virtues that were compromised. The creation of a clean heart and clear mind builds resilience in me. God wants strong souls who are solid people and leaders. That is one of the reasons I believe He doesn't fix everything for us. We are meant to struggle for our faith to become durable, to stand strong in the wake of evil, and not cave under pressure or the influence of others. The false teachings and lies from childhood about not having a voice, not deserving love, feeling guilty, and being demeaned need to be erased. I am ashamed and scared.

I need to summon courage to attend a grief support group. When I walk into the room, Amy, the group leader, greets me with open arms, kindness, acceptance, compassion, and a loving heart. We chat. Then Amy asks me, "Who have you lost?"

The wound is still fresh. Tears stream down my face. I feel embarrassed when I shouldn't be. My body's impulse is to run and hide. The old self is shaking in my shoes. But this is a safe place. For once, it is okay to cry and not be ridiculed or lambasted. Love is present.

"My loss was not a human, but rather my two animal angels, Saxon and Sadie." I don't volunteer much more information. I know that most people there lost a human family member. I am not sure if they would accept my loss. "My emotional foundation is fractured. My dogs were my family."

Here, I'm not alone in my pain. When I hear the others' stories about relatives who were murdered or committed suicide, I see that I can offer them comfort while gaining the support of community. A sense of relief and peace relaxes me. I have found what I craved my whole life. Belonging!

At home that evening, Siri and Jazzy recognize my sense of peace and settle down. What a contrast from Siri's earlier rude behavior. His unrest subsides. Going forward, their behavior will be my emotional gauge.

The Heart Surrenders

The spiritual signs and nudges prevailed. Saxon tells me so.

It is time, and you need to release us. Not for us, but for you.

My mind is racing and my body is hurting. Torn between letting go and hanging on, I struggle to find the right resting place.

In my dreams, I see where to bring Sadie's and Saxon's ashes. They will fly with the wind's updraft high upon the rolling hills south of Eau Claire. Our spirits can comingle there.

Three years after Saxon's death, stuffing it isn't working. My gut rolls and twists like intermittent dry heaves wanting to burst through the surface

The December snowfall has not come. Driving out to the site, standing atop the hillside, I try to feel the spiritual nature fitting their freedom and joy. Siri and Jazzy join me, chasing each other up and down the hill. They are free and happy here.

I can see forever in all directions. It is peaceful as the wind sweeps across the hilltops. It can lift and twirl their spirits, dancing and playing, intertwined in the updrafts toward Heaven. The wisp of the wind across my face whispers. They're saying,

Do it! It's perfect! This is a place you can visit anytime. Most of all, this is a place where we played and where you can continue to play with us.

The owners gave me permission to train on these hills. Now I need their permission to release the ashes.

"Would it be all right if I release Saxon's and Sadie's ashes on the far hill overlooking the valley of your property? It would mean so much to me and to them to be in a lovely place such as yours." I can't hold the tears back. Their response is soothing.

"We would be honored," Jerry says.

"I love watching your dogs run the hills as you train," Jeanne adds. "I am amazed at what they can do."

They understand my grief because the ashes of their Max rest out there. They are reliving the loss of their beautiful Saint Bernard.

"Like you, it took us three years to have the courage to spread his ashes."

Realizing I am not alone in grieving for as long I have grieved gives me comfort.

Jeanne tells me how she decided on this place. "Max didn't want to be confined to a box any longer. He wanted to be released with nature and move on." I can almost hear the words of Saxon.

I visualize the importance of the ashes being released and how that equates to my heart finding peace. It is both a spiritual and physical release from my body.

"Max was a big dog with a big heart, and keeping him in a box was not his style," Jeanne says. "Carrying the pain in my heart became unbearable. Pain was an addiction for my body and I sought out pain by taking on other people's emotional baggage. The cycle needed to stop." This was the same for me.

Jeanne recalls the conversation she had with Max, when she told him, "Max, today, we release you."

She and Jerry explain how they are at peace with their decision and understand this was also Max's wish.

Knowing Saxon wanted the same gave me serenity. This feels right. Any smidgen of doubt disappears when Jeanne describes how bald eagles soar over the hills. I'm confident this is where my two beloved friends will fly and dance. My decision is made. This is their final resting place. In my mind I hear them agree.

"Max's spirit still dances on the hills and he would love company," Jeanne says happily. This brings her back to the day they released Max's ashes. "It was one of the coldest, blustery days in January. Snow was up to our hips as we carried him to the hilltop. We opened Max's urn and released him to the wind and blessed him in a prayer, 'We love you and will always miss you.' When we returned to the house, this came on the radio. Vince Gill's song, 'Go Rest High.' Max's message let us know he was okay and we should be okay too."

God uses people to help others along their spiritual path. He certainly has done so here. I had to do this. It was for Jeanne and Jerry, and for me.

To be certain, on a Sunday afternoon, Siri, Jazzy, and I return to the hilltop. Armed with Frisbees ready to frolic and to go for a long walk on the land, I pause on the high ground. I stand in silence with my dogs. I turn to the four directions, feeling the breeze wash over my body. This wind speaks to my soul. I listen for a response from Saxon and Sadie letting me know that this is the ideal spot for this final ceremonial release. God's beauty abounds in these hills.

I envision the sunrises and sunsets. I know the ground will be beneath a blanket of snow that will create a rare quiet. I can picture fall's colorful canvas of leaves and magnificent rainbows in summer. On this day, eagles soar, Canada geese honk, and sand cranes do a flyover saluting God's masterpiece. I can visit this place and be one in spirit. Yes, this is the right spot.

I am nudged to proceed with the ceremony. Leaving my resistance behind and accepting the moment of reality, I drive back to the house and prepare the music.

I want to be certain that I am not undertaking an irresponsible knee-jerk act I'd talked myself into and will later be sorry for. I call Montana telling her of my decision. No answer. She calls back just as I arrive. She's frantic. "Are you absolutely sure? Will this give you peace? You have to be sure."

She reminds me this is for my soul's healing and not Sadie's and Saxon's. "They are free. They were present each moment they lived with you. You weren't. They were the faith you needed. Have you reached the point of not creating more pain for yourself and feel you are worthy to be loved?"

Her words remind me that Rosie had asked the same questions: "Are you ready to receive love, to have trust, and to find peace in your heart? You're hanging onto a lifetime of pain, abuse, disrespect, shame, guilt, unworthiness, and failed relationships."

I give Montana my pledge that this feels right and today is the right time.

Recognizing my need to tear down my own barriers delivers a victory for Sadie and Saxon. This is what they were teaching me in body and spirit. Clarity comes with knowing it was me standing in my own way to a heart and a life free from the same patterns that had controlled my mind and kept me stuck. Yes, this means a major shift for the present and years to come.

I ready myself to release Saxon and Sadie before the sun sets. Walking up the hill, I pray earnestly that God blesses these next few moments. I ask for and visualize the presence of Saxon and Sadie surrounding me and helping me relieve my pain and know joy as I dance with them in the wind swirling across the landscape. I ask their essence to materialize as the air currents carry their ashes away. But there is no wind. My mind takes over. I am uneasy and fretting. How will they be lifted? I don't want to just drop their ashes. They have to float toward Heaven with the wind. It's the way I planned it.

Happily, when I reach the hilltop, the wind is south prevailing. Dusk is near. The candle in the lantern is lit. The laptop is up and running and the CD is inserted. Most of all, the covers on the urns have been loosened.

Standing silently, I wait, breathing in God's beauty and the splendor of the moment. I pray that this ceremony is of the highest good, so that my dogs are free from the entrapment I created for them and myself. This signifies a fresh start: Learning to trust versus mistrust, deserving love and joy versus pain, accepting being in the present versus an altered mental state. I visualize my animals applauding with their paws, spinning in circles, and joyfully barking their approval with a few high fives.

Boy, she was slow on the uptake. Took forever to get around to this, but she finally got it.

They made their point. Humans are slow to change because the fear in their minds won't allow it. We stand in our own way.

The radiant sun's final descent tells me its time.

"You Raise Me Up" by Josh Groban, "Thank You" by Ray Bolz, "Go Rest High on That Mountain," by Vince Gill, and Alan Jackson's "Precious Memories," "I'll Fly Away," and "The Old Rugged Cross" play in the background as I gently take a small handful of Saxon's ashes and sprinkle him to the wind. He is sent into the four directions. A Native American ceremony and the spiritual significance of the four directions enter my mind. Turning to the west indicates end of life and also the direction from which water comes. North represents the trials one must endure and the strong cold winds that cleanse. East signifies new life. South is the direction of warmth and growth where the soul enters through the Milky Way and returns home. The green is the blessing of the earth and nourishment. The sky is for the Great Spirit that oversees all as the eagle soars across the blue.

Next I take Sadie's ashes and lift her to the four winds, blessing her life and assuring her that we will one day dance in Heaven together. Joshua Kadison sings, and "Beautiful in My Eyes" resounds softly across the hillside.

As I release their ashes, I squint in disbelief and rub my eyes to confirm what I see. It is their iridescent spirits that materialize and I am blessed. Drawn to their essence, my soul escapes my body and our spirits entwine and we dance in gaiety just above the hilltop. We spiritually are one with the universe. I feel my pain lift and a wave of overwhelming love and peace flows into my heart. I feel pure love.

God and my animal teachers, who taught me how to live without pain, smile and carry it away! More of life's painful layers will resurface, coming in waves for years to come, but the intensity will lessen with each eruption.

Their wish for me for the rest of my life is that I live with joy and in the moment, and that I remember to play. They urge me: *Don't resist what is in front of you. Accept it and find a way through it. Let go of the weight that tears you down. You can choose to live a different life. Celebrate your freedom. Dance!*

A Seismic Shift

Driving home from the hillside, washing over me, my heart felt a peaceful resolve which before was unfamiliar. Tears of joy flow for me for choosing to claim healthy life patterns. The freshness of knowing I had a choice of freeing an imprisoned heart and fearful mind by relinquishing control to God is percolating its way into my soul. Choice is something I thought I didn't have before. This day, life has taken a shift.

Now it is my mission to bring that message forward, to help others heal and find peace. It's real and a deliberate choice. My mind and my heart are crawling out of prison and seeing daylight through a faith's lens.

Siri and Jazzy are waiting for me at home. It is a quiet, reverent entrance. They realize a humility and calm in me. I sit on the floor with them on either side of me. I notice Sirius looking intently at Saxon's picture on the wall for a few moments. It is as if Saxon communicates to him.

Everything is all right for now. She is at peace for a while until another layer surfaces. You can now take care of her. This is your mission from here on out. Carry on, soldier.

Sirius is Sirius and not Saxon. His behavior has changed! He no longer exhibits anxiety, distress, restlessness, dominance, and abusive acts toward

Jazzy. He is a compassionate, calm, sensitive, and mild-mannered dog acting from the heart.

Jazzy no longer slinks cautiously in fear of flash anger. Her wariness has disappeared. She moves her body proudly. She is bright-eyed and light-hearted. They romp, play-chase, and let go. The chaotic guarded uncertainty is gone. They are relaxed. My home's rearrangement welcomes in harmony to take up residence. It's a fresh start.

My heart still has a lot of unraveling ahead, but I know I am traveling in the right directions. There will be emotional unearthings and a physical release of filtering and letting go. I'll grow stronger and healthier as toxins are shed. I hear Saxon's words.

Keep on diggin'. There's more for you to uncover. It's right in front of your eyes and you don't recognize it.

The culprit of all toxic emotions hides and intermingles through these delivery systems, which are anger, aggression, and most forms of physical and emotional maltreatment. Saxon was hinting that shame is the basis of all abuse. Knowing shame's effects would lead to releasing it from my life. Shame never entered my mind then. I've convinced myself that abuse by my parents and sibling was to blame for the poor life choices I made; a nagging need still exists to uncover more reasons behind the abusive acts. Saxon's words resonate.

Keep writing. The real reason will belch up.

Forgiveness is integral to healing wounds of the past. Here I am at the Evergreen Cemetery east of Medford, Wisconsin. I kneel with my hand on the grave of my father. I have a compassionate heart, knowing his upbringing was harsh and he was once innocent like me. My tears spill for the life my father endured as a child and the abuse that strangled him. His actions as an adult were his own. Emotionally, he was locked in his core, resisting the choice to ever let it go. I now understand why I was violated and why my animals were brutally abused. It was part of the cycle of heritable emotional abuse. He tried to create a new life for himself, just as I was passionate about changing Saxon's aggression.

Before Dad died, his physical body reflected the pain inside. Maybe the energy of my hand on his headstone touched his heart. I feel his soul soften with approval and change so he could begin to heal his soul and know a kind of love he never experienced, the love God provides. Untainted! Pure!

"I love you, Dad." It is the first time since being rejected as a child I could say this and forgive him.

Before I leave his grave, I heard him ask why I am writing my story. I have two answers. The first is, it was never my intent to hurt or blame him, but to help me understand and heal the painful events in my life. I feel liberated by speaking honestly, freely, and not fearfully. The second answer is, I want to help others know that emotional abuse passed along from previous generations can be healed through faith.

My marriages mirrored my parents'. Mine ended in brokenness, while trying to find a loving partner. I did not understand love because my parents didn't show love.

Thinking love had to be bought and paid for was wrong, when, in fact, it is freely and respectfully given. God gave me dogs to teach me what love is and is not.

When my dad died, I was too angry to cry at his funeral. More than thirty-eight years later, I cry for us both. Forgiving him freed me of his past violations that I endured.

Uncovering Shame

It's December 2018. I am struggling to pull my life together, still trying to discover the root cause that spun my life into turmoil. I turn to my care pastor to discuss how I can sort out the factors of emotional abuse.

Near the end of our discussion, she is about to pray when in pops the image of my mother on her death bed. I hear her words and I repeat them to the minister. "Always be kind and pure of heart, and remember, try to get along with your sister." The zinger. This is what Saxon wanted named. This is diggin' down to bedrock, finding the root cause, homing in on the core that led to a destructive life and fragmented soul.

"SHAME!" my care pastor exclaims. "That's shame." The light shines on the root cause. Unconscious transgenerational shame is called out. Instantly, everything across my life lines up. I understand the forms of maltreatment in my failed relationships and the reasons I was drawn to other abused people. Like me, they grew up in a shame-based family. We each had what the other needed to exist.

The behaviors imposed on my dogs, living from ego versus heart, the need to perform, chasing ribbons, having to prove myself in order to restore my lost identity, these are all learned patterns that my dogs suffered through. Forcing Saxon to achieve ribbons at all cost was done to bolster my identity and emptiness, even if it meant sacrificing his health. The real culprit was shame. The façade masking shame was avoiding and denying, feeling unworthy, unwanted, and rejected. Bitterness and anger were always at the surface, yet the need to be included or accepted was a constant longing. But there before my mind's eye it was revealed. The connection became real and toxic. I then realized there are two sides of shame: toxic and healthy. We are born with healthy shame that protects; toxic shame destroys us. The difference for those who heal is faith. It's the hope for a brighter future versus being stuck in a fearful, dismal past.

My thoughts and actions that once controlled me no longer do. My heart operates from a place of compassion, and love for people and animals and for God serving and building people up. The choice to leave the "out there" for the "in here" becomes a no man's land. Through the wanderings, a transformation emerges freeing the mind as the soul rises and shines.

This is my new way of thinking, feeling, and living as I walk in His light. But this doesn't mean happy every after. Healing and struggle is evolutionary and part of the faith process, to build a spiritual resilience.

Unexpectedly, as Pastor speaks about shame, my anger and resentment resurface toward Ma because her words held me hostage as I tried to make things right with my sister and made to feel it was all my fault all these years. Ma dismissed it as kids being kids and never considered maltreatment of an older sibling. For years, it haunted me, trying to mend feelings, when it wasn't mine to mend. Blame rolled downhill. I was faulted for my sister's instigations. I confronted her in an effort to understand her side as well as mine, which resulted in her raging outbursts, blaming me and saying I had a mental problem while she was just fine. "You're crazy and don't know what you're talking about." That gaslighting imprinted self-doubt in me, and it became who I was.

The relationship is fragile because raising the subject of maltreatment evokes shame in her. "Why are you bringing that stuff up now?" she'd say. To this day, she sees no need to be helped. Knowing you need help is the first step to healing.

I've come to realize I have a choice. Bear the grudge or release it. Forgiving my sister has allowed me to release her abuse and compassionately support and pray for her.

Learning that shame was the root cause for all maltreatment sent me researching how to heal shame. Reading two of John Bradshaw's books, *Healing Shame* and *Family Secrets,* led to my understanding that as early as the first beat of an unborn child's heart, the amygdala begins recording everything the mother feels. The answers are in us; now I know why. All of a mother's generational transferences, experiences, traumas, and mirrorings, preverbal and verbal, exist if we dig deep enough and winch it up. It's anchored in our heritage.

Now the reality that my cellular memory was shifting, healthy parameters of shame amaze me. I see faith's power and God's grace and mercy hoisting me to the other side of shame. I am overwhelmed to joyful tears and immense gratitude. I feel I am the sole survivor of my family and a survivor of my soul.

Saxon became a victim of my learned shame. From the beginning of his life to the end, he opened my eyes and heart to see myself in him. He symbolized the toxic shame. In contrast, Sadie symbolized the healthy shame, having been born into stability and love as her foundation. The stark reality as I ponder further the comparison between myself and Saxon. Neither he nor I was given the life skills necessary from birth. In infancy, we mirrored the roles, body language, and emotions. We assumed them as correct and carried them forward into our lives. Knowing love and belonging were foreign and when they presented themselves, I resisted and mistrusted based upon fear, not knowing how to receive either and feel safe. All the characteristics of healthy shame felt strange to us. Saxon was born to help me through all this.

While toxic shame will always be in me, it doesn't own me, just as Saxon's aggression no longer controlled him. I quickly can identify shame's behaviors and thinking and reject its intrusive nature. The true self never goes away. It's repressed until all of shame's layers have been peeled away and it's safe to come out.

The moment I dug out shame and pinned it on the cross for God to seal the wounding, I could now look through a new set of eyeballs with compassion for those who harmed and made me a lesser person than I was meant to be. The eyeballs are no longer inside out but look back and understand, liking who I am, a new being, not a shame-filled being. That was then and this is now. God is in the business of doing away with shame and not employing it as a weapon of punishment.

The basket of ribbons is history. It's not what identifies me now. The need to perform and prove myself has been replaced with serving the greater good, using my dogs for therapy work, teaching others the obedience skills for pet therapy and the healing of others, keeping my heart open and sourcing life from a place of love, and seeing it through God's eyes. And oh, He leads me now and I wait to find out which direction He points me to go. Needing control is no longer a factor.

Fear and love are opposing forces, just like empathy and shame. My internal critic has softened, aware I will make mistakes. But I can learn from my failure and arrive on the other side of toxic shame with a fresh perspective. Failure and falling down are okay, as long as I persist to hoist myself up, stand strong, and keep healthy boundaries by walking away from shame's trap. Now each time I face shame's outcroppings, they are shown the exit door.

Saxon and I sacrificed for one another. His body is gone, but his soul lives on. Through God's grace and with my dogs, I gratefully honor Saxon for awakening in me the importance of diggin' up the old bones. Pets we have in our lives are not there by coincidence. They are divinely orchestrated for our own salvation. They guide us to the deepest spiritual aspect of ourselves that hungers to find joy, peace and forgiveness. They are messengers, not just animals as humans often see them.

If we look beyond the surface, we can connect with our own nature, while our life perspective takes a regenerative path. Serving and loving is a pets' gift to us. They simply want to pass the torch, so we can assist others on their souls' safari and we all unite as God's creation. Animals understand this cosmic harmony.

I recently drove past the old farmstead with a renewed heart of forgiveness and gratitude recognizing where my road of healing began. The original house, machine shed, silo, and barn are gone, symbolizing to me an erasure of the past. The old pine tree far down the cow lane, deep in the pasture, by the muddy frog pond facing the westerly winds, is still firmly rooted, though worn and beaten by weather. The puzzled little girl who once sat up on the highest branch is reborn.

Toodle no longer sits waiting for me. I visualize her spirit smiling and I smile back. She is healed and free. So am I. I know healing will go on for the rest of my life. I embrace what surfaces, feel it, name it, move through it, and lift it to God by letting go. Toodle taught me to do that.

The healing process is not limited to emotional release. My body's cellular memory releases also. In the past few years, I have been ill and in pain as I let go of the old emotions. Layers of toxic shame from a lifetime locked in my body are working their way out. It's more than a decade since Saxon died in my arms. I have gained the courage to enter forbidden ground. The process has been a grueling, clouded path of self-examination and facing reality. I've learned that faith and grief are not linear and defy logic to put them in a box with a bow. Saxon's spirit walked every gnarly step of the unearthing process, prodding and showing me to dig deeper within myself to find the root causes strangling my life, even when I felt like quitting. Being showered with that much love is beyond priceless.

I did it for you, Mom.

Saxon's name means swordsman, one of the Germanic warriors who fought battles with their double-edged swords. His mission was to cut like a glowing red-hot knife, slashing through generations of shame. He was a catalyst breaking open a wounded heart and fearful mind. It's why we were supposed to be together.

His death sounded grief's battle cry, rallying it, hunting me down to manifest my destiny unencumbered. He, along with all the animals in my life, held a space of amazing love and patience for me. They are bridges, divinely built. Self-sacrificing themselves. He will always be missed as tears flow. Now out of love and gratitude versus pain and suffering, I don't allow my tears to overshadow the precious presence of my companions. Their broad wisdom and soul-filled insight astound me. They have the ability to see and read my mind.

Gradually as I awakened that I was the student in this life, Saxon was one of the great teachers. Between Him and him, I was saved from destruction, so I could go on to help others heal and pay it forward through training dogs, both privileged and abused. A learned gift and life-purpose Saxon taught me.

Siri's heart murmur is gone. He's ten now, healthy and content.

Six years ago, Jazz was diagnosed with hemangiosarcoma of the heart. A large tumor was found in the right atrium just as it was for Saxon. God gave us three additional months together. Due to the energy healing for animals that I learned with Linda, together we energetically balanced and performed a trauma release for Jazz. Her past was blinded as she released it in our hands. Energetically we wrapped etheric love around her. God swept her off her feet running jubilantly after the shot dummy in a pheasant field tumor-free. It was the way she chose death. She left this world joyfully barking. Her true self shined in the field that day, as I kissed her goodbye in my arms. Another heart cleared.

Each dog passed the baton to the next soul, relaying their purpose one after the other, taking care of me and loving me like no human ever could. As each dog ascended, another faith messenger picked up, deepening my faith and healing. Leading me further down life's spiritual path.

A month after Jazz died, Siri and I walked the hills to where Saxon's and Sadie's ashes were freed. As I held Jazzy's ashes, Siri and I together released Jazzy over the hillside as Simon and Garfunkel's "Bridge Over Troubled Water" echoed across the valley. A special piece of me left with her, for being my bridge during the most heart-wrenching times. It's just what golden retrievers do. Now every time I hear that song, I know Jazzy is near. This is her message to me:

I am still here, in the peace of your heart, watching you and blessing you from beyond. Just as our love never dies, so our connection does not end. Because I'm not with you in my physical form, I send you blessings and greetings through every little bird that sings its song, through every ray of sunshine that kisses your cheek, through the gentle breeze that catches your hair on a beautiful day in spring.

Losing Jazz crushed Siri's tender heart, and I nearly lost him too. He knew she was dying and wanted to stay with her, comforting her in her last days. But he was put on a path to be a titled breed champion and was performing in the show ring with a professional handler when Jazzy died. I had cheated him out of the chance to say good-bye and my stabbed heart bled for him. My guilt was another poignant lesson I learned from being performance driven. The combination of Siri's mourning and distaste for the conformation ring stopped me cold in my tracks. It forced me to rethink my core values. This was the final straw. I promised Siri the ribbon chase was over. The rest of his life would be lived in harmony and from the heart doing what he was born to do—love and help people heal. He is holding me to my promise.

It's Not Your Fault

Mia came to me shortly after Jazzy died. I was grieving and wary. Mia wasn't the dog I had in mind. In the breeder's home, as she relaxed on the carpet chewing on her bone, our eyes met, and the energy exchange between us immediately cinched the feelings in my heart. For the short time we were together, we reversed roles as teacher and student.

Mia, an eight-month-old golden retriever, was returned to the breeder because she was biting the children and parents. They were first-time dog owners, having three children, ages three, six, and nine, who begged to have a puppy. They had no knowledge of dog behavior or pack structure. They mindlessly expected the dog to know what to do, to be a fixture and a cute family addition. A disaster in the making.

The children taunted, screamed, chased, harassed, swung her by her tail, and dragged her around the yard like a toy, pounding on her with a plastic bat. They pulled and pinched her ears, and jumped on her while she slept. They yanked her until she yelped. They stole—and even played in—her food bowl while she tried to eat. Mia was kicked in the head by the parents, and then thrown into her kennel and yelled at for biting the screaming three-year-old. She never found her place in the family or had a moment of peace. She never felt safe. Boundaries, order, and unity were nonexistent. From her first fear period, at six to twelve weeks old, the children's harassment inflicted an imprint on her. The parents took her to one training class and thought that could fix her for life. She lived a life of chaos and abuse. Rage built up in her. She couldn't take it anymore. She was in a constant defensive state of rage—fight-or-flight-freeze response to survive. Mia was blamed and found guilty.

Mia came to my home on a trial basis. When I called the breeder, searching for an older female golden, they thought her last hope was with me.

Her ability to stabilize and maintain her life line was severely impaired because of her head injury and environment. At the same time, my emotional barriers held her at a distance. Her training with me began with leadership, followed by a combination of obedience and desensitization. Then came counter-conditioning and operant and clicker-treat training, the same behavioral modification techniques I used with Saxon. Despite energetic healing multiple times a day, she was unable to hold the balancing. Her entire energy field was impaired.

Her wild, raging, empty animal eyes, stiff body, and defensive nature told the emotional horror roiling inside her. The slightest body movement caused her to flinch and spring into attack mode like a feral animal. Many times, in the process of teaching her how to trade items, she lunged at me and gouged my hand. Every minute of the day was chaos. I kept her tethered to her kennel for our safety. It was a living example of what would be upheaval for years, an unhealthy life that was cruel for all of us. It was an encore of patterns in my life that I didn't want repeated. I wanted to help for a short time with both of us needing to move forward.

I put her on my back porch to be alone with a bone to chew on. I'd crack the door open, and she'd snarl that guttural growl. Her angry body language and whale eye signaled a fearful attack warning. Over time, when I tossed some steak near her through the kitchen window to build a positive association to me, she'd step away from the bone she was gnawing on to where she trusted me and we could exchange items. She had the ability to learn basic commands, but beyond that, her broken soul was irreparable.

Realizing how being with nature and running in open fields freed my dogs, I took Mia and Siri to the pheasant farm to run the same paths there as Sadie and Saxon had. This was also the place where Jazzy died. Mia was on a long line first. After teaching her to come on a whistle, I let her run free with Siri. Her soul was fed to know nature. She was an entirely different dog out there. The ecstasy she experienced to live as one with her universe was foreign.

In the house, her outbursts escalated, her mind snapped. She attacked Siri, who realized how unbalanced Mia was and tried to help right her. Siri became sick from the unrelenting upheavals. Siri was my priority and Mia knew that. She intentionally elevated her aggression. Siri was reaching a breaking point. She was forcing my hand.

Mia suffered deep sorrow. Every night in her kennel, she moaned and howled. Life for her felt hopeless. Any attempt to love her was met with rejection and she pushed it away. It's a feeling I understood all too well. In essence, she was telling me she didn't want to be saved.

So stop trying so hard. Let me go. I'm damaged.

The trial period was three weeks, but I extended it to five, making sure no medical reason existed. I didn't want to miss anything if there was the slightest chance of saving her. Wrestling with my decision to return Mia, knowing her life was in my hands, was heartbreaking. There was no point in comparing this brokenness to Saxon's aggression. He wanted to be saved. Rehabilitation was not in Mia, and to let her live in agony, isolated from anyone else, was cruel. Hers would continue to be a life of abuse. That's wrong.

We took a long walk alone and then with Siri. Mia ran free one last time, seeing the pheasants and feeling the crisp winter breeze on her face, letting her ears fly in the wind with a smile on her face. Walking to the spot where Jazzy died, we sat together as she felt my heart open. She felt love and tears poured out, so new to her. I showed her my vision of Jazzy who decided to die in a full-tilt retrieve. Jazzy got to choose; that's all Mia ever wanted. Surprisingly, compassion rose up in her and we briefly bonded in the field, feeling Jazzy's spirit near.

Mia had learned to eat from my hand, and in the field I reached for a treat without her flinching, and she gently took it from me. Yet, I knew it took everything in her muscle memory to trust me, letting her guard down, risking more pain and betrayal.

The short glimmers of love, kindness, and freedom gave Mia a chance to realize that a part of her was normal, but it was not sustainable. Knowing I had to let her go didn't stop the enormous guilt I carried when I took her back to the breeder. I knew her life would end, and she did too. On the last night, energetically she held her life balance long enough so she could be wrapped in her own love and transition peacefully.

This was our last conversation. Tears covered my face as I sat beside her and spoke to her. Siri supported us, lying quietly on the floor, holding a space of love. Mia listened.

"Mia, this is a decision I dreaded making, but in my heart I know it is the right one. All of my options to help you have been exhausted. If you choose to escalate your anger and continue biting people, your physical life will end. If you are placed in another home, your life could be one of abuse and maltreatment because they may not understand you. Now, you get to choose. I know God will catch you and help you heal in Heaven's safe harbor. Peace will come over you. When your life ends, I wish your spirit will come to me and let me know you are safe." Mia affectionately licked the wounded hand she bit. She was sorry for hurting me that way.

"Your anger was not your fault and you have reminded me that in my childhood it was not my fault either. We were wrongly blamed and forced to carry the guilt. Forgive yourself. Healing will come by letting it all go. The Mia that played and ran free in the open fields is my lasting memory of you. Remember the good times, Mia."

I reached for her paw. She gave me it to me and let me kiss it. Praying over her, I lifted her being to God, blessing and keeping her as His own creation. The words that came to me for her were meant for my understanding.

When we arrived around noon, the breeder came out and attached a leash to Mia's collar. She never looked back. Mia faced death head-on and transitioned without fear, knowing her death meant peace and not a life of terror. This is a good lesson for humans: Death is not to be feared.

Mia was dispatched the next morning with a single gunshot. Her spirit came to me and I knew she was safe. My decision to return her to the breeder hurt like hell. But sometimes all can't be saved. Mia lived nine months. We taught each other about fault and guilt, and that this life is just another transition to eternal life. Mia and I broke a multiple generational cycle. Having carried blame through our lives, guilt's weight was lifted from us both. Forgiveness, love and gratitude liberates and heals the life we leave behind.

Mia's soul lives on. We were together for the time needed to teach one another. There are no coincidences. She helped me seal shut the life I didn't want repeated. I gave her seeds for a healthy reincarnation. She will come back on her own terms, manifesting her destiny. She will realize her false start and know she is salvageable. And, one day, come back to be a therapy dog, If that happens, I hope to be privileged to train her. She experienced true love and compassion.

What makes it all right for humanity to abuse innocent children and animals, to blame them and not take responsibility? It's what society does. And we wonder how things go off the rails. I feel Mia's essence wanting me to convey this message to humanity:

Be responsible, people. Stop abusing the innocent, for I am one of many damaged animals reflecting your ignorance and irresponsibility.

A Soul Restored

Siri has a new companion. Her name is Grace, which means God's gift. She fills our hearts with joy and forces me to live for the moment, appreciating life as it comes our way. She is an alpha who will push me at every turn, keeping me on an honest path and reinforces healthy boundaries.

She brings much joy as she leaps delightfully through the air like a gymnast across the warm, sunlit alfalfa field, chasing and barking at butterflies because life has been transformed for us all. We are free to be ourselves, a lighthearted, peaceful loving pack that hangs out together. I can *just be*, and all is well with my soul. We three are a pack.

Siri, a therapy dog and God's ambassador, is living out his soul purpose, holding his red stuffed heart toy in his mouth, wagging his tail, and serving as the church greeter, assisting on the prayer team, and providing comfort for children of divorce. He opens wounded hearts and pours out his love, making church a safe place to find healing. He serves the greater good, breaking down emotional barriers, and bringing comfort to those who walk in heavy-hearted, just like I used to. I stand aside, watching how his heart is fulfilled loving and comforting people. I am blessed to tears as he walks beside me when we take communion, and he then rests contentedly during the service under my chair.

As for me, the purpose I now serve is the fulfilling of the promise I made to Saxon when he took his last breath in my arms and the prophecy that the spiritualist Grace Angel envisioned. Grace's words were, "Make compassion your passion." And I have.

With Spirit's help, I am assisting emotionally damaged and abused dogs in healing from human cruelty. I use the energy healing techniques including trauma release, grounding and focus, clearing negative energy, energetically rebalancing the chakras, and blinding a dog's past life. These protocols allow the dog the opportunity to have a mended silver cord. Once they are spiritually reconnected to the universe and all chakras are open, their ability to function is restored. The actual obedience training, healthy boundaries, and life skills can advance quicker because the dog's being has become whole and is open to learning. Some rise to become therapy dogs that I continue to train using all the obedience skills I acquired training Sadie, Saxon, Jazz, Siri, and Grace. Training my dogs compounds the highest good. It's how I pass the torch. I am honored to work with new therapy teams that serve others for the greater good. Because of Saxon, I have received a purpose-filled gift for the rest of my life.

A shackled prisoner to toxic shame, I'm not, but I am a survivor. I am empathetic for those who are still ensnared. No shopping spree, drug, alcohol, ribbons, exotic travel, or psychologist can fix shame. At the heart of reaching for temporal satisfaction is a spiritual vacuum built in us.

With full surrender and believing, my eyes fixed on Christ, taking a step of faith, hoping not to fall in the abyss, trusting, I take His hand, never looking down. I relinquish control and walk across the bridge realizing faith supports me. It's the cross Christ died on bearing the shame for me and all humanity. Not only am I saved, He's made me a believer and I am all in, focusing on Him. The choice is mine to make, and I choose God. In return, my turmoil from shame is erased.

The lack of belonging is replaced by being included in the open arms of God's family. Whatever comes my way, I know faith will carry me through, lifting my concerns up to Him. I don't fear being alone. Hand in hand, Spirit walks beside me and is in me, guiding me. I am listening to what He has in store for me. Our connection is stronger than any steel.

I found my peace, my hope, and I am comforted by joy's presence. I am content, accepting that He's in charge of my life. God's grace holds me now. I know what it means to be born again. I have chosen baptism by emersion, symbolizing burial of the old nature and retrieval of my soul for a restored spiritual life.

I believe our world would be healthier if we dealt deliberately with toxic shame and flushed it from our lives, so it could not be not replicated. Toxic shame is far-reaching, weaving into every facet of society. We don't connect its evasive, illusive, and destructive effects. It dodges and disguises itself in most families. It's often overlooked as it stares us square in the face. It is the core culprit of all kinds of violence in our world. Shame's shucking and jiving roots itself with anger, division, resentment, belittling, and berating as its camouflage.

Shame may be one of the seedbeds of the mental illness germinating in our society, targeting the most vulnerable. Though my innocence and that of my animals were stolen, we united and stood strong in the midst of the harsh chaos, elbowing and shouldering through the violations. We chose not to remain victims but to be survivors taking back the stolen parts of our souls. Each of us is only one, but we can make a difference if we choose. It's a choice about overcoming shame's mental entrapment. Because words matter.

My hope is to give the reader a new direction for disentangling the inner turmoil that shame instigates. The answer for me, inspired by Saxon, was an introspective soul search and completely trusting God's plan for my life. He gave me the courage to let those lies I fed myself, go.

He is the Great Physician. Because of fear and disbelief, God proved to me that His way is the right way. Once I stopped wrestling with The Holy Spirit and trusted Him, the internal conflict subsided. The outer and inner image pair-up. I chose complete surrender and believing. No more a fractured soul but healed and made whole.

I am grateful to each dog that carried the torch, prodding me to keep diggin' up bones until I crossed the bridge of faith. God bless your spiritual discovery with His amazing grace, forgiveness, courage, gratitude, and love. Shalom!

Epilogue

It concerned me how my years of grief overshadowed Siri during this writing and spiritual healing process. Siri sat with me daily as I wrote and rewrote, cried, and clawed my way through grief and all the uprooting. Finally, the epiphanies reached the other side of shame, and I was reborn.

I learned and was shocked by Siri's amazing, forbearing love. Recalling him as a puppy gazing in silence heavenward, I intuitively learned how a tandem collaboration between Saxon and Siri was formed. Siri listened intently for his instructions as the scepter was passed. Arriving home, he delivered it to me. This explains the King of Hearts card. Saxon walked in step while I was discovering my spiritual path and life purpose, and Siri walked at heel humbly, loving and supporting me.

My humanness got in the way of my interconnectedness that animals naturally understand. Everything they know, live, and feel comes from a place of loving one another, not from ambition or awards. They seek only the benefit of another without anything in return. This pure love is freely given.

I am grateful to each dog that steadfastly and selflessly supported me. They showed me hope in the dark valleys. Their wisdom far exceeded my understanding. I stand amazed that they are not just a dog. They are God's perfect design and part of a divine plan.

Humans see themselves as separate, living small, outside their existence. Maybe this is our downfall and prevents us from living in harmony. Individualism works to a certain point but becomes destructive when blown out of proportion. Animals naturally understand that everything in life is interconnected, coming from a place of love and matters of the heart—the greater good.

In the hierarchy of dogs, each member is uniquely designed to have a purpose for the survival of the pack. So it is that God has a divine plan in our creation. We all have a purpose in life and are formed to have a role to carry out according to His design. Humans are not meant to be separate from the animal world. It's a lesson that animals are desperately trying to convey about our imbalances.

If we live from a place of love and share that love, love's power will overcome the anger that festers into disease. Love unites and heals while chaos divides and destroys.

So imagine a world where shame and guilt are nonexistent and the mistreatment of animals is replaced with love and respect. When humans find the same interconnectedness as animals, so that animal shelters and safe houses will no longer be needed.

We are meant to be the world's steward and to love one another. Our animal steward guides are in our lives as teachers for our spiritual elevation. If we are to truly heal ourselves, we must forgive others, while aligning our inner and outer lives, while following God's plan for our life.

Blessings from the heart and peace to your soul. Sirius

Believing, go forward trusting faith is by your side.

Acknowledgments

Immense gratitude to my Lord above who patiently walked with me through a plethora of life struggles to trust my faith and free me from shame. His love came down and grace holds me now.

My mother who seeded in me the compass of a faith-based life.

Bill Barten who believed in Saxon and changed his life as Saxon changed mine.

Saxon's veterinarians who compassionately supported him medically, behaviorally, emotionally, and spiritually.

The many dog friends and trainers I came to know while achieving Saxon's hunt test ribbons.

To the dogs and cat in my life: Toodle, Brandy, Sadie, Jazzy, Saxon, Mia, Siri, and Gracie who supported and taught me valuable life lessons through each rung of my spiritual growth. Divinely orchestrated as one transitioned, they passed their torch to the next dog to carry forward.

Beyond this were the many true friends and spiritual teachers I called upon in the process of writing and healing who answered and clarified my distorted thinking.

Pastor Paul of Jacobs Well Church who over the years spoke messages which zeroed in on shame's disguises and how it destroys the soul. He provided a healing road map that was going to take much introspection and tough emotional work.

Rosie who demanded me to journal when I thought it was silly, trying to blow off her insistence.

The late Montana Grey who believed my story could help others. She inspired confidence to write what my heart buried and I couldn't voice. She began the rough framework of the memoir from my journal.

My brilliant writing coach and friend, Marion Roach Smith, who brought structure, challenge, and the xyz who helped me put order and clarity to this book.

To my invaluable copy editor, Rob Brill, who has a deep spiritual understanding, edited without judgment, cared, challenged, and took this very personal manuscript from something rough to a smooth, concise, poignant read, never knowing his thumbprint was there.

Gratitude to you all for being in my life. May God bless you beyond measure.

About the Author

Bonnie Wright has trained performance dogs for twenty-four years. Harnessing evidence-based research, continuous study, intellect, and spiritual intuition with the goal of passionately improving the lives of dogs and educating the public. Over the years the dogs taught her to take an individualized holistic approach.

Her high standards, respect, compassion, and science are knitted across her life's work.

She is a certified animal behavior instructor forming the All Star Dog Training Company, LLC in 2013. She established the SS Safari All-Star Fund to provide community grants through the Eau Claire Community Foundation. When Saxon, her own dog, was diagnosed with inter-dog fear aggression at five months old, she rehabilitated and trained him to achieve an AKC Master Hunter title, participating in the Master National Retriever Championship event. She never realized the behavior modification methods she taught Saxon were predestined to uncover and set free her life of unconscious transgenerational shame. *Diggin' Up Bones* is a memoir showing the reader this inspirational life-changing story. The memoir's intent is to serve the greater good and support charitable organizations.

Bonnie graduated from the University of Wisconsin at Eau Claire with a BS degree in education, with a minor in early childhood education. She completed her MBA from Cardinal Stritch University at Milwaukee, Wisconsin.

She retired in 2012, serving the healthcare industry, after a successful thirty-five-year career with a major pharmaceutical corporation. Currently, she trains therapy dogs for reading programs and the local Mayo Health System. She and Siri volunteer for their church. She remains an active board member of the Blackhawk Retriever Club 501(c) 3 and an AKC performance field judge. She enjoys long walks in the country with her dogs, bicycling, field training, and writing.